W9-CES-849

The Dow Jones-Irwin Guide to
COMMON STOCKS

The Dow Jones-Irwin Guide to
COMMON STOCKS

Chris Mader
The Wharton School
University of Pennsylvania

Robert Hagin
Hagin Capital Management
La Jolla, California

LIBRARY
BRYAN COLLEGE
DAYTON, TENN. 37321

 DOW JONES-IRWIN   Homewood, Illinois   60430

58695

© DOW JONES-IRWIN, 1973 and 1976

All rights reserved. No part of this publication may be
reproduced, stored in a retrieval system, or transmitted,
in any form or by any means, electronic, mechanical,
photocopying, recording, or otherwise, without the prior
written permission of the publisher.

This publication is designed to provide accurate and
authoritative information in regard to the subject matter
covered. It is sold with the understanding that the
publisher is not engaged in rendering legal, accounting, or
other professional service. If legal advice or other expert
assistance is required, the services of a competent
professional person should be sought.
*From a Declaration of Principles jointly adopted by a Committee
of the American Bar Association and a Committee of Publishers.*

2 3 4 5 6 7 8 9 0 K 5 4 3 2 1 0 9 8

Previous edition published under title
What Today's Investor Should Know about the New Science of Investing

ISBN 0-87094-108-9
Library of Congress Catalog Card No. 75–43167
Printed in the United States of America

Preface

The stock market strategies developed and explained in this book are easily understood and applied. They combine what is *known* about investing with what is successfully *practiced*. Part One's four chapters guide you toward your personal financial plan. Then Part Two, Understanding the Stock Market, explains what we really know, and don't know, about how to invest in common stocks. Part Three, Personal Investing Strategies, develops step-by-step procedures for investment success.

Here you will find the condensed results of hundreds of research studies, conducted by both investment professionals and university researchers. From them we now know that many widely held investment beliefs are, at best, mythical, and, at worst, counterproductive. Unfortunately, most investors have yet to benefit from the explosive growth of knowledge about common stocks.

Poor capital management, and repeated bear markets, have hurt most investors. Pessimism has driven many out of the market—the number of shareowners in the United States dropped from over 30 million in 1970 to only 25 million by 1976. Still others have shifted funds into low-interest savings accounts or nonliquid deposits. They may have concluded that the only way to make a small fortune in the stock market is to begin with a *large* one!

But with no appreciation possibilities—with no equity holdings— investors have no escape from ongoing inflation. At stake are the financial security and future independence of literally millions of American families.

Hundreds of people have contributed to this book by contributing to the literature on investing. *You* are also a participant in this project. Your collective involvement in the market determines its behavior; you finance American business; and you help assure a prosperous future for yourself and others. We wish you success in investing and we welcome your comments and inquiries: Write to Chris Mader, The Wharton School, University of Pennsylvania, Philadelphia, Pennsylvania 19104; or Robert Hagin, P.O. Box 2033, La Jolla, California 92038.

March 1976   **Chris Mader**
                                                                Robert Hagin

Contents

Part Three
Personal Investing Strategies

part one
Your Investment Objectives

1

Successful Investing

For thousands of years, millions of intelligent men and women have spent billions of hours searching for profitable investing strategies. What, then, can this book offer you that is either new or useful? Here you will find a readable explanation of the startling *new* knowledge about stock market investing and how you can apply this knowledge for personal profit.

During the past 15 years, sophisticated investment studies more than doubled our knowledge of how to invest. Existing concepts—such as price charting, earnings forecasts, and diversification—were thoroughly investigated. And new concepts—such as the random walk, the efficient capital market, and betas—were added to the professional's jargon.

Unfortunately, many investors assume that these concepts are difficult to understand and apply. To correct this notion, Part One guides you in setting your investment objectives. Then we have condensed the new knowledge into everyday language in Part Two and have translated it into step-by-step investment strategies in Part Three.

This three-part outline reflects the way people *should* approach investing. For example, you probably rank financial security among your more sought-after objectives. Yet, most investors pursue this goal with a mixture of hasty guessing and hopeful thinking. In the often frantic search for the new investment *news,* they ignore the new investment *knowledge.* But wait. If you know what information is useful—and then how to apply it—investing can be both easier and more profitable. We hope to make it so for you.

Why Invest?

You invest to make a profit from this effort, just as a well-managed company does. Presumably, you would expect such a company to weigh its performance against explicit short- and long-range plans. Yet, few investors properly plan and manage their own investments with similar attention.

Think about your own—probably fragmented—capital structure. Typically, a family has a checking account, probably a savings account, perhaps a home (possibly with a mortgage), and life insurance—maybe including a long-standing policy, more recent ones, and an employee group plan. Retirement income, one of the most ignored and least understood parts of personal wealth, is somehow to be derived from Social Security, complicated pension rights, and available retirement funds. The will, if there is one, may be outdated.

Upon this fragmented foundation, the typical family erects a hodgepodge of investments: savings bonds, mutual fund shares, common stocks, and so forth. Once a year, everything is pulled together just long enough to figure out the income tax, and then left for another year. This is fragmented capital management. It results from looking *individually* at your assets—such as real estate, insurance, savings, and securities—rather than seeing their total structure.

And what of the capital you *do* choose to invest in securities? Is it subjected to uninformed decision making—such as unplanned impulse buying and selling? Too few investors know what can reasonably be expected from common stock investing over some period of time, much less how to apply this knowledge to their own needs and objectives. Too few weigh the risks of different securities instruments, such as speculative stocks, securities of seasoned companies, convertible bonds, warrants, and stock options. Thus, most investors just buy common stocks without relating them to their own capital structure or judging how much profit to expect, how soon, and the downside risk.

When the market pushes to new highs, the emotional urge is to jump on the bandwagon. When it sags, investors see stocks selling at fractions of their old highs, and gloom pervades. In between is a mixture of hope and fear, of impulse and indecision, of nearsighted planning and fragmented capital management.

How to Invest

The solution to these related problems is to invest:

1. In terms of your personal financial objectives and capital structure.
2. By applying the known "odds" of common stock investing.

To help you analyze your financial objectives and capital structure, Figure 1–1 shows a triangle divided into four layers. The base layer represents your *foundation capital,* such as equity in a home, cars and personal property, ready cash and checking balances, insurance, and Social Security and retirement benefits. These assets provide your current standard of living and protect you and your family against short- and long-term contingencies.

We call the next layer *core investments.* They are low- to moderate-risk investments with long-term objectives. They include mutual funds with average or better performance, common stocks of large

FIGURE 1–1

Composite Capital Structure

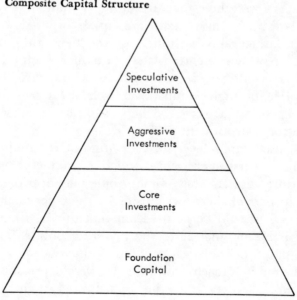

companies, high-grade bonds, and so forth. Note that the top three layers are labeled as "investments." Their purpose is to provide for your *future* standard of living, and they are directly under *your* control. Successful investing—or the lack of it—can affect your material well-being for a lifetime.

The next layer represents *aggressive investments*. These include good- to medium-quality investments with shorter-term performance goals and somewhat higher risk. The top and smallest layer represents *speculative investments,* such as historically volatile stocks, speculative bonds, and call options. Viewed in this way, your otherwise fragmented capital forms a composite structure that you can shape to meet *your* personal needs and objectives.

To invest successfully, before you buy individual stocks you must set realistic objectives that balance your current and future financial needs. The next two chapters help you set such specific investment goals and the investment amounts needed to reach them. This eliminates confusion and temptation by insuring that the role of each investment is clearly understood.

Know the "Odds"

Most people like to keep up-to-date on their investments. They buy newspapers with closing stock prices and routinely turn to the financial pages to see how they are doing. Paradoxically, few who follow the latest price movements are equally up-to-date on knowing the significance and usefulness of the news they read. How *should* the latest news be translated into meaningful investment strategy? What would you do, for example, if your favorite stock increased in price, on high volume, over each of the past five trading days? Modern research, reviewed here, indicates how to use such news for personal investment profit.

Investors also search feverishly for innovative companies with knowledgeable management and distinctive products. Yet, in their quest for future winners, these same people may overlook the latest knowledge in part of their own business—their personal investing.

In fairness, it should be pointed out that this new knowledge is often unavailable or unclear to the investing public. The institutional orientation or statistical content of much good research puts it beyond the public's reach. Ironically, the very depth and rigor that make such work acceptable to the sophisticated often make it unsuitable to the majority. In the deluge of current *news*, little new *knowledge* has filtered down to individual investors. As a result, many who keep abreast of the market use out-of-date knowhow in arriving at investment decisions. They may be basing their future prosperity on strategies now known to be worthless, while simultaneously ignoring what is *genuinely useful*.

This serious lag between scientific discovery and widespread understanding has three main causes. First, it is difficult to accept facts that are often counter to intuition. Psychologically, we rely on "gut feel" in the face of uncertainty. Yet, as we will demonstrate shortly, in today's competitive markets intuition is not enough.

Second, investors have not absorbed the new knowledge because its meaning and significance have not been adequately interpreted to them. University researchers, in particular, are remiss in couching important findings in overly scientific jargon. This communications gap was colorfully depicted in *The Money Game* with the assertion that "no random-walk theoretician has managed to write a complete paper in English yet, and most Wall Streeters cannot read those little Greek symbols lying on their sides inside the square-root symbols." [**162**, p. 159]*

Third, some Wall Streeters believe it is against their interests to disseminate the new investment knowledge. For example, since your broker earns a commission for executing transactions, it follows that he needs reasons for you to buy and sell. Similarly, investment advisers clearly must advise. But much of the new knowledge casts doubt on the popular reasons and techniques some brokers and advisors use in trading stocks. Also, some Wall Streeters show little interest in serving individual investors when large institutions trade more frequently and generate bigger commissions. The broker or advisor you should pick, of course, is one who rejects these attitudes

Whatever the cause (be it your psychological resistance, poor communication due to professional rhetoric, or some firms' reluctance to promote individual investor knowledge), the purpose of Part Two, Understanding the Stock Market, is to spell out the meaning and significance of the latest investing knowledge. We want you to *know the odds*. Specifically, we will analyze the merits and demerits of both "technical" and "fundamental" approaches to investing and caution you about some misleading market folklore.

---

* Boldface numbers refer to bibliography entries in the back of this book.

Part Three, Personal Investing Strategies, then develops step-by-step strategies designed to reach your goals. We will explore the issue of performance versus risk and examine the role of various stock market instruments—common stocks, mutual funds, warrants, options, and so on.

Conclusion

In any stock market strategy, investors must rely on Wall Street professionals for varying degrees of *information* and *advice*. The distinction is important. Many brokers and advisers relay significant news to their clients. Thus, their role as "news monitor" is an important one. Still, the more important task is drawing inferences from such information and taking investment action. Here, modern research has revealed many *do*s and *don't*s that will help you know what news is useful and then how to apply it to your stock market decisions.

2

Setting Objectives

Nearly everyone is concerned about money, but few people carefully plan their financial future. As an example, most of us spend more time working on, or worrying about, our income tax than on our personal financial plan. All too frequently, vital decisions on investments and major family expenses are made without considering their impact on one's *financial lifeline*. In broad terms, your financial lifeline predicts your accumulation and dispersal of wealth throughout your lifetime. It involves three interrelated issues: the destination, the road map, and the vehicles.

The important first step of successful investing is setting realistic objectives. The second step is using those objectives as a road map or investment plan. Too often, bad investment decisions, or good ones turned sour, cause detours that inhibit reaching well-defined objectives. The third and final step is to select the combination of insurance and investment vehicles that will carry you to your financial destination.

This chapter is designed for those who, while pursuing their businesses and careers, have neglected the "business" of their own economic future. Most individuals' investment objectives and financial plans are too vague. Hence, before we tackle the major subject of "how to make money in the stock market," you must first decide *how much you want to make.*

The old adage "It takes money to make money" is true. You cannot profit from investments if you do not *invest!* More specifically, after you have defined your objectives, it is possible to determine how much you should be setting aside each year to attain them. *How much* you invest can be as crucial as *how well* you invest.

Comparing Performance

The goal of a well-run investment portfolio—like that of a well-run business—is planned profit. By contrast, haphazard investing usually leads to volatile performance. The penalty for this can be illustrated by the results of a sequence of investments made by a hypothetical Mr. Adams: up 20 percent, up 40 percent, up 20 percent, down 50 percent. This performance might look acceptable, but it's not. After the excitement of three good years, Mr. Adams is even after the fourth.[1] Also, changing the sequence of these gains and losses does not change the overall result. Unfortunately, such erratic performance is more than an exercise in percentages. Practically speaking, this has happened to millions of investors!

The results of volatile performance can be illustrated further by contrasting the three records shown in Table 2–1. Which investor has the most appreciation at the end of five years? As we have seen, Mr. Adams' performance stands roughly even after four years. Suppose he then makes a comeback in the fifth year. Mr. Baker's performance shows less volatility—exactly half the upside return of Mr. Adams in the good years, but a lesser decline in the bad year. Mr. Clark, by contrast, plods along at 7 percent per year—hardly anything to dazzle the gang at the country club. The surprising fact is, however, that *the three investors have practically the same overall returns, but Mr. Clark also enjoys stability instead of the risk of catastrophic loss.*

The significance of Table 2–1 is that seemingly outstanding investment records, if interrupted by periodic sizable losses, usually wind up average or below over the long haul. Investors with such bouncy portfolios should realize that one bad period can erase the

---

[1] Overall performance *cannot* be measured by adding 20, 40, and 20 percent and then subtracting 50 percent, because of period-to-period compounding. The "period" can be days, weeks, years, or any other interval. Using years, the period-to-period record is shown below:

Start	*End of Year 1*	*End of Year 2*	*End of Year 3*	*End of Year 4*
$100.00 (+20%) =	$120.00 (+40%) =	$168.00 (+20%) =	$201.60 (−50%) =	$100.80

heady performance of several good ones. Unhappily, in the good times we must often tolerate the shortsighted braggadocio of haphazard, but lucky, investors. During bad times the subject of investments is somehow ignored!

This brief comparison of returns from speculative versus conservative investing does not imply that one posture is better than the other. Both have a place in most people's capital structure. But it is essential to strike a balance in light of the investing opportunities and *your* proclivity for risk. Lacking such perspective transforms investing into a pattern of gambling and hoping.

TABLE 2–1

Comparison of Three Hypothetical Performance Records

Investor	Annual Percentage Gain or Loss					Annualized Percentage Return
	Year 1	Year 2	Year 3	Year 4	Year 5	
Adams...........	+20	+40	+20	−50	+40	+7
Baker............	+10	+20	+10	−20	+20	+7
Clark...........	+ 7	+ 7	+ 7	+ 7	+ 7	+7

Impulsive forays into the market are likely to produce losses. Many investors, such as Adams and Baker, get disheartened by their performance and leave the market, never knowing that the way they played the game subjected them to inordinate and unnecessary risks.

Investing by Objectives

Investing by objectives, using a reasoned mixture of investment vehicles selected for their return and risk characteristics, with performance monitored against planned goals, is the surest road to financial success. Unfortunately, most personal investment programs are not managed within the context of a plan tailored to individual needs. Instead, decisions often originate from attempts to fit today's hot investment products to the customer, regardless of his or her unique requirements.

This obvious flaw in the way people manage their money stems from the understandable tendency of both investors and professionals to focus on the fun side of the job—the exciting concepts, the creative new products, the hot growth areas, and so forth. Facing such an array of seeming opportunities, it is difficult to remember to ask, "How does *that* relate to my investment objectives?" A physician, for example, recently asked an investment adviser for an opinion on writing Polaroid calls. One might as well have asked the physician, "Should I take penicillin or aspirin?" *No investor, and no investment adviser, should recommend medicine before he judges what the patient requires—no matter how exciting or revolutionary the medicine may be!*

A suitably tailored plan is not enough. Success is rarely achieved by chance. A plan must be executed in a businesslike fashion by organizing, staffing, directing, and controlling the resources required to accomplish the plan. *Organizing* defines the authority-responsibility relationships among those carrying out the plan. *Staffing* involves selecting qualified people to implement the plan. *Directing* means leading and effecting the plan's implementation, while *controlling* audits the results. Let's look at these steps in terms of your personal responsibility as an investor.

First, you must *plan to invest!* Some people mistakenly assume that investing is something for "good times" or when one gets "a little bit ahead." Such an unplanned approach can spell fiscal disaster for you and your family. "Scarlett O'Hara investors" say, "I'll worry about that tomorrow," and spend all of their current income —and sometimes more—with scores of rationalizations about present needs. Yet, the harsh fact is that spending everything precludes the capital accumulation required to educate your children, purchase a vacation property, enter a personal business venture, assure a worry-free retirement, or fulfill whatever dreams you may have. "Scarlett O'Hara investors" forget one of *Gone with the Wind's* major themes—the struggle to retain Tara. It was Tara, Scarlett O'Hara's estate, that assured her financial tomorrow through war, death of husbands, and economic depression. Without investment, tomorrow *is* another day—for which you may not be prepared.

If Your Goal Is $250,000 . . .

The benefits of early investment (although it is never too late) cannot be overemphasized. Suppose, for example, your goal is to have a quarter-of-a-million dollars at age 65. There are several ways to reach this goal. Assume that your investments earn an after-tax rate of return of 7.5 percent each year. With that rate, Figure 2–1 shows three ways to arrive at your target of $250,000 at age 65.

Figure 2–1 confirms the maxim that it helps to be born rich. Under Plan I, a one-time $14,000 investment that is allowed to compound for 40 years at an after-tax annual rate of return of 7.5 percent will grow to $252,619. Barring the good fortune of having $14,000 to invest at age 25, an alternative is to invest a certain sum each year. Plan II shows that investing $1,200 each year from age 25 to 65, with the same after-tax performance of 7.5 percent annually, will bring you $272,708 at age 65.

FIGURE 2–1

Three Ways to Obtain $250,000 by Age 65

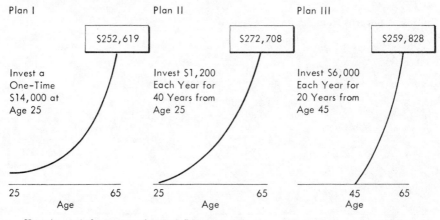

Note: Assumed after-tax rate of return is 7.5 percent each year.

The shorter the investment period, the greater the yearly commitment must be in order to reach the goal.

This is shown by Plan III. If one does not start investing until age 45, $6,000 per year must be set aside to reach the goal of $250,000 by age 65.

One's ultimate capital (say, at age 65) depends on four factors:

1. The initial invested amount.
2. The annual additional investments.
3. The annual after-tax rate of return.
4. The number of years remaining until the goal (say, until age 65).

Turning again to Figure 2–1, it should be noted that the after-tax rate of return—7.5 percent per year on the average—is approximately that obtained from holding a well-diversified portfolio of common stocks. These comparative graphs show that the three plans provide roughly equivalent results. Whether it is possible to invest two years of your spouse's income before starting a family, or whether it is possible to start investing $100 a month at age 25, or $500 a month at age 45, is a personal matter. From an investment point of view, however, the conclusion is clear—*start investing as much as you can, as early as you can!*

More ebullient investors may feel that the assumption of an approximate historical after-tax rate of return of 7.5 percent is too

FIGURE 2–2

Improved Returns from Astute Investments

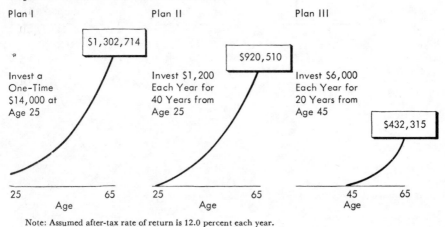

Note: Assumed after-tax rate of return is 12.0 percent each year.

conservative. Suppose performance can be improved to 12 percent annually after taxes. Figure 2–2 projects the results of the three previous investment plans, using this superior rate of return. In each case, the totals are up dramatically. But the early investor (Plan I) gains the most—a mere $14,000 will grow to $1,302,714 in 40 years. Even the start-small-but-early investor (Plan II) more than doubles the performance of Plan III. Clearly, it pays to start investing as early as possible!

After Planning—Organize, Staff, Direct, and Control

Once you have set realistic financial goals and devised a plan for attaining them, you must organize your *income-spending-investing* pattern in accordance with this plan. Very personal priorities and decisions are required to assure the planned flow of investable funds. Again, however, the responsibility is yours, and new investment knowledge can only be applied when investable funds are made available.

Income in excess of spending is the only source of investable funds. This formidable fact, coupled with the desire to live the good life and keep up with the neighbors, explains the failure of most to attain financial independence. In the classic words of Adam Smith, the famous 18th century economist, "Parsimony, and not industry, is the immediate cause of the increase of capital. But whatever industry might acquire, if parsimony did not save and store up, the capital would never be the greater." [161, p. 320] To paraphrase this concept in modern English, "In the long run, the difference between those who become wealthy and all the rest is not the size of their income, but how much they save and how well they invest it." The value of parsimony is still recognized, as confirmed by the motto of many Wharton School graduates: "Happiness cannot buy money!"

Remember,

1. To attain a meaningful financial goal, you must invest.
2. The more you invest, and the earlier you invest it, the larger your capital should become.
3. The only source of investable funds is money that would otherwise go for current expenses.

It is helpful to contrast two approaches for providing these investable funds: a commonly accepted one that does not work and a simple one that does. The first begins with the premise that investable funds are those "left over" after expenses. But such an orientation is backward because it looks upon investing as "How much can I spare?" instead of viewing it as "What are my objectives, and how will I attain them?" The flaw in this first approach is that investing is continually forced to compete with our desire to consume, with the result that investing is too often postponed.

The second approach starts from the subtly different point of view that both insurance and investing fulfill imperative family objectives. Insurance is meant to guarantee the economic functioning of the family unit even without its income. It is more likely, however, that the present pattern will go on, in which case investments must be the vehicle for reaching financial objectives. This consideration, plus the enormous advantage of investing as early as possible, dictates a simple, but sensible, approach to financial planning: *insure, invest, and spend the rest!*

This approach begins by estimating the cost of providing for your dependents in your absence, and by using this estimate as a benchmark for determining reasonable insurance against contingencies, such as death, disaster, or disability. The second step is to invest enough, soon enough, to make the attainment of your financial goals a reality. These two steps secure your financial future. How to spend the remaining income is a matter of personal preference. The important point in this approach is to prevent the flow of investable funds from continuously being funneled into such things as a new car, a swimming pool, a vacation, or what have you, at the expense of attaining the financial future most people profess to want more, but mistakenly think they can postpone.

Staff, Direct, and Control

Few people can, or should, determine their insurance needs or manage their investments alone. Not since the Renaissance of the 1600s has one person been capable of being truly expert in all known areas. Today, there is almost infinitely more to know and life is much more complex. Estate planners, tax consultants, insurance specialists, investment counselors, and brokerage firms are available to aid investors in the myriad, specialized facets of financial management. For instance, your last will and testament (and everyone should have one) has tax and insurance implications, and vice versa. Your age, in turn, bears on the urgency and terms of your will, your income-earning ability and its duration, your insurance needs and costs, and your investment risk preferences.

Your personal financial plan and its management can benefit from the diverse skills of experienced professionals. This does not mean, however, that you can then divorce yourself from this task. In any organization, the staff must be both directed and controlled by management—in this case, you.

Toward this end, your annual tax return can become more than a necessary evil. It can also be your "annual financial checkup." This required annual accounting can pinpoint deviations from objectives that may cause you to change your investment plan. Thus, the concept of a financial lifeline helps you decide your financial objectives and lets you monitor planned performance.

The Responsibility Is Yours

Neither generals, managers, nor individuals can delegate responsibility. While you can give authority to others for action in your behalf, this does not relieve you of ultimate responsibility. This pervasive management principle was recognized as universal in the 1916 writings of the French industrialist Henri Fayol. For the modern investor, it means that the final responsibility for the business of your personal investing is yours alone.

3

Your Personal Financial Plan

Your Personal Financial Plan should be much like a security prospectus, which describes a company's current position and business objectives. It details your present financial status and aims. As shown pictorially in Figure 3–1, it helps you translate vague goals and uncertain contingencies into realistic investment objectives. Once these are set, *and not before,* you are prepared for more knowledgeable investing.

FIGURE 3–1

Preparing a Personal Financial Plan

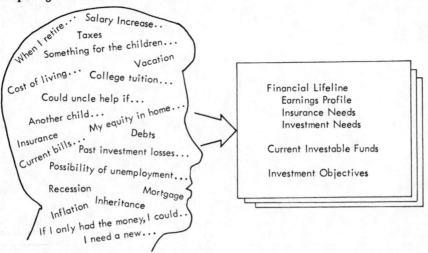

Financial Lifeline

Your financial lifeline is a "best guess" estimate of what is likely to occur. But being a "guess" does not destroy its usefulness. Once established, this projection provides important benchmarks against which to measure your future income and investment performance. Knowing whether you are on target, or above or below your forecast, tells you where you stand. But the projection should change when unforeseen events occur, such as the birth of triplets. Then you must replan in light of the "new developments."

Just as your forecast financial lifeline can change, so should your Personal Financial Plan. It is not to be dipped in bronze and forgotten. It deserves review, probably annually, and modification as facts and assumptions change.

Heads of households—whether single or with a family—have different responsibilities throughout the course of their financial lifeline. These are typified in Figure 3–2. In addition to providing income for current needs, a head-of-household's obligation to his or her family continues as long as there are surviving dependents. Thus, your Personal Financial Plan becomes a blueprint for meeting varying needs through all phases of your lifeline—with or without your earnings. The latter kind of protection is normally provided by insurance. In the more cheerful and probable event, your investments will be counted on to meet your needs, say, at retirement.

Because of the complexities of pension and Social Security income, expenses for college tuition, financing a home, and so forth, forecasting calls for specialized expertise and some calculations. For this reason, some firms offer detailed, computerized forecasts that plug in children's ages and education plans, retirement ambitions, pension rights, potential inheritance, and in some cases almost "the day you

FIGURE 3–2

Phases and Extraordinary Needs in a Typical Financial Lifeline

Phase 1	*Phase 2*	*Phase 3*	*Phase 4*	*Phase 5*	*Phase 6*	*Phase 7*
Dependent upon family	Employed, single head-of-household	Marriage and parenthood	Growing children	Children's education	Countdown years	Retirement
Personal education expenses	Acquire personal property	Home and related assets	Growing expenses, vacations	Multiple tuitions	Buildup for retirement	Secure lifetime income and capital base

trade the Cadillac for a three-wheel Schwinn." But for now, this chapter develops ball-park estimates of your earnings profile, insurance needs, and investment needs. We then help you assess your current investable funds and set a realistic objective.

Earnings Profile

One way to ascertain your insurance and investment needs is to calculate how much you are worth alive. Your total earnings between now and retirement represent the maximum economic loss your dependents would sustain by your premature death. The present value[1] of this lifetime earnings profile can be estimated from:

1. Your current employment income.
2. Your expected growth in employment income.
3. The number of working years until retirement.
4. An appropriate discount rate.

To simplify this calculation, we have used data from the U.S. Bureau of the Census to approximate your probable lifetime earnings. For people from ages 25 through 65, these representative earnings data have been discounted to their present value. The results, shown in Table 3–1, are based on:

1. Various levels of current employment income.
2. Actual income growth experienced by male college graduates of the various ages, as determined by the U.S. Bureau of the Census.
3. An assumed retirement age of 65.
4. A discount rate of 6 percent per year.

Using Table 3–1, you can approximate the present value of your remaining lifetime earnings by referring to your current age and income level. For example, if you are 25 years old and earning $15,000 annually, the discounted present value of your remaining income before retirement at age 65 is $378,930, assuming that your

---

[1] The present value of future money is defined as its value now. Regardless of inflation considerations, money obtained today can earn interest and thereby grow to a larger future amount. Thus, the present value of $1.00 to be received in one year, when discounted at 6 percent interest, is only 94.3 cents today. Stated another way, if you invest 94.3 cents at 6 percent today, you will have $1.00 (before taxes) one year from now. Hence, the present value of future income is found by discounting the amounts expected in the future back to their value today.

TABLE 3-1

Approximate Discounted Present Value of Remaining Lifetime Earnings

Current Age	Current Annual Income (from Employment)				
	$ 10,000	$ 15,000	$ 20,000	$ 30,000	$ 50,000
25	$252,620	$378,930	$505,240	$757,860	$1,263,100
26	236,610	354,915	473,220	709,830	1,183,050
27	223,160	334,740	446,320	669,480	1,115,800
28	211,660	317,490	423,320	634,980	1,058,300
29	201,650	302,475	403,300	604,950	1,008,250
30	192,790	289,185	385,580	578,370	963,950
31	184,820	277,230	369,640	554,460	924,100
32	177,580	266,370	355,160	532,740	887,900
33	170,930	256,395	341,860	512,790	854,650
34	164,790	247,185	329,580	494,370	823,950
35	159,060	238,590	318,120	477,180	795,300
36	153,680	230,520	307,360	461,040	768,400
37	148,600	222,900	297,200	445,800	743,000
38	143,780	215,670	287,560	431,340	718,900
39	139,160	208,740	278,320	417,480	695,800
40	134,730	202,095	269,460	404,190	673,650
41	130,440	195,660	260,880	391,320	652,200
42	126,260	189,390	252,520	378,780	631,300
43	122,150	183,225	244,300	366,450	610,750
44	118,090	177,135	236,180	354,270	590,450
45	114,050	171,075	228,100	342,150	570,250
46	109,990	164,985	219,980	329,970	549,950
47	105,920	158,880	211,840	317,760	529,600
48	101,790	152,685	203,580	305,370	508,950
49	97,570	146,355	195,140	292,710	487,850
50	93,270	139,905	186,540	279,810	466,350
51	88,840	133,260	177,680	266,520	444,200
52	84,300	126,450	168,600	252,900	421,500
53	79,600	119,400	159,200	238,800	398,000
54	74,720	112,080	149,440	224,160	373,600
55	69,640	104,460	139,280	208,920	348,200
56	64,330	96,495	128,660	192,990	321,650
57	58,750	88,125	117,500	176,250	293,750
58	55,790	83,685	111,580	167,370	278,950
59	47,200	70,800	94,400	141,600	236,000
60	40,640	60,960	81,280	121,920	203,200
61	33,650	50,475	67,300	100,950	168,250
62	26,170	39,255	52,340	78,510	130,850
63	18,130	27,195	36,260	54,390	90,650
64	9,430	14,145	18,860	28,290	47,150

Source: Table derived from Census Bureau data in *Current Population Reports, Consumer Income, Annual Mean Income, Lifetime Income, and Educational Attainment of Men in the United States, for Selected Years, 1956 to 1966*, Series P–60, No. 56, August 14, 1968.

income growth equals that achieved historically by male college graduates. A 42-year-old currently earning $30,000 a year also has essentially this same present value of income if he or she works to age 65 and makes typical progress. Use Table 3–1 to approximate the current value of *your* remaining lifetime earnings. This figure provides a useful benchmark for evaluating your life insurance needs.

Insurance Needs

Life or income insurance is designed to finance a dependent's consumption in the event that the household head is unable to provide such support. Insurance sustains the financial lifeline without income from the insured.

Both the number and type of one's dependents influence the amount required in the absence of this income. A young couple with two small children, and burdened by the debts of household formation, have different insurance needs than a childless, high-salaried couple. In the former case, the economic impact of the husband's premature death would be severe, whereas a working wife is already self-sufficient and might easily remarry, especially if she is without children. As Professor John Bowyer of Washington University put it, "The amount of life insurance a man carries should be in an inverse relationship to the relative attractiveness of his wife." [12, p. 27]

The present value of your future earnings, estimated from Table 3–1, represents the *maximum economic loss* that your family would suffer if your income stopped today. It is not necessary, *or prudent*, to insure yourself against this maximum potential loss. First of all, the purpose of insurance is to make sure your dependents are cared for. Without any dependents, you do not, for example, need life insurance in excess of your estate expenses. Moreover, even if you have several dependents, not all of your future earnings would have been used to support them. A significant percentage of this projected income would have to go for taxes, insurance premiums, investments, and the portion consumed by you. Furthermore, sources of income other than earnings, such as dividends, interest, pensions, Social Security benefits, or the liquidation of assets, also offset the need for insurance.

In formulating your insurance program, remember that the primary objective of insurance is to guard against an unexpected loss of earnings. Many forms of insurance supply this protection plus an investment return. For example, a whole life policy builds up cash values. But while both insurance and investment represent true financial needs, the policy that provides the best insurance usually does not also provide the best investment.

This conflict is too often overlooked because the sale of insurance and the sale of other investment instruments have traditionally been handled by different groups of salesmen. From both an economic and a consumer-investor point of view, this is an artificial separation. A sound financial plan needs elements of both insurance and investment and not the conflicting interests of competing salesmen.

Insurance is a complex subject, and a thorough analysis of it is helpful. But at the risk of incurring the wrath of the insurance industry, you can easily make a ball-park estimate of your needs. If you have no dependent relatives or children needing support, a strategy of *minimum* (burial expenses) insurance and maximum investment is appropriate. The other end of the spectrum is typified by a young,

FIGURE 3–3

Approximate Percentage of Remaining Lifetime Earnings That Should Be Protected by Insurance

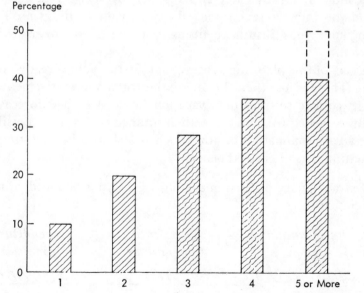

Number of Dependents (without other foreseeable means of support)

Source: Table

large family without investment or pension income to help offset their insurance needs. After subtracting income taxes, insurance premiums, savings, investments, and head-of-household consumption from such a family's current income, the remaining consumption by dependents might amount to 50 percent of the family's gross income, hinging mainly on family size.

The percentage of remaining lifetime earnings that should be protected by life insurance can be approximated from Figure 3–3. A person with no dependents has no need for insurance beyond estate expenses. The addition of a spouse, or aged relative, usually implies an insurance burden. And the addition of successive children increases the need for insurance in two ways. First, the required child care can prevent the surviving spouse from seeking employment, or child-care costs can erode the income obtained from employment. Second, each new child adds to expenses. The large family's needs taper off, however, when the older children become independent or can even make a contribution.

Investment Needs

The successful attainment of your investment objectives is made much more likely by early and regular investing. But how much should you invest? Having looked first at your earnings profile and having met your insurance needs, you are ready to answer this question.

As part of this planning process, look first to your already-invested funds. Then adjust them by any extraordinary preretirement costs, such as college tuitions or a vacation home. Detailed forecasts are clearly very helpful, but, as with insurance needs, it is possible to make an approximation of how much you should be investing. One such estimate is illustrated below:

1. Extraordinary preretirement objectives (not financed from current earnings) :

Extraordinary Item	Years until Expenditure	Expenditure Amount
Son's College	10	$20,000
Daughter's College	15	$20,000

2.   Retirement objective (in excess of pensions, etc.) :

Years until
Retirement   *Goal*

<u>25</u> $250,000

These objectives can be balanced against the return you expect
from your investments in order to determine:

1.   Whether your current investments will fulfill your objectives.
2.   The size and urgency of needed new investments.

In gauging your current investments against future expenditures,
care should be taken not to compound funds you do not have. Sup-

TABLE 3–2

**Value of Each $1,000 of Lump-Sum Investment
Compounded Annually at an After-Tax Return of
7.5 Percent**

Years Invested	*Value of Investment*
1	$ 1,075
2	1,156
3	1,242
4	1,336
5	1,436
10	2,061
15	2,959
20	4,247
25	6,098
30	8,755
35	12,569
40	18,044

pose, for example, that our illustrative family has current investments of $20,000. As shown, they would like to have $20,000 for
their son's education ten years from now. Table 3–2 shows the
future value of a lump-sum investment. In ten years, with a 7.5
percent compounded annual after-tax return, a present investment
will roughly double. Thus, $10,000 of the family's current holdings
needs to be earmarked for the son's education. (Note: This analysis
also gives you valuable information about the risks you are willing
to take with money designated for various planned extraordinary
items.)

In our example, the daughter will be of college age in 15 years.
One might reasonably expect the current value of an investment to

triple by then. Assuming that the $20,000 college cost is again valid, roughly another $7,000 of the family's current investments must be earmarked for the daughter's education. Suppose the father is 35 years old and expects to retire in 25 years, at age 60. By then, the nonearmarked $3,000 in his current portfolio should grow about sixfold, according to Table 3–2. This produces $18,000 by his retirement. Almost certainly, additional investments will be necessary.

To give an idea of the cumulating benefits of ongoing investment, Table 3–3 shows the value of routinely investing $1,000 per year over various numbers of years. Again, an after-tax rate of return of 7.5 percent annually is used for the projections. Table 3–3 shows

TABLE 3–3

Value of Yearly Investment of $1,000 Compounded Annually at an After-Tax Return of 7.5 Percent

Years until Goal	Value of Investment
1	$ 1,000
2	2,075
3	3,231
4	4,473
5	5,808
10	14,147
15	26,118
20	43,305
25	67,978
30	103,399
35	154,252
40	227,257

that a person with 25 years until retirement can expect to augment his retirement nest egg by about $68,000 by routinely investing $1,000 each year. But if retirement goals are higher, one must invest more. In the case of our illustrative family with virtually all of its current investments earmarked for the children's college educations, the goal of $250,000 at retirement calls for ongoing investments of over $3,400 per year—attainable probably, but requiring adherence to a *plan*.

Current Investable Funds

Many investors, as well as investment advisers, make the mistake of rushing to look at the income statements and balance sheets of prospective investments before analyzing the comparable facts about the prospective investor. Every publicly owned company is required to prepare a certified annual report that summarizes its assets and income. By contrast, most investors—even those who carefully monitor their stocks in daily newspapers—lack accurate measures of their personal investment performance toward realistic goals. Before deciding where you are going, and how you are going to get there, determine where you are *now* by assessing the amount of your investable funds.

In determining your current investable funds, it is important to separate the foundation layer of your capital structure from the three investment layers. Individuals own property to fulfill a variety of requirements, including the need for living accommodations (houses, furniture, cars, and so forth) , the desire for items that bring aesthetic appreciation and, in some instances, capital appreciation (art, antiques, jewelry, and so forth) , and the desire for pure investments. Foundation assets are rarely sold to finance the future. They make life more comfortable, while investments are designed to take care of the future. Your current investments should not be confused with your seldom-sold foundation capital.

More important, such an evaluation forces consideration of special events, such as death or retirement contingencies. Say, for example, that Mr. and Mrs. Dow, a couple in their late 40s with two teenage children, own a $100,000 house. What is its:

1.   Net sale value for financing the children's education?
2.   Net sale value in the event of Mr. Dow's death?
3.   Net sale value at retirement age?

Looking at foundation-level assets in these terms forces one to think beyond their current value. Will the house be sold to finance the children's education? Probably not. What will Mrs. Dow do with the house if her husband dies unexpectedly? She might *plan* to sell it and buy a $60,000 house. They could then reasonably put a planned net sale value of $40,000 on the house in this event. What will they do with the house when they retire? If they keep it, its planned net sale value would be zero.

Investment Objectives

Finally, you now have enough information about your needs and means to determine sound, realistic investment objectives for *you*. Given your financial lifeline and current investable funds, you can plan a course of action likely to reach a meaningful and attainable goal. After you have insured adequately, and assessed the long-term value of your current holdings, achieving your goal depends on:

1. Your ongoing investment amounts.
2. Your overall after-tax rate of return.

You must make the commitment to provide the first. Then this book will help you increase the second.

You have taken step one of successful investing by deciding on your personal investment objectives. Step two translates these objectives into your plan for reaching them. It acts as a road map to guide and monitor your investment performance, with replanning as necessary. The third step—and our focus from here on—is selecting the combination of vehicles that will carry you to your financial destination.

Summary

Let us briefly review the important points of the last two chapters, as they are crucial to financial success. Before investing, or even trying to improve your results with new knowledge, gain an accurate perspective on your investment objectives. These depend on your *financial lifeline*—a composite of current and future income until retirement (or some other time). Then, estimate your and your dependents' future needs. After insuring, set your investment objectives and work out a realistic plan for attaining them. Your plan will depend on your current investable funds, the annual amounts you invest less any extraordinary expenses, the length of time before your goals, and the after-tax rate of return you achieve on your investments. The balance of this book will help you improve that important final factor—*the rate of return on your investments!*

4

Investing—Art or Science?

Is successful investing an *art* or a *science?* This question captures the philosophic difference between the "old school" and the emerging practice of capital management. The old-school view has been expressed (by a well-known money manager) something like this:

I've been in this business for 45 years, including managing O.P.M. [Other People's Money] since Tarzan was a boy. No one can tell me it is a science. It is an art. Now there are computers and all sorts of statistics but they have not improved our understanding of the market. It is still personal intuition and the sensing of market patterns.

If, as an investor, you do not find that quotation alarming, consider what would have happened if Wernher von Braun, the respected space scientist, were quoted as saying:

I conducted my first experiments with liquid-fuel rockets at Berlin-Ploetzesee in 1930. I have been spending other people's money ever since. No one can tell me it is a science. It is an art. Now there are computers and all sorts of statistics but they have not improved our understanding of rockets and space. It is still personal intuition and the sensing of cosmic patterns.

Computer-based analysis and research have contributed to knowledge in innumerable fields. Isn't it reasonable to suppose that they have also helped our understanding of investing in common stocks and related instruments?

For a fact, the combined efforts of hundreds of researchers, augmented by modern computer technology, have substantially increased our understanding of the stock market. Yet, people who do not know about this recent research or do not know how to apply it, may debate this point. They contend that investing is an indefinable art. To such people, "personal intuition" is the cornerstone of the art of investing. But in this era is intuition good enough?

Intuition

Suppose someone offered you an even money bet that 2 of the next 25 people you meet will have the same birthday. You would quickly reason that, excluding leap year, there are 365 possible birthdays and, at most, only 25 days could be represented by 25 people. You might even calculate that 25 is only 6.8 percent of 365. Intuitively, it seems unlikely that two of these people would have been born on the same day. Would you take a bet that will double your money if no 2 people out of the next 25 you meet have the same birthday? Would you take the same bet for the next 50 people? The next 100? The next 180?

The answer is that you should not take any of the bets! With 25 randomly selected people, it is more likely than not that 2 of them have the same birthday.[1] This is counter to most people's intuition, but true. Yet, in the face of uncertainty, people tend to trust their intuition. Furthermore, the analysis of our birthday bet involves combinatorial probability theory, which is difficult (and uninteresting) for most people.

These same characteristics mark much of the recent scientific stock market research. First, many of the findings contradict our intuition. Second, it is difficult for most investors, as well as many market professionals, to evaluate these findings because the underlying research relies heavily on mathematics and statistical inference. As a result, most investors and many market professionals are uncertain about

---

[1] The birthday wager can be explained by noting that each person you meet has a *progressively better chance* of causing a birthday match. Some rather unintuitive results of the relevant mathematical calculation are summarized below:

Number of people	10	20	22	23	25	30	40	50
Likelihood of two matching birthdays (in percent)	12	41	48	51	59	71	89	97

Hence, with as few as 23 people it is a better than 50–50 bet that 2 will have matching birthdays. With 50 people, you have a 97 percent chance of having 2 with the same birthday. Unintuitive, but true.

the meaning and significance of the findings. Yet, such research has made positive contributions to sound investing—and will continue to do so.

As with the birthday wager, you will find that much of the information here is contrary to your intuition, the age-old tenets of Wall Street, or both. Thus, to understand and use this new knowledge effectively, you should try to adopt the totally fresh viewpoint of the unindoctrinated. You should strive to set aside what you "know" about the stock market and instead take an objective look at what has been learned in the last 15 years. If you have difficulty doing this, you might consider taking your intuition and money to Las Vegas—where you will no doubt have more fun losing both. But whether you decide to go to Las Vegas or to invest, it will be helpful to look at the "laws of chance" that underlie both gambling and the stock market.

Laws of Chance

The phrase *laws of chance* appears contradictory at first glance. On the one hand, "laws" implies predictability, while on the other, "chance" implies unpredictability. We expect laws to state that something will always happen in a certain way. For example, the law of gravity states that all objects, regardless of their weight, will fall toward the center of the earth with the same rate of acceleration. This law is readily accepted because it is invariant and can be easily demonstrated by an experiment.

Yet, even this basic law was not accepted before Galileo's investigations in the early 1600s. Before his time, the accepted intuition of the "old school" had obscured the facts. Consider for a moment the following quotation from a popular physics text:

Galileo's . . . work can be considered a turning point not merely in the history of physics but in the history of the natural sciences as well. Theretofore, people were attempting to philosophize laws of nature out of some vague, often meaningless "principles." They often drew perfectly logical conclusions from wrong premises and "derived" "natural laws" which were in contradiction to experience. Since no one made efforts to check these "laws" by experiment, they were accepted and dominated "scientific thought" for well over a millennium.

Aristotle's assertion that "bodies fall faster in proportion to their weight" provides a classic example of such "laws of nature." This statement is wrong, and Aristotle could have easily disproved it by trial. But the experimental method, which appears natural to us, evidently was not obvious to him or to most of his contemporaries and followers. Aristotle's contributions to science and philosophy are monumental in fields involving pure reasoning and observation. They are for the most part worthless or lacking in fields such as physics where the acquisition of knowledge must depend on experimentation. In fact, his [Aristotle's] authority in physics dominated thought for many centuries and materially blocked progress in this field. [**93**, pp. 16–17]

Galileo had the temerity to question the wisdom of Aristotle and, in so doing, changed the course of history. His experiments showed that, contrary to popular belief, heavy objects fall no more rapidly than do light objects. In fact, unless impeded by air resistance, all objects fall to earth at the same rate regardless of their weight. What had been intuitively correct for generations of mankind, as a result of their observing falling feathers and rocks, was wrong!

In recent years, many researchers have similarly dared to question Wall Street's traditional "laws of nature." They have sought to verify the worth of Wall Street's investing techniques by rigorous experiments. In so doing, they have challenged the intuitive shibboleths of the investment profession—thus preaching heresy in the view of some—which makes the comparison to Galileo complete. As students of history will recall, Galileo was condemned by the Inquisition for heresy—a sobering thought for the authors!

Although the law of gravity long eluded our understanding, its truth can be verified by experiments. Indeed, a feather and a rock were simultaneously dropped from the same height by an astronaut on the moon. As was televised to the world, in the absence of air resistance both fell at the same speed.

The laws of chance, by contrast, are disturbing because they appear to vary. How can laws govern chance or random behavior? Laws of chance would seem to be lawless by definition! Fortunately for Las Vegas and Monte Carlo, events governed by chance do not vary in a haphazard fashion. Their behavior can be specified quite precisely.

Knowing the Odds

You know, for example, that in Las Vegas the customers lose and the house wins. Otherwise, the roulette wheels would not keep spinning night after night. Nonetheless, many people believe that certain individuals, like lucky old "Aunt Sarah," can win at roulette.

And it may be true that Aunt Sarah *has* won at roulette. Winning in the past, unfortunately, does not improve the odds that Aunt Sarah, or anyone else, *will* win the next time.

Statistics tell us that no system can be devised to succeed against a fair roulette wheel. But statistics also tell us that some people will win. It's just that the odds are that any one person will lose. And, importantly, the longer you play, the more certain it becomes that you will lose! If no amount of evidence can make you *really* believe this, then you are an incurable optimist. Yet, in spite of this awesome certainty of losing in the long run, some people like to play roulette. Las Vegas and Monte Carlo—like certain investing strategies—persist even though the odds are unfavorable.

A far more exciting game than roulette is the one the famous economist John Maynard Keynes referred to as "the game of professional investment." An intriguing aspect of this game for the 25 million shareholders playing it is the fact that, unlike in gambling, the odds of winning are *in their favor!* Unhappily, this fact alone does not guarantee successful investing. The "game" of professional investing is played with a myriad of investment instruments and selection techniques. The informed player should know the "odds" of each.

The research examined in this book calculates those odds. It does not rely on "intuition" or on what people "think" about the market. The conclusions distilled and reported here were derived from modern tools of scientific inquiry and statistical inference. As presented here, the conclusions can be understood and applied by any investor. But to enable you to appreciate the research more fully, it will be helpful to cite three related laws of chance.

The first law states that chance occurrences are individually unpredictable. (In academic parlance, such events are said to be statistically independent or random.) The second law states that, while random events are not individually predictable, one can accurately predict the average of many such events (called the "expected value" by statisticians). The third law states how much variation from this average we might reasonably expect.

Implications for Gamblers

Let's return to the question of the gambler's odds. Gamblers often devise betting schemes based on a streak of similar events. After observing a sequence of one result, say, two consecutive blacks in roulette, they adopt a particular betting strategy. Some reason that three blacks in a row is relatively rare and bet against another black. Conversely, others reason that the game is "running hot" and that black has a better-than-normal chance on the next spin. *These are both useless betting systems,* assuming that the roulette wheel is fair and unbiased. *Any* system would be useless—random events are unpredictable. The fascination lies in hoping that the events are *not* random, and then discovering a system to predict them.

Statistical techniques have indeed been used to determine whether a roulette wheel is "fair." Some readers may remember pictures of Albert Hibbs sipping milk at a Las Vegas roulette table while his partner, Roy Walford, tabulated the frequency of various wins. By studying a wheel's performance for several days, Hibbs and Walford were able to detect nonrandom behavior patterns on certain wheels. Once they had established with a high degree of reliability that certain nonrandom events were happening, they were able to translate this nonchance behavior into a winning strategy. While in no case could they predict the "next event," they were able to say that, because of biases in the mechanical performance of the wheel, certain numbers occurred more often than would be expected if the wheel were mechanically perfect.

Implications for Investors

You may be asking yourself: "What does roulette have to do with investing?" Simply stated, understanding the difference between chance occurrences and predictable events will help you accept, despite your intuition, some important research results described in upcoming chapters. For example, some studies have begun by asking: How would stock prices behave if each day's price changes were completely independent of previous price changes?

To find patterns in roulette wheel performance, one first assumes that the wheel's outcomes will be purely random. Then, actual performance is measured against this benchmark. Similarly, stock price changes can be studied for variations from normal behavior. We might find *price patterns* or *economic facts and forecasts* that do allow us to predict future stock prices with a useful degree of accuracy.

This kind of research—explained and applied here—has uncovered *knowledge that can positively help investors.*

part two
Understanding the Stock Market

5

Common Stock Investing

Why buy common stocks? Nine people out of ten—and maybe all ten—would say something like, "Because you hope they will go up!" Most investors strive for capital gains. It's glamorous. Growth is the vogue objective. The best stories are of supergrowth; the worst, of capital losses. Either way, the stock market's constantly moving prices can fascinate, and at the same time terrify, investors.

What causes these stock price movements? The simple answer to this question is "supply and demand." But this trite reply omits some important details—such as *who* of the millions of shareholders are buying, *why,* and *what prices* they will pay for *which companies* from among the over 3,000 listed on the major exchanges plus the well over 10,000 unlisted public companies. To some, the stock market's complexity is part of its challenge and appeal. Arcane techniques for predicting price movements, espoused by various would-be financial wizards, are part of the folklore.

Total Return

Of course, there is another reason to buy stocks. Dividends. When dividends are combined with capital gains or losses, they tally up to what is called *total return.* For example, a stock bought at $20 might pay $1 in annual dividends for a 5 percent yield. Suppose the stock's price bobs around for a year and ends at $22, which is up 10 percent.

Then, the investor's total return equals the 5 percent yield plus the 10 percent capital gain—or 15 percent for the year.

The fact is that stock prices fluctuate much more than dividends. So price change usually accounts for most of total return—one way or the other. Yet, on average and in the long run, dividends have contributed nearly *half* of the total returns on stocks. Even with the possibility of more rapid inflation than in past decades and of corporate capital needs that may restrain dividends, dividends will probably account for at least a third of future total returns. Not in every year or for every stock, but across the market and over a decade or so.

Investment Horizons

Who invests for a decade? Well, perhaps surprisingly, many companies' shares are held for ten years or longer. Only 6 percent of AT&T's outstanding shares trade in a typical year, and only 9 percent of IBM's, to cite the world's two most valuable corporations. And while it is true that smaller firms often have higher stock turnover, the NYSE as a whole takes about five years to turn over its share ownership.

Even if you invest just for next month, when you sell, the buyer will be looking ahead from there. So will the buyer to whom your buyer sells, and on it goes. In theory, a stock's price today reflects all that is expected of it—*forever*. In practice, you only worry about *your income* while holding plus *your selling price*. But that price depends on what the next buyer expects to get, and around we go again.

It all comes down to a simple formula:

*A stock's long-term total return is that provided by **all** its future dividends.*

Since forever's stream of dividends is a bit hard to discern, a simplification is commonly made:

A stock's long-term total return is its current dividend yield plus its long-term dividend growth rate.

This formula is far easier to deal with. You first compute the stock's "current dividend yield"—the annual dividend stated as a percentage of the stock's current price. For our $1 dividend on a $20 stock, it is 5 percent. Then you must forecast the stock's long-term dividend growth rate. Since dividends flow from earnings, the issue is often recast as an estimate of the earnings growth rate. For how long? Sorry you asked—*forever* again.

On a Clear Day . . .

Lacking such foresight, mortals often choose another simplification toward estimating a stock's total return. They impose a reasonable time horizon and predict the stock's likely price at that time. Suppose, for example, that we expect our $20 stock to pay $1 dividend initially, with increases of 10 percent annually over the next five years. In line with this growing dividend, the stock price is also projected to grow at 10 percent annually. The results are shown in Table 5–1.

TABLE 5–1

Computing Total Return

Year	Annual Dividend	Year-End Stock Price	Annual Profit (dividend + gain)	Total Return (profit/price)
1................	$1.00	$22.00	$3.00	15%
2................	1.10	24.20	3.30	15
3................	1.21	26.62	3.63	15
4................	1.33	29.28	3.99	15
5................	1.46	32.21	4.39	15

The year 1 profit is $1 in dividends and $2 in capital gains. This $3 profit represents a 15 percent total return on the $20 initially invested—stemming 5 percent from dividend yield and 10 percent from capital gains. In the second year, the dividends and capital gains increase, thus increasing that year's profit to $3.30. But this still represents a 15 percent total return on *that* year's beginning stock price of $22. The dividends at 5 percent plus steady growth at 10 percent provide a total return of 15 percent compounded annually.

What happens if we suspect that dividend growth will not be steady? Or if the stock price grows faster or slower than dividends? We approach our pocket calculators as the plot thickens. We might also compute the total return resulting from several different—but possible—selling prices. We might even estimate the probability of each price occurring. All this is fine theory, but let's review the typical investor's real decision problem.

Relevant versus Irrelevant Information

The linchpin of investing is decision making. The decision constantly facing every investor, or potential investor, is whether to buy, sell, or hold. Success in these decisions depends on how well you separate the *relevant* from the *irrelevant* information.

Most people assume that decision makers suffer from a lack of relevant information. After all, the most common decision is "decide now." But in the last 15 years, the decision process has been subjected to intense scrutiny by managers and schools of management alike. As a result, many business practitioners and educators contend that understanding the role of information in decision making is the vital skill—not only in investing, but in any profession.

In fact, the real problem most decision makers face is how to deal with an *overabundance of information,* most of it irrelevant. Effective decision making then depends on the knowledge and ability to differentiate between what is relevant and what is not. It is the *quality* of information that counts, not the quantity.

Investors provide the classic example of decision makers who face this overabundance. Using the same basic data, corps of security analysts provide literally tons of research reports to legions of brokers. They, in turn, pass out a constant flow of recommendations to an army of investors. Thus the daily battle between buyers and sellers is one between people who have access to the same information—but disagree. Consequently, the key to superior decision making is knowing what information is relevant and then how to apply it to your personal investing.

Why Stock Prices Move

If we had to express why stock prices move in one word, it would be *expectations.* Whether supported by theory and statistical analysis or just a hunch, a decision reflects what we expect will happen. And since stock price rises or slumps contribute so importantly to total return, especially in the shorter run, we naturally form these opinions in terms of stock price movements. Opinions like "Polaroid will bounce back" or "Upjohn has had it" may or may not prove correct, but they are the kind of beliefs that investors form—and act upon.

Predicting stock price movements is a major topic in this book. But even after you knowledgeably use the right information, events can still differ from your expectations. As investor expectations change, a stock's price will change—and it may do so without any intervening transactions at all. How *certain* must you be in order to buy or sell? In part, this depends on the cost of you changing your mind.

The Cost of Change

Transactions cost is the economist's term for what Street people call "the cost of doing business." To invest in common stocks, you must employ a stockbroker and pay his fee. Brokerage commission rates, on major exchanges, were specified for most trades until May 1, 1975. Then, bending to pressure from the Securities and Exchange Commission and some leaders within the industry, the exchanges began to allow price competition in all stock brokerage charges.

The result is that you can now buy stocks with or without such related services as research, custody of certificates, loans collateralized by your securities (margin accounts), or portfolio accounting. The brokerage commission you pay may vary accordingly.

Generally, however, transactions costs to buy or sell are roughly 1 percent of the total invested for high-priced stocks bought in 100-share lots. For example, buying 100 shares of a $60 stock costs about $60 in commissions. The "round trip" cost of both buying and selling is therefore 2 percent. It takes about a 1¼-point price gain in the stock to cover this two-way commission.

For low-priced stocks the percentage commission climbs. A $10 stock times 100 shares is only $1,000, yet the broker's effort and paperwork are essentially the same as for the $60-stock transaction. The commission might be about $30 to buy or sell 100 shares of this $10 stock. The round trip cost is therefore $60, or 6 percent, of the total invested. Hence, you have to be even *more certain* about your trades in low-priced stocks because of the higher portion that goes for commissions.

Over-the-counter stocks (stocks not listed on a major exchange) can be even more expensive to buy and sell. They are quoted with a *bid* and *ask* price, for example, 5 bid and 5½ asked. This half-point difference—called the *spread*—is also an element of transactions costs. A round trip can easily cost 10 percent or more of the total invested in such a stock.

Large investors, especially institutions, have the advantage of proportionally lower commission costs due to their large-volume orders. However, they sometimes disrupt the market with their big orders, often adversely affecting their own results. (We will discuss this *liquidity* issue later.)

The point is that, because of transactions costs, both individuals and institutions should generally avoid rapid turnover. As mentioned, most people actually hold a few years, and many hold indefinitely. Still, to participate you must pay commissions. And there are many good reasons to sell what you once bought. Some transactions costs must be expected. Remember, however, that on Wall Street they say that short-term traders don't get rich, but their brokers do. *Your* objective is to make *you* wealthy.

What Can You Expect?

Many people expect miracles from stocks and from other forms of investing as well. Surveys have disclosed this systematic optimism. So it is wise to learn the true odds early.

Fortunately, we can uncover such historical facts because of the quantitative nature of stock prices and the standardized, centralized, and publicized markets for them that have been developed. Each day the *Wall Street Journal* lists well over 10,000 numbers recording stock price movements. Over months and years, and with computers to do the donkeywork, we can tally the average behavior of stock price movements.

The first such comprehensive tabulation of long-term common stock returns was developed in a classic and often-quoted study published by Lawrence Fisher and James Lorie of the University of Chicago. [50] They showed that the typical rate of return on New York Stock Exchange common stocks between 1926 and 1960 was nearly 10 percent per year. Clearly, however, there were variations from year to year and from stock to stock.

A follow-up study selected individual stocks and measured their total rate of return over various holding periods within the 1926–60

FIGURE 5-1

**Frequency Distribution of Rates of Return on Investment in Each Common Stock
Listed on the New York Stock Exchange, 1926–60, Using All Possible Combinations
of Month-End Purchase and Sale Dates (based on 56,557,538 cases)**

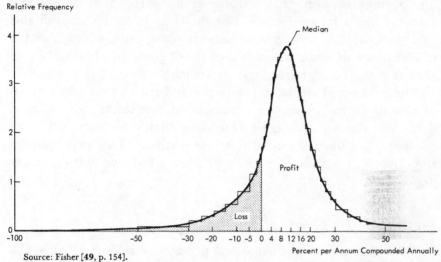

Source: Fisher [49, p. 154].

time span of the available data. In all, 56,557,538 combinations of
stocks and holding periods were tabulated. (Not even graduate
students would stand for that, so computers were used.) The range
of results—showing that 78 percent of these transactions produced
profits—are shown in Figure 5–1.

Expect the Unexpected

Investing involves the future. But after an investment has been
made, the in-advance odds no longer apply—by then, a particular
outcome has occurred. This can be a frustrating side of the stock
market that detracts from the fascination felt by many investors. For
example, the morning newspaper unremittingly shows us the winners we missed and "what could have been." But don't forget that
the biggest percentage gainers for a day are 1 in 1,000 and that your
holding horizons are a good deal longer than a single day's gyrations.

Part of knowledgeable investing is knowing the odds of the *unexpected* as well as the average. The study results depicted in Figure
5–1 involved fairly long holding periods—usually a decade or more.
Most stocks do provide positive returns over such a long time span.

The economy rarely slumps for a whole decade, and the company's management has time to change its strategy—or be changed.

By contrast, when stocks are held for only a year, the odds change. The average, on average, is still the same (except that transactions costs become a bigger factor). But the chances for an unprofitable trade go up. Held for very short periods (days), stocks have about as much chance of going *down* as they do of going up. It is only over time that their long-term trend exerts itself.

The *number* of stocks you hold also influences your likely range of results. Investing an equal amount in five stocks, for instance, draws you closer to average performance than does being subjected to the typical fluctuations of just one of them. This principle has important implications for *diversification,* which we will discuss in depth later.

Getting Rich Gradually

Table 5–2 provides an updated perspective on the returns produced by investing in common stocks compared to other vehicles. Note that "Savings" have provided a modest, but always positive, total rate of return. "Long-Term Bonds" fluctuate in price and often return less than their face interest rate, unless held to maturity. "Stocks," as represented by the Standard & Poor's index, show good gains in most periods but meager results in others. Having the highest average return, stocks also exhibit the most *risk,* or variation in rate of return.

The 1926–1973 average stock market return was *9.3 percent per year compounded.* What does this mean for individual investors? First, it means that few years and few stocks will return exactly that

TABLE 5–2

Annual Total Rates of Return and Inflation (*total return* includes both income and capital gain or loss)

	Savings	Long-Term Bonds	S&P Stocks	Inflation
1926–29	4.0%	4.4%	19.2%	−0.6%
1930–39	0.8	6.9	−0.1	−2.1
1940–49	0.5	3.0	9.0	5.5
1950–59	1.9	0.9	19.2	2.0
1960–69	3.8	1.3	7.8	2.3
1970–73	5.2	9.3	4.6	5.4

Source: [75].

rate. Early in both 1975 and 1976, stocks roared ahead at several times that rate of gain. So a 9.3 percent historical average may sound rather mediocre to some. But this rate doubles your money in less than eight years (before taxes). It quadruples capital in 15.6 years. And in the 35-year span of a typical career, capital growing at 9.3 percent compounded annually expands by over *20-fold*.

Fallacy of the Short Run

The game of patience and percentages can be nicely, if not wildly, rewarding. Unfortunately, some investors think only about the short run. Indeed, in the view of some, "the action begins again at 10 A.M. tomorrow," and "a long-term hold" means until after lunch. But trying to succeed consistently in the short run is difficult—despite the powerful *intuitive* appeal of parlaying several small, quick gains into a fortune. For example, what would a year's subscription to *tomorrow's* newspaper be worth?

Suppose an investor begins the year with $1,000. Further imagine that he is able to pick *tomorrow's best-performing NYSE stock* each day for a year. If he could buy unlimited amounts at the day's open and sell at the day's close, at year-end even with commissions our investor would *own the world!* No one has come close yet. Investing to get rich gradually is more certain, if less exciting, than trying to get rich quickly.

6

Trends and Patterns

The techniques used to analyze stock price movements are broadly classified as either *fundamental* or *technical*. Fundamentalists attempt to predict stock price behavior from factors which are "fundamental," or internal, to the company, its industry, or the economy (for example, earnings, products, management, competition, consumer spending, and so forth). A market fundamentalist might buy if a company has shown good year-to-year earnings increases, is in an industry that he believes will grow faster than the economy, and yet its stock sells at a historically low multiple of earnings and book value.

Technicians, on the other hand, hold that all such fundamental factors are reflected in the stock's price behavior. All data of importance are internal to the stock market itself. Thus, pure technicians contend that future stock prices can be predicted from diligent study of past stock prices and trading volume. A market technician might, therefore, buy based on a particular pattern of recent price and volume changes.

Many security analysts rely on a combination of fundamental and technical information. In fact, a study guide used by brokers to prepare for securities examinations asks, "Which kind of analysis should be used to select stocks?" and provides as the standard answer to this question, "both fundamental and technical." (See Loll [107, p. 110]) Despite the widespread acceptance of both analytic methods, raging differences of opinion exist on their usefulness and accuracy. We will examine the research evidence supporting or refuting each approach.

46

Technical Analysis of Price Movements

Technical analysis, in its strictest definition, uses past stock price patterns in an attempt to predict future stock prices. Knowing future prices would be enormously useful, but can it be done?

A price *chart*—sometimes including trading volume, a market trend line, or still other indicators—is the technician's principal tool. Charts are a useful visual record of a stock's past performance. Financial newspapers print charts on the overall market each day, and research publications depict the individual movements of thousands of stocks. Figure 6–1 shows a representative bar chart for the

FIGURE 6–1

A Stock Market Price Chart

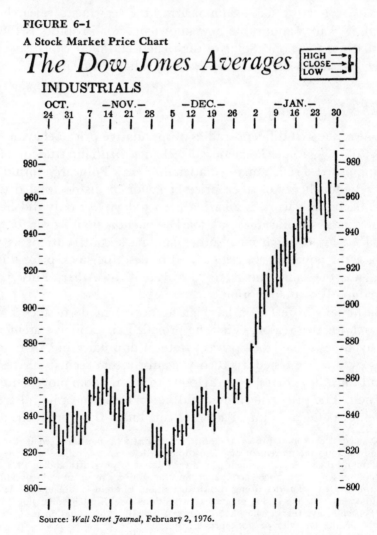

Source: *Wall Street Journal*, February 2, 1976.

Dow Jones Industrial Average's daily high, low, and closing prices.

Chart devotees draw lines on these price graphs and apply a set of rules to determine when extraordinary or predictable price patterns seem to be developing. We have already confirmed one pattern—on average, stocks rise moderately in price. To derive extra benefit from technical analysis, we must decipher which stocks can be expected to stray from this average or whether the market itself is doing better or worse than average.

We should expect long-run success with or without price charts. We want to know whether the charts can provide any *extra* profit from investing. Rather than take a technician's word on this issue, we will review the facts. Summarizing the legitimate research and distilling it into applicable new knowledge for investors is the key approach of this book. Some of the richest and most conclusive findings concern this very issue, so let us see what is *known*.

In the Beginning . . .

One of the first diligent studies of speculative price behavior dates back to 1900. Louis Bachelier [5], then a brilliant student of the distinguished French mathematician Henri Poincaré, formulated and tested a theory of stock price behavior in his doctoral dissertation. Bachelier's work is amazing even today. Not only did he discover a most significant stock market phenomenon—over 75 years ago—but his research made other landmark contributions as well. In fact, the equation Bachelier used to describe stock price fluctuations was the same one later "discovered" by Albert Einstein for describing Brownian motion.[1]

Bachelier's dissertation has significance in modern stock market research for two reasons. First, he provided an explicit statement of the hypothesis that stock prices gyrate in unpredictable, or random, ways. Second, he tested his theory against actual security prices and found that they corresponded closely to his random-movement supposition. The prices he studied did *not* move in meaningful trends, waves, or patterns. Thus, Bachelier concluded that recent historical

---

[1] Named after Robert Brown, the Scottish botanist who first observed it, Brownian motion connotes the movement of microscopic particles as they collide with the molecules around them. This movement is of great interest to physicists, and in 1905 Albert Einstein presented his renowned paper on the subject. In it he "discovered" the mathematical equation describing Brownian motion. Einstein is said to have felt that this discovery was one of his greatest contributions. Yet Einstein died not knowing that Bachelier, five years earlier, had discovered that the same equation could be used to describe the behavior of stock prices!

price data were useless for predicting future price changes. Either because Bachelier's work was so counter to intuition, or because it took an Einstein to understand it, his research findings fell into obscurity for nearly 60 years.[2]

An important lesson to learn from Bachelier's work is that a person with an intellect comparable to Einstein's could spend years studying the stock market, and could even develop knowledge that sparked intellectual excitement decades later, but could not also succeed in changing the investment behavior of his period. Apparently, in 1900, as today, researchers quietly applauded the achievements of other researchers but made little effort to bridge the gap between theory and practice. There are lessons to learn from this history. Hopefully, we will learn them!

In 1927, the Russian economist Eugen Slutsky [160], who was not aware of Bachelier's work, constructed some sample price charts by recording chance events. The results looked like actual price changes and appeared to exhibit cycles and other patterns. Unfortunately, ten years passed before Slutsky's work was translated into English. Even then, it did not spark the intellectual interest of either academicians or practitioners.

Before the Fall . . . and after

Stock market technicians proliferated during the boom of the 1920s, but there were no careful attempts to verify technical analysis. After the 1929 debacle, virtually all enthusiasm for investment advice was dampened during Wall Street's "era of disrepute."

Investors then had persistent memories of Black Tuesday, frightening stories of stock manipulation by investment pools, and many suicides. Nor could the public forget the corruption exemplified by Richard Whitney, scion of a wealthy family and ex-president of the New York Stock Exchange, who was convicted in criminal court for misusing company funds and sentenced to Sing Sing. Wall Street bore the stigma of these events for nearly three decades, during which the general public, and qualified researchers had little to do with the market. In fact, only two significant studies on common stocks were reported in the United States between 1930 and 1959.

In 1934, Holbrook Working [183], of Stanford University, noted that speculative price patterns might be chance occurrences since even artificially generated series of price changes form apparent

---

[2] The first modern-day reference to Bachelier's work appeared in 1959 [138].

trends and patterns. He later challenged "a skilled and close student of prices to distinguish reliably which is the real and which is the artificial price series." [**184**, p. 1435]

Working's studies, however, lacked both the mathematical rigor and the empirical evidence needed to impress impartial observers. So in spite of this early research by Bachelier, Slutsky, and Working, in the late 1930s no one could seriously doubt the basic tenet of technical analysis: Stock prices move in discernible patterns that are useful for prediction.

In 1937, Alfred Cowles and Herbert Jones [**30**], distinguished researchers of the Cowles Commission (now Foundation) for Research in Economics, reported that stock prices move with predictable trends. These findings, *withdrawn in 1960 after an error in the analysis was discovered,* stood at first as confirming evidence supporting technical analysis. Intuition had seemingly been proven correct. The widespread belief that Cowles had silenced the skeptics turned would-be researchers away from the subject for nearly 20 years.

More Seeds of Doubt

In 1953, at the London School of Economics, Maurice Kendall [**86**] found, to his surprise, that price changes behaved almost as if they had been generated by a suitably designed roulette wheel. That is, each price move was statistically independent of past prices. Using periods of 1, 2, 4, 8, and 16 weeks, Kendall reported that when price changes were observed at fairly close intervals, the random changes from one price to the next were large enough to swamp any systematic patterns or trends which might have existed. He concluded that "there is no hope of being able to predict movements on the exchange for a week ahead without extraneous [that is, something besides price] information." [**86**, p. 16]

In contrast to the widely quoted (but later shown to be erroneous) research by Cowles and Jones, Kendall's 1953 work was published in the rather obscure *Journal of the Royal Statistical Society* and received little attention. So, while there was scattered evidence of doubt, prior to 1959 no one seriously questioned the doctrine of technical stock market analysis.

The Renaissance of Investment Research

We have asserted that man's understanding of common stocks has mushroomed in the past 15 years. This new knowledge is due partly to modern, high-speed computers. It is astonishing to recall that the first of the now-ubiquitous computers was built in 1946 by Presper Eckert and John Mauchly at the University of Pennsylvania. Moreover, it was not until 1954 that General Electric installed the first computer in a commercial firm. Yet this relatively recent tool has already impacted on the stock market as a spectacular growth industry and as a much-needed aid in both investment research and back-office processing.

In 1959, two widely read technical papers were published by Harry Roberts [146], of the University of Chicago, and M. F. M. Osborne [137], an astronomer at the U.S. Naval Research Laboratory in Washington, D.C. These studies kindled interest in using computers to study stock price movements. Then, around 1960, Haloid (now Xerox) machines began running off copies of Bachelier's 60-year-old dissertation, which had just been discovered by Professor Paul Samuelson and others at M.I.T.

After reviewing the research of Working and Kendall, Professor Roberts showed that randomly generated price changes look very much like actual stock data. Even chance behavior produces trends and patterns. Roberts was the first modern author to conclude that "probably all the classical patterns of technical analysis can be generated artificially by a suitable roulette wheel or random-number table." [146, p. 10]

Earlier Research Refuted

Other vital research was reported in 1960 and 1961 by Working [185] and Sidney Alexander [3]. Each had discovered independently that results based on weekly or monthly stock price *averages* could show erroneous correlations not present in the unaveraged prices. This statistical effect refuted Cowles' earlier research, which had been based on price *averages*.

Accordingly, Cowles [29] revised his 1937 conclusions about the apparent predictability of monthly price changes. He withdrew his earlier finding and redid the study. Revision revealed *no evidence* that correct price data could be used to predict future prices. An important support for the tenets of technical analysis was ripped away with the publication of these new results. The reinvigorated seeds of controversy grew into debate on what has become known as *the random walk*.

7

The Random Walk

The *random walk* description of stock price behavior is a controversial—and often confusing—issue. But practitioners as well as scholars have come to recognize its importance. It has even spawned a best-seller—*A Random Walk down Wall Street*—by Professor Burton Malkiel [110], now on the President's Council of Economic Advisers.

What the Random-Walk Model Says

The random walk model asserts that future stock price changes cannot be predicted from the pattern of recent price changes. The random walk is sometimes called a "drunkard's walk," and the parallel is apt. In a comedian's drunkard routine, you cannot forecast either the size or the direction of his next staggering step. Similarly, if stock prices do follow a random walk, knowing past price movements is no help in predicting either the size or the direction of the next price movement.

Various researchers have hypothesized that stock price changes occur in a random sequence. Then they compared the movements of *actual* stock prices relative to such behavior. When the researchers could not discern significant differences between the actual and the random price patterns, they had to conclude that stock price changes —like random numbers—are not predictable from past prices.

The random-walk issue boils down to one basic question: Is the price and volume news printed daily in newspapers useful for predicting future price movements? Those who support the random-walk model say "No!" But, *intuitively,* that does not "seem" correct. The daily stock tables *are* interesting to many—are they no more significant than results from roulette?

Professor Clive Granger, of England's University of Nottingham, studied the random-walk model for more than a decade. He observed: "The opponents of the random-walk feel instinctively that there is something wrong with the model." [62, p. 91] But, as we have seen, instinct or intuition can be a poor guide. Surprisingly, even though the random-walk model has been around for years, most investors have not examined and understood its meaning. Instead, they have been content to rely on instinct and intuition. This is not merely unwise—it is often dangerous.

What the Random-Walk Model Does NOT Say

Professor Granger, in his article with the above title, noted one point of confusion for some people. These people feel that if the random-walk model is valid, then all security analysis must be futile. This is *not* true. The model states only that predictions based solely on historical *price movements* are futile. This does not necessarily preclude the validity of predictive approaches based on *other* historical data.

Professor Granger emphasized, for example, that "the question of whether or not future prices can be predicted using all the world's available information, such as earnings, dividends, expectations, indices of business confidence or even prices of other stocks, is a much wider question than the one raised by the random-walk model." [62, p. 91]

Another problem is the unfortunate use of the word *random.* The Merriam-Webster New Collegiate Dictionary lists the following synonyms for random: *haphazard, casual,* and *desultory.* These words imply "happening by accident," "at the mercy of chance," "working without intention or purpose," and "ungoverned by a method or system." It should be emphasized that the random-walk model of stock prices does *not* imply that stock price changes "happen by accident" and are uncaused. Indeed, the forces of supply and demand interacting on stock exchanges cause price movements. This is not a random or chance process.

The random-walk model does not *assume* anything—it is a statement alleging how prices move. While competitive or efficient markets might *explain* what we observe, their existence, or their absence, does not alter the assertion of the random-walk model that price changes occur without meaningful trends or patterns. Also, the random-walk model does not deny the possibility that "experts" (or even lucky dart throwers) might achieve higher-than-average returns. It only says that historical price data are useless in this endeavor.

Whenever you hear of "the random walk," you should remember that:

1. The random-walk model has nothing to do with the market mechanisms that *determine* period-to-period price changes—it only describes their alleged behavior, not its cause.
2. A rising trend of stock prices is not inconsistent with the random-walk model.
3. The random-walk model is unaffected by the fact that the prices of some stocks appreciate or depreciate more than the prices of others.
4. The validity of the random-walk model does not deny the possibility of superior investment performance from information *other than historical price data.*

The random-walk model if correct, means that you should not try to predict future price movements from historical price information! Now let's determine whether this momentous assertion is correct.

Testing the Random-Walk

The random-walk concept holds that *any price change is independent of the sequence of previous price changes.* For example, one can test the validity of the random-walk model for daily (day-to-day) price changes, monthly (month-to-month) price changes, or any other interval. The time span between price observations is called the "differencing interval." The daily price quotations in newspapers represent a one-market-day differencing interval. The quotations in the financial weekly *Barron's* have a one-week differencing interval.

Differencing intervals can vary from minute-to-minute transactions to extremely long intervals of a year or more. Thus, the research question becomes, Is the random walk valid for some particular differencing interval? That is, is there a random relationship between day-to-day price changes? Between week-to-week price changes? Between month-to-month price changes?

The early random-walk experiments by Kendall and Osborne showed that a series of weekly or monthly price changes were of no help in predicting future price movements. But suppose a prediction scheme relies on certain "events," such as large price changes or specific chart patterns, which occur at *variable*, rather than *fixed*, differencing intervals?

There are myriad forms of variable-time intervals, but they all monitor a series of price changes in search of some extraordinary "event." One common variable-time scheme is the basis for *point-and-figure charting*, a method of technical analysis of stock prices. This method observes and records the event of a stock's price moving by some predetermined amount. Thus, at the variable times when a stock's price moves by a specified amount, say, one dollar per share, these chartists plot X's for rising prices and O's for falling prices. Variable-time charts are meant to reveal complex price patterns that elude fixed-time differencing intervals.

Technical analysis assumes that the market repeats itself in *some* pattern and that historical data about price movements are useful for prediction. But there is no single pattern underlying all technical analysis. Consequently, only the commonly used techniques—be they fixed- or variable-time schemes—have been classified and explicitly tested against a random walk. And no one can ever refute *all* patterns without subjecting them all to rigorous tests.

Hope for Technicians?

In 1961, Alexander [3] of M.I.T. reported the first scientific analysis of variable-time stock price behavior. Alexander tested what is called a *filter technique*.[1] He contended that if his filter

---

[1] Filter techniques are based on the assumption that trends exist in stock prices but that these trends are obscured by insignificant fluctuations, or market "noise." With a filter, all price changes smaller than a specified size are discarded or filtered out. The remaining data are then examined. A typical filter rule might be: If the stock price advances 5 percent (signaling a breakout), buy and hold the stock until it declines by 5 percent (signaling the start of a reversal). At that time, sell the stock held and sell short an equal amount until the stock again moves up 5 percent. Under such

technique could show above-average profits, then this would indicate nonrandom price movements. He evaluated his filter technique with Kendall's data and reported profits better than those obtained from a buy-and-hold strategy. This success led him to conclude that "price changes appear to follow a random-walk over *time,* but a move, once initiated, tends to persist." [3, p. 26] And, "it must be concluded that there *are* trends in stock market prices." [3, p. 23]

Alexander said, in effect, that the random-walk model does describe week-to-week, or month-to-month, price movements, but that it does not describe his filter rule. He thereby lent support to technical prediction schemes based on filters. This conclusion was good news for Wall Street technicians who search historical price data for variably timed beginnings of "moves."

In another 1961 paper, Harvard economist Hendrik Houthakker [74] also reported favorable experiences with a variable-time decision rule applied to commodity futures. In effect, Houthakker advanced the hypothesis (cf. Darvas [37]) that changes in prices are characterized by long "runs" (that is, a series of price changes in the same direction). If such a hypothesis were correct, standing sell orders, called "stop orders," could be used by a speculator to sell when adverse runs were beginning. But the standing sell order would not be triggered by favorable runs.

For example, if a trader wished to limit his losses to, say, 5 percent, he would place a stop order to sell at 5 percent below his purchase price. If price fluctuations were not random, and if a price fall were likely to lead to a further fall, such a trading policy would reduce losses without affecting the upward runs of profits. Hence, average profit would increase.

Houthakker's test of his trading rule on wheat and corn futures proved quite successful and led him to say, "I feel that . . . [the results] indicate the existence of patterns of price behavior that would not be present if price changes were random." [74, p. 168]

Bolstering Random-Walk Research

Both Alexander's and Houthakker's results were quite surprising, since experiments with variable-time decision rules by other re-

---

a rule, trend reversals of less than 5 percent are ignored. Filter techniques seek to discover "significant moves" by studying price changes of a given magnitude, irrespective of the length of time between them. In short, the filter technique substitutes the dimension of the "move" for the dimension of "time." This precept is also the basis of the point-and-figure chart technique.

searchers met with failure. In the early 1960s, one of the authors [68] conducted tests with many variable-time decision rules, using a four-year file of daily data on 790 actively traded stocks. Tests of the usefulness of moving averages, filters, thresholds, and so on, consistently showed no reliability. Similar discouraging results were reported by Barney [8], Bauer [9], Johnson [80], and Levine [97]. Investigators less willing to report their failure to find successful trading strategies doubtlessly exist. But how could the research of Alexander and Houthakker be explained?

As other scholars became intrigued, they discovered several problems. Professor Paul Cootner [25], of M.I.T., first noted a procedural error in Alexander's computations. And while Alexander's results were impressive, Alexander did not state what statistical confidence one should place in them. Thus, the likelihood of obtaining similar results purely by chance, or "dart board" selection, was not known.

Similarly, Houthakker's work was based on tests using prices of *commodities futures*—not stock prices. Commodities futures have been shown to have seasonal patterns. Upon careful examination, it is clear that Houthakker's "trends" could have been derived from seasonal movements, not behavior inherent in the prices themselves.

Pro and Con

In 1962, academic debate on the validity of the random walk accelerated—although it was still almost unknown on Wall Street. Cootner [26] published an extensive study of weekly data on 45 stocks. Essentially, he reported that at one-week intervals prices appeared to move randomly. But he also found evidence of trends in the same data at 14-week intervals. Thus, Cootner's research showed that for longer differencing intervals, such as 14 weeks, the random-walk model was *not* valid!

Further evidence that studying weekly price changes was futile came from a 1962 doctoral dissertation done at the University of Chicago by Arnold Moore [124]. Moore's research verified random-walk behavior for *weekly* price changes, using a sample of 33 representative stocks from the New York Stock Exchange.

Eugene Fama [42] did a 1965 doctoral dissertation at the University of Chicago that remains one of the most definitive studies of the random walk ever conducted. He tested data covering daily to two-week differencing intervals for the 30 stocks in the Dow Jones

Industrial Average—spanning periods from five to seven years. Fama reported no evidence of trends in stock prices for any differencing interval he tested. The conclusion: *Information on short-term stock price changes is useless!*

Hope Revived?

In 1966, *Fortune* ran an article entitled "The Case against the Random Walk," reporting on the doctoral dissertation of Robert Levy [98] at the American University in Washington, D.C. *Fortune* described Levy's research as a "decisive refutation of the random walk." [192, p. 160] Levy found that stocks with relatively above- (or below-) average price performance in the past six months tended to maintain above- (or below-) average performance in the next six months.

This finding in support of longer-term trends was not new. For example, Cowles reported in 1937 that, "taking one year as the unit of measurement . . . the tendency is very pronounced for stocks which have exceeded the median in one year to exceed it also in the year following." [30, p. 285][2] And there was Cootner's work revealing trends in 14-week price data. Interestingly, Levy also found that "short-time [*sic,* with a one-month differencing interval] results did not reveal any discernible pattern." [98, p. 181]

Seeking further clarification of this important issue, Michael Jensen [77] showed that Levy's work contained an error by overstating the returns earned by his "relative strength" trading rules (see [99] and [100]). Still, some of Levy's decision rules showed more profit than could be attained from a buy-and-hold strategy.

What perplexed Jensen was that Levy tested 68 different decision rules on the *same body of data* and that 20 of his decision rules actually produced returns higher than would a buy-and-hold investment policy. And Jensen pointed out that, when the correct rate-of-return calculations are used, none of Levy's "profitable" trading rules showed returns *after transaction costs* that exceeded the correct buy-and-hold returns. At best, Levy was reporting evidence of a subtle form of long-term, nonrandom behavior that apparently could not be used to beat the market average.

---

[2] Cowles' article had the statistical error cited earlier. It should be noted, however, that the above quotation is not affected by this error.

Victor Niederhoffer [129, 130, 131], individually and with Osborne [132], studied the other end of the differencing interval spectrum. Niederhoffer and Osborne analyzed the most basic discernible stock market data—successive transactions on the ticker tape. They reported that stock market ticker transactions display four nonrandom properties:

1. There is a general tendency for price reversal between trades.
2. Reversals are relatively more concentrated at integers where stable, slow-moving participants offer to buy and sell. There is a concentration of particular types of reversals just above and below these barriers.
3. Quick-moving competitors cognizant of these barriers can take positions at nearby prices, thus "getting the trade" and hoping to make a profit.
4. After two changes in the same direction, the chances of continuation in that direction are greater than after changes in opposite directions. [132, p. 914]

Unfortunately, such short-term and small-percentage movements, although statistically observable, provide no successful trading strategies when transaction costs are included. Thus, a sequence of progressively more rigorous, computer-based investigations, reaffirmed by each researcher, *upholds the random-walk model when the differencing interval is between one day and three months.*

Technicians Still Can Hope

In deference to technical analysts, one must admit that the statistical tools (serial correlation, run tests, and so on) used up to this point were inadequate to detect the complicated patterns (for example, head-and-shoulders) which are reputed by some chartists to serve as predictors. Furthermore, research on the random-walk model had generally neglected trading volume information. Yet, many technicians contend that volume is a necessary adjunct to historical price data.

Limited acceptance of the random-walk model also stemmed from the fact that "randomness" can only be defined negatively. There is no single test for randomness. A conclusion of randomness can be drawn only when one is unable to discover any systematic price movement. Thus, when research does not reveal predictive price patterns, one can only conclude that those *particular* price changes are random. Consequently, each test must carry the proviso that some other test on some other price data *might* be able to detect a meaningful pattern.

How About All Stocks, Trading Volume, and Chartists?

To overcome the limitations of earlier research, one of the authors [68] posed the research question: Does the random-walk model hold for *all* actively traded stocks? His findings from a large variety of computer programs and statistical tests were quite conclusive: There was no systematic behavior in stock prices that could be used for profitable prediction when the data were studied with differencing intervals between 1 and 16 days. Further, there were no systematic differences that would allow profitable prediction when the findings were segmented by stock price range, stock exchange, or industry.

Is it true, as many technicians contend, that it is the *combination* of price and trading volume data that provides useful predictive information? This question was also investigated. In sum, the results reaffirmed that short-term (less than 16 days) stock prices move in random, hence unpredictable, patterns. The introduction of the previous period's trading volume data does not enable one to improve, even slightly, prediction of the direction of future stock price change.

There are two kinds of chartists: bar chartists (cf. Edwards and Magee [40] and Jiler [79]) and point-and-figure chartists (cf. Cohen [19] and [20], and Tabell [174]). Both kinds of chartists plot price on the vertical scale. On bar charts, the horizontal scale is uniformly divided into fixed-time periods. On point-and-figure charts, the units on the horizontal scale are used to indicate reversals in the stock price's direction. These, of course, occur at variable-time intervals.

Once the stock's historical record has been charted, the technical analyst visually studies the configuration for predictive signals. While it is unlikely, it must be conceded that chartists might be able to detect visually complex patterns that traditional statistical tests would be unable to perceive.

Again, research by one of the authors [68] sought to emulate the chartists' vision. Chartists look for specific kinds of patterns, such as head-and-shoulders, saucer bottoms, and triple tops. A computer was instructed to "look for" the mathematical equivalent of what a chartist hopes to find visually. Next, the occurrence of any of these patterns was recorded, and the stock's succeeding price behavior was noted. Finally, a statistical analysis was conducted to determine whether these patterns did precede certain kinds of price action. The study found no evidence that the commonly used chart patterns actually forecast price changes.

A second research approach sought to have the computer derive original predictive patterns from the data. In this approach, charts were grouped by the computer on the basis of price behavior *following the chart*. For example, all chart patterns that appeared before dramatic price increases were grouped. Then these patterns, which all preceded similar kinds of price movements, were studied for similarities. Again, *this research found no evidence that predictable stock price movements followed any visually detectable chart pattern.*

Doesn't Technical Analysis Work "Sometimes"?

For some readers the evidence presented here may seem contradictory to their personal experience. Such people "know" that technical schemes based on historical price and volume work. But do they? The answer is quite clear. There is *absolutely no evidence* that knowing the price and volume movements of a stock over the recent past is meaningful in predicting the future price behavior of that stock.

Yet, many practitioners persist in using this kind of technical analysis. They must occasionally feel successful; otherwise, they would not continue the practice. Success in the stock market, however, must be gauged against a realistic benchmark. One would *expect* a certain level of results even if technical analysis is indeed useless. Stated another way, the benchmark for comparing investment performance should be the results one would expect from unskilled stock selection.

Suppose that, instead of basing investment decisions on the results of elaborate technical analysis, an investor selected stocks by throwing darts at the financial page of a newspaper. Further, suppose transaction dates were chosen by throwing darts at a calendar. What investment outcome would result from such random stock selection?

Fisher and Lorie's work [**50**] revealed that the *median* rate of return from *random* investment in common stocks was 9.8 percent compounded annually during the period from 1926 to 1960. Also, using random holding periods averaging several years, they found that *78 percent of such transactions were profitable.*

These findings become especially interesting when you consider that technicians generally claim to be accurate only some of the time. For example, Edmund W. Tabell, considered the dean of chartists until he died in 1965, said that he was right only about 70 percent of the time. Admittedly, the longer a position is held, the more likely that it will become profitable, and Tabell made no statement as to how long or short a time it took for him to be "right." Also, the annual rate of return achieved on overall investment is usually more important than the percentage of individual buys with profitable outcomes. Nevertheless, *it is our conclusion that people who give credit for their success to technical analysis have, in fact, not been aided by it in any way. They have merely obtained normal results, as could be had from random investment.*

Can Performance Be Explained?

Of course, investment performance is the record of what has happened in the past, and not what will happen in the future. In investing, as in the business of life, major decisions preclude getting the results of some alternate choice—both paths cannot be traveled. Yet, there in the morning paper appear the investment "could have beens."

Before using past performance data, one must first ask, "Is the future going to be like the past?" Richard Brealey, in his outstanding book *An Introduction to Risk and Return from Common Stocks,* has cautioned his readers that "the fact that a trading rule would have been profitable in the past does not necessarily indicate that it will offer a valuable investment tool. A formula that is capable of explaining past events may owe its success to coincidence." [**13**, p. 37]

One such classic decision system that has been suggested is not at all complex. The rule simply says, "Buy stocks whose names end in *x.*" In the 1962–69 market rise and technology-glamour boom, this rule gave good performance—Ampex, Magnavox, Memorex, Syntex, Tampax, Telex, and, of course, Xerox (maybe it was the two x's that did it). But the more recent fortunes of these "x-rated" stocks have, in some cases, dwindled. The good mechanical or "technical" rule of one era may not work well in the next. If 10,000 people using Ouija boards predict market swings, some of those people will, by sheer weight of numbers, be correct in their predictions. But there will be scant rationale to believe that their technique will work *again*.

Academic research, which has no vested interest in holding out false hopes of prediction, is in overwhelming agreement—technical market prediction schemes based on price and volume movements over the recent past appear to be useless. Most market practitioners will react to this statement by asserting that they only use such technical analysis "sometimes." This is ridiculous! The evidence is overwhelming that such analysis should *never* be used. Isn't it strange that a hospital patient who will literally trust his life to a computer's ability to read his electrocardiogram will not listen when told that the same pattern-detection techniques fail to find useful patterns in stock price data?

Nonetheless, "technical" jargon remains an integral part of Wall Street's vocabulary. Financial pages make frequent references to such things as a "technical correction," even though few commentators agree on its definition or occurrence. Most of this gobbledygook appears to serve the purpose of the psychiatrist's inkblot—to project meaning into nothing.

For example, one well-known technician's soothsaying was quoted in the *Wall Street Journal* as follows: "It may be well to assume that the major stock indexes will either keep fluctuating erratically within the current, comparatively narrow, trading range (roughly, 780–850 on the Dow Jones industrial average) or else stage false breakouts in one direction or the other, or both, during the weeks ahead." [204] In other words, if the market doesn't stay steady, it will probably go up—or down—or both.

Epitaph

It should be emphasized that technical analysis, as discussed here, refers to recent price and/or volume information. Some technicians use "secret" formulas to calculate other indicators, such as percentage strength, moving and geometric averages (see James [76]), advance-decline lines, net upticks, and the like. No analysis can ever encompass all of the possible schemes. But for now, an important *don't* of successful investing is: *Don't rely on technical analysis based on recent historical price or volume information.*

It's nice to look at a stock's price chart—even fun if it points up and you own it. But for predictive significance, short-term price and volume data have nothing credible in their favor. It would appear that William Shakespeare wrote a fitting epitaph *(Macbeth,* Act V, Sc. v.) for this kind of market forecasting.

> It is a tale
> Told by an idiot, full of sound and fury,
> Signifying nothing.

8

What Causes Price Movements?

Evidence supporting the random walk does not mean that price changes are uncaused. Price changes result from the combined actions of buyers and sellers which shift the market's equilibrium between demand and supply. For example, when the demand for a stock increases, relative to its supply, this imbalance causes a price rise that is sufficient to attract sellers who create enough additional supply to restore the market to economic equilibrium.

Since price changes are caused by changes in either the net supply or demand for investments, above-average investing strategies can be developed if one can:

1. Determine what causes people to change their minds.
2. Act on this information before it is fully reflected in the price of the investment.

This logical approach to achieving above-average rates of return introduces the issue of the "efficient capital market theory."

The Efficient Capital Market Theory[1]

The setting for an "efficient capital market" is a market in which many people, with similar investment objectives and access to the

---

[1] Some authors, such as Lorie and Hamilton [109], distinguish among three levels of "efficient" markets. They define the "weak form" as a market in which historical price data is efficiently digested and, therefore, is useless for predicting subsequent

65

same information, actively compete. The stock market certainly provides this setting. Many people—both professionally and privately—continually search for undervalued securities. Also, in their quest for wealth, investors have similar basic objectives. Everyone prefers a high rate of return to a low one, certainty to uncertainty, and so forth. Furthermore, the law requires that both parties in a securities transaction have access to the same material facts.

Scholars have hypothesized that in such a market setting—with many people playing the same game and having similar objectives and equal access to information—it would be impossible for any investor to have a consistent advantage over the market, which reflects the composite judgment of its millions of participants. This hypothesis is known as the "efficient capital market theory" or the "fair-game theory." "Efficient" means that the market is capable of quickly digesting new information on the economy, an industry, or the value of an enterprise, and accurately impounding that information into the price of the stock. "Fair game" means that participants in such markets cannot expect to earn more, or less, than the average return for the risks involved.

The efficient capital market theory hypothesizes that all available information is continually analyzed by some among the literally millions of investors. It holds that in this kind of market, news of, say, an earnings increase is quickly and accurately assessed by the combined actions of investors and immediately reflected in the price of the stock. The purported result of this efficiency is that, whether you buy the stock before, during, or after the earnings news, or whether you buy another stock, you can expect a fair market rate of return commensurate with the risk of owning whatever security you buy. (Risk is discussed in detail in later chapters.)

It is important to note that this theory might be true for one kind of information, say, earnings, but might not be true for other types of information, say, dividend changes. Similarly, it might hold true for information on particular instruments, say, widely held stocks, or in certain markets, such as the New York Stock Exchange, but not for other instruments or markets. We might reasonably expect, for example, that the efficiency of widely held stocks is different from

---

price changes. They distinguish this from the "semistrong form," in which all publicly available company-related data is assumed to be fully discounted in the current price of the stock. Finally, they discuss the "strong form," in which not even those with privileged information can secure superior investment results.

that of stocks of smaller firms having far fewer investors. Thus, when you refer to the efficient capital market theory, you must specify the "information," the "instrument," and the "market."

This theory does not deny the profitability of investing. It merely states that the rewards one earns from investing in well-organized, highly competitive markets will be fair, on average, for the risks involved. But this theory also holds that acting on publicly available information *cannot* improve one's performance beyond the market's assessment of a fair rate of return.

If the stock market is a fair game, much of the hope for skillfully achieved extraordinary gains is removed. Of course, this still would not lessen the importance of investing. *The efficient capital market theory, if valid, would merely change the underlying philosophy from one of trying to beat other investors to one of assuring a fair and stable rate of return consistent with personal objectives.*

If You Want Above-Average Performance . . .

The efficient capital market theory focuses our search for useful market predictors on that information which might cause people to change their minds about investment values. Thus, the theory is a useful guide. From its perspective, researchers can determine which information is "efficiently" and "inefficiently" processed by competing investors in various markets and for various investment instruments. They can hypothesize cause-and-effect relationships and study how efficiently a particular security and market digest a particular kind of information.

Investors tend to focus on one market (NYSE securities), one instrument (common stock), and one or two categories of news items (earnings and dividends). It is likely, therefore, that other fruitful areas exist where investor information processing is *not* efficient. Those who can discover and accurately assess these inefficiencies can profit from their differential knowledge. But as such unrecognized knowledge is disseminated among competing investors, its value to users is destroyed by the equalizing forces of an efficient capital market. Even if research can pinpoint news items which *are* efficiently processed for particular instruments in particular markets, such knowledge enables investors to avoid analyzing this useless, fully discounted information—*an important decision in itself.*

To consistently attain above-average investment performance, an investor must *know*

1. the *odds*
2. that certain *information*
3. will influence certain investment *instruments*
4. in certain investment *markets*
5. in known *directions*
6. by approximate *magnitudes,* and
7. must act on the information *before other investors do.*

If this cannot be done, investment analysis becomes an expensive exercise in hopeful thinking! The fact that over 50,000 professional security analysts, brokers, and portfolio managers—not to mention the millions of investors—are all trying to do the same thing makes the game of investing *very competitive.* In this league, an above-average batting record comes down to having a game plan and knowing when to swing and when not to.

Dissecting the Causes of Price Movements

Several kinds of information can precipitate price movements of various instruments in various markets. Three broad categories of such information are:

1. *Market-related information.* General economic news typically affects the market as a whole. On days when several hundred stocks reach new lows, while only a few reach new highs, it is clear that even the stocks of well-managed companies in growing industries cannot withstand a bear market.

2. *Industry-related information.* Instead of affecting the general economy, news sometimes has an impact only on a particular industry. For example, the 1975 one-time tax credit for certain new homes helped resuscitate the home-building stocks, at least temporarily. Similarly, industry-wide strikes affect only firms in particular industries.

3. *Company-related information.* News about a company's earnings, dividends, forthcoming stock splits, patents, merger offers, new discoveries, and so forth—with little or no bearing on its industry or the general economy—can prompt a change in the price of a company's stock.

If you are trying to predict price movements, a logical first step is to discover the relative importance of each of these three basic kinds of information. For example, if the relative importance of information related to the company, the industry, and the market is about equal, it might behoove analysts to allocate their research efforts to these three areas equally. Similarly, if 80 percent of a price movement is caused by movement of the market at large, or by industry-level effects, an analyst who devoted major attention to company-related information might be grossly misled. In such a situation, variations in company performance would be swamped by the effect of market or industry swings.

Benjamin King [**89**], in his doctoral dissertation at the University of Chicago, sought to determine the relative importance of the following underlying causes of price movements: the market, the basic industry (such as metals), the industry subgroup (such as non-ferrous metals), and the company. After studying 403 consecutive months of data (1927–60) for 63 NYSE stocks, King reported that:

1. There is a strong tendency for stocks to move with the overall market.
2. Stock price comovements correspond closely to industry classifications.
3. Only a minor proportion of stock price movement can be attributed solely to company-related factors.

King's research is startling in its consistency. First, his findings parallel earlier but less comprehensive results reported by Granger and Morgenstern [**63**] and by Godfrey, Granger, and Morgenstern [**60**]. Second, the market and industry comovements were remarkably consistent, especially when you consider the industry changes that doubtless occurred over the more than 33 years spanned by King's study. In the most recent period he examined (1952–60), King showed that, on average, price changes were attributable to the investing public's reaction to four factors in the following proportions:

1. The market as a whole—31 percent.
2. The basic industry—12 percent.
3. The industry subgroup—37 percent.
4. The particular company—20 percent.

Thus, on average, 31 percent of a stock's price movement was ascribable to general economic factors influencing the market as a whole. Practically half of the movement was traceable to the influence of a firm's basic industry and its industry subgroup—12 percent and 37 percent respectively. After these market and industry comovements were accounted for, only a scant 20 percent of the total price movement could be attributed to the individual company!

These aggregate figures do not present the entire picture that King developed. There were some interesting differences within the composite averages. These differences are summarized in Table 8–1, using King's most recent data.

TABLE 8–1

Classification of Price Comovements by Industry Membership

	Percentage Movement Explained by:			
Industry Membership	Overall Market	Basic Industry	Industry Subgroup	Individual Company
Railroads.................	47	8	26	19
Metals....................	46	8	31	15
Petroleum................	37	20	28	15
Utilities..................	23	14	41	22
Retail stores.............	23	8	42	27
Tobacco..................	9	17	49	25
Average..................	31	12	37	20

Source: Derived from data in King [89].

These data show that the shares of railroads, metal companies, and petroleum firms rank highest in overall market dependence, with the stocks of tobacco firms being relatively insensitive to overall market swings. The industry columns confirm King's statement that the "general adherence to the pattern of industry comovement is ineluctable. . . . the strongest industry effects are those for petroleums, utilities, and tobaccos—the weakest for metals, [retail] stores, and rails." [89, pp. 203–4]

King's research made three major contributions. First, it showed that, on average, roughly one third of a stock's movement can be traced to general market swings. Second, it showed that there are clear industry differences. In the tobacco industry, for example, King could trace only 9 percent of stock price variations to general market swings. By contrast, he could attribute nearly half of stock price movements to general market swings in the more cyclical railroad and metals industries. Third, it provided evidence that this relationship between stock swings and market swings is consistent over time. Thus, for example, even today there is reason to believe that tobacco stocks are not as sensitive to general market swings as metals stocks.

King's research was expanded and updated in 1968 by Marshall Blume [11] in his doctoral dissertation at the University of Chicago. Blume, who studied 251 securities, demonstrated quite conclusively that there is an overwhelming tendency for certain stocks to move with the market, and that this relationship is persistent over time. That is, stocks that are very sensitive—say, those which tend to move 1.5 percent for every 1 percent change in the market—tend to maintain this level of sensitivity over time. Similarly, stocks that are insensitive to market swings—say, those which tend to move only 0.5 percent when the market as a whole moves 1 percent—continue to behave in this fashion. Thus, Blume's dissertation undeniably confirmed that *individual stocks tend to establish and maintain a consistent relationship to overall swings in the market.*

How Wall Street Organizes Its Research

These findings are significant in view of the way many Wall Street professionals "pick stocks." Traditionally, brokerage firms, bank trust departments, and investment advisory services organize their research departments around industries. The rationale for this approach is that, by concentrating his or her efforts, each analyst can become an expert on both the industry and the companies within that industry.

But it is often difficult for security analysts to balance their in-depth company analyses with an assessment of their industry's comparative attractiveness, not to mention the overall condition of the market. Thus, many analysts spend most of their time trying to select the best stocks within their industry specialty. The dominance of this company-level research often blinds investors to the *more important* general market and interindustry impacts.

Security analysts should discipline themselves to balance in-depth company studies with both general economic and interindustry analysis. It is important to remember that, on average, almost one third of a stock's price movement can be attributed to overall market forces. Furthermore, the consistent differences among industries lend themselves to different approaches for each industry. Metals and rails, for example, tend to move with the overall market, while tobacco firms do not. Also, basic-industry associations are more important in petroleum and tobacco than in rails, metals, or retail stores, and so forth. Practically speaking, with 85 percent of the movement of petroleum stocks tied to the market and the industry, little effort need be expended on choosing *between* the stocks of oil companies. *The real question is whether or not to be in the market and if so, in which industries.*

How to Distill Useful Information

When placed in the context of the efficient capital market theory, the foregoing research should prompt us to look for useful information by:

1. Specifying the investment "instrument" that interests us (for example, common stock).
2. Defining the "market" to be studied (for example, the NYSE).
3. Tabulating the kinds of "information" that *might* affect the value of the investment instrument at the four levels the market, the basic industry, the industry subgroup, and the particular company.

When *possibly* useful information is placed in the perspective of Figure 8–1, one can assess how efficiently information is processed at each hierarchical level. If the information is quickly and accurately impounded into the instrument's price, the market would be deemed economically "efficient." But if for some reason the market does not fully react to a certain kind of news, or reacts slowly, the discovery of this economic "inefficiency" will permit one to profit in excess of a "fair game."

It should be reiterated, however, that one does not have to discover market inefficiencies to profit from investments. An efficient market is one in which everyone can expect a "fair return" for his risks. If such a market is efficient at digesting earnings information, for instance, it would mean that acting on such information could not increase your expected return above a fair-game return. Importantly, and unlike the situation in Las Vegas, this expected return is a positive and profitable economic reward for investing.

We will use the framework shown in Figure 8–1 to explain the

FIGURE 8-1

The Investment Analysis Function

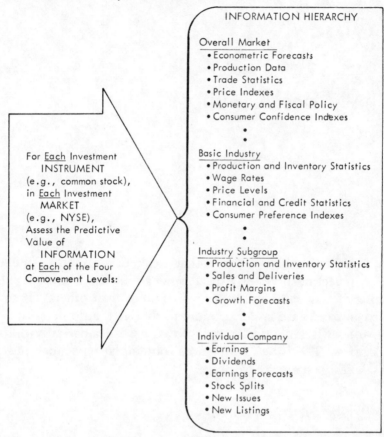

research bearing on the usefulness of various types of information for predicting company-, industry-, and market-caused price changes. We will first single out *earnings* information and discuss what price gets paid for such earnings and whether earnings levels are predictable.

9

What Price Earnings?

A wealth of evidence shows that stock prices tend to move together, reflecting investor expectations about the overall economy. In spite of this, some stocks are worth more than others. Of course, some companies are larger or more profitable than others. But even companies with identical earnings can have dramatically different stock prices. The issue for investors contemplating a stock purchase (or sale) is: What price earnings?

What Constitutes Worth?

When you buy a share of stock, you forgo present spending in exchange for expected future benefits. Since you know today's stock price, investing involves a certain sacrifice for an uncertain benefit. These uncertain future returns come from the firm's earning power, which will determine the extent of its future dividend distributions and, to varying degrees, the future selling price of the company's stock. A cornerstone of *fundamental security analysis* is that a share of common stock is worth the present value of the future income its owner will receive. Since the income from dividends and the eventual selling price are to be received in the future, their worth must be discounted to reflect interest rates and risk. The price the next buyer is willing to pay, in turn, hinges on that buyer's own perception of his or her returns and eventual selling price.

Thus, in buying common stock, an investor acquires the legal right to share in the company's future earnings through dividends and growth. The price investors will pay for the company's future is generally many times its annual earnings. For example, a bank savings account might earn 5 percent annual income. It takes $20 to earn $1 at that rate, so such an investment costs 20 times its annual earnings.

Price/Earnings Ratios

A stock's price-earnings ratio is a crucial benchmark. It is simply the ratio of the stock's current price to its annual earnings. The earnings may be those for the preceding 12 months, those projected for the current year, or those projected for some future year.

Since 1961, the P/E for the 30 Dow Jones Industrials has averaged about 14 times the prior year's earnings and has ranged from under 7 to over 24. Knowing the market's P/E, measured by this index or others, facilitates comparisons between the P/Es of individual stocks. Table 9–1 lists representative P/Es. Two recent dates are shown for comparison—the first corresponding approximately to the market's high in 1973 and the second to the market's status in late 1975.

Note that a P/E could not be calculated for Litton Industries or Penn Central in 1973 because neither had positive earnings. In December 1975, Litton again had earnings and its P/E was 8, but Penn Central was still rolling downhill.

Note that the 1973 P/Es range from a high of 78 for Polaroid to a low of 8 for the Ford Motor Company. This means that investors occasionally evaluate some companies' earnings at almost *ten times* those of other companies. These two companies also illustrate the volatility of P/Es. Ford's rose from 8 to 48 when earnings slumped. Polaroid's sagged from 78 to 23 with the general market decline.

Over time, P/Es change for the overall market and for individual companies as well. For example, P/Es dropped sharply in 1973–4 but recovered partially in 1975. Higher P/Es stem from the fact that investors anticipate more growth and/or certainty in the earnings of particular stocks, and are willing to pay a higher price for a share in the future of such stocks. Market P/Es similarly reflect the economy-wide outlook and rates on competing investments, such as bonds. Thus, high P/Es reflect investor optimism.

The P/Es in Table 9–1 also show that in early 1973 investors were four times as optimistic about the future of Xerox, with a

TABLE 9-1

P/E Ratios for 35 Large Companies on February 6, 1973, and December 5, 1975

Company	1973 P/E Ratios	1975 P/E Ratios
Aetna Life & Casualty..................	11	13
Asarco..............................	10	10
AT&T..............................	11	10
Avon Products.......................	60	20
Chase Manhattan.....................	12	4
Coca-Cola...........................	45	22
Continental Can......................	10	9
Delta Airlines.......................	22	22
duPont..............................	20	39
Eastman Kodak.......................	46	27
Exxon...............................	13	7
Ford................................	8	48
General Electric......................	24	15
General Foods........................	12	12
General Motors.......................	10	14
Gulf Oil.............................	11	5
IBM................................	39	18
IT&T...............................	13	7
Kennecott Copper....................	9	28
Litton Industries.....................	—	8
McDonnell Douglas...................	10	7
Mobil Oil...........................	12	6
Penn Central	—	—
Philip Morris.	27	15
Polaroid............................	78	23
Procter & Gamble....................	31	23
Safeway............................	11	9
Sears, Roebuck......	29	27
Tenneco.......	11	6
Texaco.........	12	7
Texas Utilities......................	16	10
Union Carbide.......................	13	8
U.S. Steel...........................	10	5
Weyerhaeuser........................	21	24
Xerox...............................	48	16

Source: *The Wall Street Journal,* February 6, 1973, and December 5, 1975.

P/E of 48, as they were about the future of Mobil Oil, with a P/E of 12. And optimism about the future of different oil companies was remarkably consistent, as represented by Exxon (P/E = 13), Gulf Oil (P/E = 11), Mobil Oil (P/E = 12), and Texaco (P/E = 12). By 1975, the market's P/E had dropped, but the general P/E relationships remained. For example, Xerox had only a 16 P/E, but the P/Es of the four oil companies ranged from 5 to 7.

The market's relative optimism about the future of any listed company can be estimated from the P/E ratios published daily in the *Wall Street Journal* and other major newspapers. These ratios are calculated from the previous day's closing price and the most recent 12-month earnings.

Some analysts like to turn P/E ratios upside down so as to express current earnings as a percentage of current price. The British call this inversion of the P/E ratio the "earnings yield." Thus, a P/E of 10, which is 10/1, can be converted to an earnings yield of 1/10, or 10 percent. This means the stock's earnings currently yield a 10 percent return on their purchase price. Similarly, a stock selling at 20 times current earnings provides only a 1/20, or 5 percent, earnings yield.

Why do people buy stocks whose current earnings are only 5 percent of the purchase price, when they could buy other stocks that earn 10 percent or even more? The reason is that they expect the future earnings of high P/E stocks to grow faster and/or to be more stable. *The key to using P/Es is to realize that they reflect the market's expectations about the growth and certainty of future earnings.*

What Price Growth?

How much should you pay for growth? *Growth stocks* are stocks that are expected to outgrow the economy at large by producing annual earnings gains of, say, 15 percent or more. And certainly growth stocks have been the darlings of investors in the last two decades, particularly among the increasingly important institutions. Whether they are called the "top tier," the "favorite fifty," or just "glamour stocks," growth companies are supposed to multiply capital in rabbitlike fashion. Sometimes they have. But the question is: Will they again?

Some theory on what growth is worth provides a helpful context for the review of the evidence that is given below. For example, if the market averages a 12 P/E, we might ask, "What growth rate is required to justify a 24 P/E for a particular stock?" Remembering that total return is calculated as the dividend yield plus the growth rate, we might at first think that only the difference in dividend yield would have to be made up in extra growth by the growth stock. Thus, if the average stock yields 4 percent and grows at 5 percent, then a growth stock yielding only 1 percent but growing at 8 percent should provide the same 9 percent total return.

The matter is not so simple. The above calculation assumes that the P/Es of both stocks will remain unchanged and that their 5 percent and 8 percent growth rates will go on indefinitely. In fact, no company can outgrow the economy forever, or it eventually *will be the economy*. As growth slows down with large size, we might expect the company's P/E to decline, reflecting its slower growth.

Therefore, one method of analyzing growth stocks assumes that they will outgrow the average for some given number of years and thereafter be average themselves. For example, it would take our 8 percent growth rate company nearly 25 years of outgrowing a 5 percent market average to compensate for a P/E that declined by half (to the market average) during that period. Clearly, this is a rather long time, so we must look for faster growth to shorten this time horizon.

What is 15 percent annual growth worth when compared to a 5 percent market growth rate? Such a rate of growth would have to persist for over seven years to compensate for a P/E that declined by half. Even then, the growth stock's yield would probably have been less than average. Also, the investor would have received no extra rate of return for any extra risk in buying the high P/E stock. [See 101] In summary, we can probably say that a double-the-market P/E implies that shareholders expect superior growth from the company for a decade or more. Now let's turn to the evidence supporting this theory.

How Much Should You Pay?

Probably the most widely read study of growth rates and P/E ratios was published in 1963 by Volkert Whitbeck and Manown Kisor [182], at the Bank of New York. They sought a definitive answer to why IBM was then selling at 35 times earnings while General Motors was selling at about 18 times earnings. Their analysis showed that IBM had experienced an annual earnings per share growth rate of 16.1 percent. During the same period, GM had experienced an average annual growth rate of only 5.3 percent. In addition, Whitbeck and Kisor demonstrated that IBM's expansion was not only more rapid but also more stable. They reported that "IBM commands a higher price/earnings (P/E) ratio, not because of its past performance, but, rather, because the market, on balance, expects more *in the future* from IBM than it does from GM. As investors, we buy common stocks not simply for records prior to purchase, but, more fundamentally, for what we anticipate from them after our commitment." [**182**, p. 337]

Here, then, is the issue. Theoretically, a stock's price is governed by its future stream of earnings. In reality, investors have different expectations about the future earnings ability of different companies. A share of stock is worth what someone will pay for it. And investors value current earnings differently, depending on the company. To predict which stocks are the best buys, you have to predict future Es and P/Es—that is, what will the company earn, and how much will the market value those earnings? We will first discuss the evidence on P/Es and then, in the next chapter, see whether earnings can be predicted.

Do Expected Earnings Growth Rates Explain P/Es?

The researchers at the Bank of New York concluded that differences among expected growth rates explain about 60 percent of the differences in normal P/E ratios. Similarly, John Cragg, of the University of British Columbia, reported that anticipated growth in earnings explained, on the average, 67 percent of the differences in P/E ratios.

Richard Crowell [**33**], in his doctoral dissertation at MIT, studied the relationship between expected earnings and P/E ratios in different industries. Of the 12 industries analyzed, Crowell demonstrated that, at one extreme, 69 percent of the differences in the P/E ratios for bank stocks could be explained by differences in anticipated growth rates; at the other extreme, only 5 percent of the differences in the P/E ratios accorded steel stocks could be traced to expected growth differences.

Further research, reported by Cohen, Zinbarg, and Zeikel [**22**], quantified this general relationship between P/E ratios and expected growth rates. These researchers first determined analysts' opinions on the expected growth rates for 30 selected large firms. The growth forecasts were then correlated with P/E ratios. Two periods were investigated: the market's bottom of 1970 and its recovery high of 1971. The average result—naturally subject to variation—was that the large firms selected carried P/Es approximately equaling *four plus twice their annual growth rate.* Thus, a company expected to grow at 7 percent annually would sport an average P/E of 4 plus 2 times 7, or 18. It should be reemphasized that these results are for *large,* hence relatively stable, firms and that they reflect higher market P/Es than have existed more recently.

Combined, this research confirms that *differences in the relative P/E ratios of various stocks can be significantly explained by differences in each company's expected earnings growth rate.*

High P/Es versus Low P/Es

High P/Es correlate with high expected growth rates. But what if you can't predict growth rates—or think the market can't? Then, presumably, you would prefer to buy low P/E stocks and to shun high ones. That would entitle you to share in more company earnings, for some fixed invested amount. And that, in turn, would allow more dividends or more retention of earnings to finance company growth.

This line of reasoning prompts the question: Are low P/E stocks better investments than high P/E stocks? Paul Miller [122], then of Drexel & Co. and since cofounder of another firm, researched this point, using data covering 1948–64. Focusing on larger companies (annual sales over $150 million), he found that stocks having low P/Es at year-end did show significantly better price increases over the following year. The higher the P/E, the worse the stock tended to perform thereafter.

William Breen [15] did a similar study for the years 1953–66. He first confined his selections to higher-growth stocks—those showing compound annual growth in earnings per share of over 10 percent for the prior five years. He then computed the returns (price appreciation plus dividends) for portfolios with the lowest P/E stocks among this group and with the lowest P/E stock in each industry. Breen concluded that "low price/earnings multiples measured either relative to the whole population, or to industry classification . . . give portfolio performance which in most years is superior to the performance of randomly selected stocks." [15, p. 127]

These studies imply that if you don't care to forecast earnings growth, or if you set minimum standards for acceptable past earnings growth, then you are better off with low P/Es than with high P/Es.

Note, however, that in selecting stocks the studies used earnings figures for the year, which to some extent are not immediately available at year-end. Also, the studies spanned a generally rising market and did not adjust for the risk of unstable prices.

What Price Stability?

The other issue theoretically affecting P/Es is the *stability* of the rate of return. Investors dislike risk. Uncertain, unpredictable earnings get valued less than do stable earnings of the same level. Thus, we see that large diversified companies often sell at higher P/Es than does the average small firm with similar growth expectations. (Naturally, there are exceptions, notably the conglomerates, which are seen as *too* diversified to be managed or *too* leveraged to be stable.) Cyclical stocks, which exaggerate the effects of economic cycles, also get downgraded. Consumable goods face a more stable demand than do durable goods, and their makers' and marketers' common stocks usually do too. People can slow down on auto buying, for example, but usually do not cut back much on food or soap.

Still other factors affect P/E ratios. Common stocks compete with all other alternatives for the favor of investors. And outlooks for growth and aversions to uncertainty can change over time. For one thing, the general level of interest rates partially determines P/E ratios. When quality long-term bonds yield 9 percent and lower-grade bonds yield 12 percent, as they have of late, this puts pressure on P/Es. Such pressure resulted in unusually low P/E levels in 1974, which rebounded when interest rates relaxed in 1975 and early 1976.

We must conclude that, while it would be extremely useful to be able to predict future shifts in P/Es, to a great extent they depend on predictions for earnings themselves. Therefore, the next chapter discusses this fundamentally important topic.

10

Predicting Earnings

Modern research has shown that there is a strong, but not perfect, relationship between stock prices and earnings. The question remains: If you could forecast earnings, could you then forecast stock price changes?

Suppose for a moment that you had the ability to forecast earnings with complete accuracy. Could such information be used profitably? Henry Latané and Donald Tuttle [94], of the University of North Carolina, sought an answer to this question. They compared changes in a stock's earnings with changes in its price for 48 stocks over a 14-year period. They found large year-to-year differences among the proportion of price changes that could be explained by changes in earnings. This proportion of explained price variations ranged from 64.5 percent to 0.8 percent, and *the correlations were all positive*. That is, increases in stock prices were associated with gains in company earnings. Likewise, decreases in stock prices were, on the whole, associated with decreases in company earnings.

In some years, this tendency was almost eliminated by other factors, while in other years the influence of earnings on prices was quite strong. Latané and Tuttle reported that, over the entire 14-year period studied, only 17.4 percent of all price variations could be explained by earnings changes. Thus, a surprisingly small proportion of stock price movement was traceable to changes in company earnings. Nonetheless, Latané and Tuttle observed that "perfect knowledge of future earnings would be of great value in selecting stocks." [94, p. 347]

Richard Brealey expanded on this work to determine just how much benefit could be realized by such "perfect knowledge of future earnings." Commenting on Latané and Tuttle's research, Brealey stated that the average annual price appreciation of the 48 stocks was 12.2 percent. If, however, at the beginning of each year, an investor had been able to select from this group the stocks of the 8 companies (out of the 48 studied) that were to show the greatest proportion of earnings increase, his average annual profit would have been 30.4 percent. [13, p. 85]

Thus, two conclusions are well supported in the research literature. First, P/E ratios reflect, to a major degree, the expected growth in company earnings. Second, if *one* could accurately forecast future earnings, an above-average investment strategy could most certainly be devised. Use of the term *one*, however, is more than literary impartiality. Indeed, if *many* could predict future earnings accurately, the profitable strategy of *one* would succumb to an efficient capital market.

Surprising Earnings Changes

Further research relating earnings to stock prices was reported by Professors Philip Brown and Ray Ball. [16] For selected companies, they adjusted stock price changes to eliminate the movements of the general market. Then they studied these "nonmarket" stock price changes for 12 months before, and 6 months after, the date of each company's reported earnings. They found that, when a stock's actual earnings were better than its forecast earnings, the price of the stock would typically rise during the preceding 12-month period, and that the rise faltered in the 6-month period after the actual earnings announcement. This is depicted in Figure 10–1, where "0" on the horizontal scale denotes the official earnings announcement.

They also reported that stock prices declined during the months preceding and following unexpectedly poor earnings announcements. Figure 10–2 traces the average stock price movement when actual earnings were below the forecast level.

This information is very revealing. It shows what typically happens to a stock's price in the months that precede and follow a surprising earnings performance. Note that *by the time the earnings*

FIGURE 10-1

Average Price Movement during Months before and after the Earnings Announcement of Stocks of Companies Producing Unexpectedly Good Earnings*

Price Change Not Attributable to Market Change

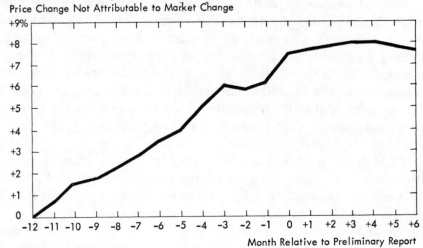

Month Relative to Preliminary Report

* After Brown and Ball [16].

FIGURE 10-2

Average Price Movement during Months before and after the Earnings Announcement of Stocks of Companies Producing Unexpectedly Bad Earnings*

Price Change Not Attributable to Market Change

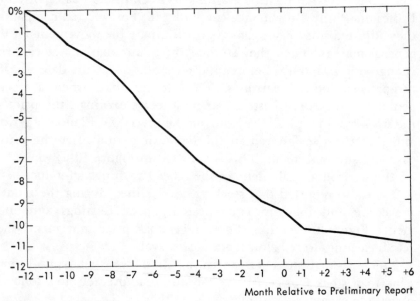

Month Relative to Preliminary Report

* After Brown and Ball [16].

report was issued, the market had almost fully anticipated the report. Also note that *the stock price made little adjustment after the announcement of either favorable or unfavorable earnings.*

This research indicates that, on the average, stock prices react well in advance of the reported annual earnings of companies— when the results are actually occurring. As noted, the theoretical worth of a share of common stock is linked to its future stream of earnings. Research indicates that the process by which the market anticipates this earnings stream is both steady and accurate. The market action, combining the separate actions of millions of investors, does a remarkably efficient job of digesting this information.

Can Changes in Earnings Be Predicted?

There are many reasons to expect that companies with consistently strong earnings records should continue to be capable of producing good earnings in the future. Similarly, companies with low profitability in the past *intuitively* seem likely to have such difficulties in the future. Some of the supergrowth stocks of the past, such as Avon Products, IBM, Polaroid, and Xerox, enjoyed a certain monopolistic advantage in rapidly expanding markets, enabling them to post consistently good earnings performance. It therefore seems reasonable that companies with satisfied customers and large, successful investments in product development, personnel, plant, and equipment should have a competitive advantage that is likely to persist.

Do good earnings records persist? Brealey [13] sought to answer this question. By studying the earnings changes of approximately 700 industrial companies over a 14-year period, he found that, contrary to intuition, year-to-year earnings changes do *not* tend to persist! In fact, they even show a slight tendency to reverse.

Brealey even classified his findings separately for 62 different industries. Still, he found no evidence that period-to-period earnings changes occur with discernible patterns or trends. In fact, after rigorous tests, he reported that "a good year or succession of good years was more frequently followed by a poor year and vice versa." [13, pp. 94–95]

Similar findings have been reported by Joseph Murphy, Jr., who studied the earnings of 344 companies in 12 industries during 38 different time periods. Murphy's research, conducted at the University of Minnesota, reported that there appears to be little significant correlation between relative rates of growth of earnings per share in one period and relative growth in earnings per share in the next period. Only rarely did companies which recorded superior growth in earnings per share in one period show more than an even chance of recording above average growth in the next period. [126, p. 73]

Thus, if we *could* make accurate forecasts of future earnings changes, such forecasts could undoubtedly lead to above-average investment returns. Caution should be exercised, however, to avoid predicting future earnings changes solely on the basis of past earnings.

Trends in Earnings?

John Lintner and Robert Glauber [103], of Harvard University, studied the earnings of 323 companies over varying periods of up to five years in an attempt to discern predictive patterns. Somewhat surprisingly, while there is evidence of long-term patterns in price movements, Lintner and Glauber were unable to detect consistent patterns in long-run earnings that could be used to produce above-average investment results.

Manown Kisor and Van Messner [90] studied earnings changes over six-month intervals. They first showed that, *if* they could calculate the *direction* of earnings changes six months hence, *irrespective of the amount of the changes,* they could outperform the market. But using a sample of 813 industrial companies, they found only *one* pattern that could be used to predict the direction of subsequent earnings changes. That pattern, which they called "increased momentum in relative earnings," shows *acceleration* in the rate of change in a company's earnings relative to the earnings performance of the general market.

Thus, Kisor and Messner showed that, when the path of a company's relative earnings assumes the shape depicted in Figure 10–3, the likelihood of some increase in earnings for that company over the subsequent six months is significantly better than it is for the market as a whole. This evidence parallels the findings of Levy [98] and one of the authors [68] that stocks which advance in *price* substantially ahead of the market in one six-month period tend to have above-average price appreciation in the following six-month period. But with the exception of the pattern of *accelerated* earnings growth, as depicted in Figure 10–3, there is overwhelming evidence that future earnings changes cannot be forecast solely from past earnings.

Does anyone really *try* to predict earnings from historical patterns? Yes!!! There is much evidence that investors, as well as Wall Street professionals, rely heavily on historical earnings to predict future earnings because doing this seems intuitively correct. John Cragg and Burton Malkiel [31] have studied earnings estimates made by professionals who specialize in bank trust management, investment banking, mutual fund management, general brokerage, and

FIGURE 10–3

Pattern of Earnings Changes with Useful Information Content

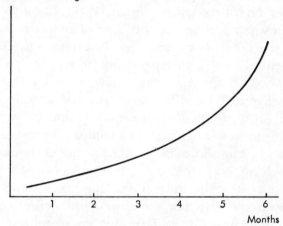

*That is, after removing the performance of the market.

the investment advisory business. Their remarkable conclusion was that when these experts were asked to forecast earnings, the overwhelming tendency was to base their predictions on recent changes in historical earnings. Even more startling was the fact that the predictions of the top analysts were "no better than the simplest strategy of the naive investor—who simply believes the company growth will parallel changes in gross national product." [158, p. 43]

It should be emphasized that this research does not mean that earnings cannot be forecast from information other than historical earnings. Thus, a vital question is: Do forecasts gain value from such facts as balance sheet items, sales estimates, and computerized cash-flow simulations. To answer this question, we must first define what is meant by "earnings."

What Are Earnings, Anyway?

The concept of corporate earnings would seem to be simple enough. Since the securities legislation of 1933, the certified public accounting (CPA) profession has had to certify the authenticity of earnings reported by publicly owned companies. This requirement of CPA-certified financial statements was intended to imbue stockholders' information with a kind of "Good Housekeeping 'Fiscal' Seal of Approval." Unfortunately, CPA-certification of earnings has not meant that the earnings were calculated in a manner easily comparable to previous years' earnings or to the earnings of competitors.

Most people assume that accounting is a profession dedicated to exactness. This image is propagated by the accounting profession's proclivity for reporting a firm's financial condition to the nearest dollar—even when dealing with millions. The fact is, however, that accounting statements have traditionally been prepared within the broad guidelines of so-called generally accepted accounting principles, and the resultant statements have been far from precise or comparable. Even CPA-audited earnings statements have sometimes been downright misleading when people assumed that the earnings of different firms were calculated in a comparable fashion.

Companies that appear to be similar because of common products, size, and so forth can, from an operating point of view, elect to manage their assets quite differently. One manufacturing company might, for example, purchase the newest production equipment. A competitor might lease it. Still another competitor might elect to sustain old equipment through heavy maintenance outlays. The accounting for these different operations can vary the reported earnings of different companies substantially. More important, however, is the fact that under the "generally accepted" guidelines even identical operating decisions can be accounted for differently.

This flexibility, plus the reality that businesses hire their accountants, troubles the client-accountant relationship. Accountants, by and large, are ethical people with high professional standards of honesty and integrity. Within the relationship between the client and the CPA firm employed as its financial watchdog, the issue has often become "what the accountants will accept and certify." In this decision, the professional ethics of the accounting firm have rarely been compromised. Yet, *within* "generally accepted" accounting practices, there are a myriad of "accepted" precedents that can confuse the reported earnings. This problem was articulated in a *Forbes* Special Report:

Accounting rules which, under the guise of affording management legitimate choices, result in distorted earnings figures. In all too many cases the question is not whether a given accounting treatment fits, but whether the companies' accountants can be convinced to accept it.

Toward this end companies and their auditors, too, will go to great lengths to seek out precedents. . . . A single precedent, perhaps backed by the threat of the company "to take our auditing business elsewhere," can be enough to make a questionable accounting treatment "generally accepted." [191, p. 5]

"Smoothing" Reported Earnings

The cases of abuse, irregularities, and just plain confusion from mixing "apples and oranges" on certified financial statements have resulted in lawsuits against each of the Big Eight CPA firms. Numerous artificial increases in reported earnings through changes in depreciation schedules, flow-through of investment credits, and the pooling treatment of mergers have been documented in the accounting journals. Further, evidence from Barry Cushing's [34] doctoral dissertation at Michigan State University supports the widely held belief that companies smooth out fluctuations in their periodic earnings. But, for all the confusion such accounting variations generate among the public, and for all the grief they cause corporate officers and their CPAs, the market is remarkably efficient at properly reflecting the *true worth* of a company.

Corporate executives who contemplate changes in their investment credit or depreciation accounting should first consult Robert Kaplan and Richard Roll's [83] study of the impact such changes have on securities prices. They concluded:

Earnings manipulation may be fun, but its profitability is doubtful. We have had difficulty discerning any statistically significant effect that it has had on security prices. . . . firms that manipulated earnings seem to have been performing poorly. If this is generally true, one would predict that earnings manipulation, once discovered, is likely to have a depressing effect on market price because it conveys an unfavorable management view of a firm's economic condition. [83, p. 245]

Yet, in spite of the market's apparent economic efficiency, problems arising from subtle differences embedded in the reported earnings of similar companies have long complicated the job of both money managers and security analysts. The *Forbes* Special Study, for example, noted:

> Sun Oil elects to charge off its drilling costs for new wells right away, while competitor Continental Oil capitalizes the costs of successful wells and writes them off gradually. . . . Delta Air Lines depreciates its planes over ten years, while United Air Lines, at the other end of the spectrum, writes off its 727 jets over as long as sixteen years. Douglas Aircraft elects to record some of its aircraft development costs as assets, while competitors may charge similar expenditures against current income. [191, p. 4]

What and When to Report

When translated into a particular year's earnings, differences in accounting policy can certainly vary the reported results (if not the ultimate stock price). For example, Eunice Filter, a brokerage house industry specialist, adjusted the accounting practices of major computer companies so as to achieve comparability. She determined that the reported earnings of some firms should be *halved* in relation to Digital Equipment and IBM, the two firms with the most conservative accounting policies. Since these differences do emerge in the longer run, she concluded that this discrepancy "points up the extent of potential vulnerability of future earnings." [48, p. 44]

Delaying the reporting of earnings is another accounting policy deserving scrutiny. Remember the joke line, "I have some good news and some bad news . . . First, the good news." Well, corporations do that too. Alan Abelson [1], the author and financial detective, has stated that "companies that do well generally tend to report earlier than those that do poorly."

This assertion was confirmed by Victor Niederhoffer and Patrick Regan. [133] Of the 50 best-performing and the 50 worst-performing NYSE stocks during 1970, they found that "only 40 percent of the bottom 50 companies announced their earnings within two months of the end of the fiscal year, whereas 88 percent of the top 50 did so." Apparently, late reporting is prima facie evidence of a problem.

Accounting Standards

Recognizing the problems that arise from accounting differences, and facing the threat of a more active Securities and Exchange Commission, the nation's CPAs adopted new rules on March 1, 1973. The new rules—the first retooling in more than 50 years of the standards under which accountants operate—require that CPAs certifying financial statements follow the opinions of the Financial Accounting Standards Board. For example, one rule requires that all research and development costs must now be expensed, no matter how promising the results. Another rule requires that newly selected auditors must consult with their predecessors about possible procedural disputes underlying the change in auditors.

Reported earnings are, in reality, the composite of hundreds of assumptions that have been distilled into one number—net earnings. This single, certified figure provides irreducible simplicity. That simplicity, coupled with the view that earnings contribute much to common stock values, has caused the investment community to adopt net earnings (usually stated per share) as its key indicator.

Company Earnings Forecasts

Several observations can be made concerning "official" earnings forecasts. First, there is little doubt that such forecasts, especially if in accord with SEC guidelines, have an influence on stock prices. For this reason, it would be useful to know the *accuracy* of such forecasts. If insider forecasts are not accurate, they will confuse, rather than serve, the public.

Second, even the most expertly derived forecasts are *sometimes* wrong. To insure against lawsuits in such a situation, in the opinion of U.S. District Judge Jacob Weinstein (in a shareholder suit against Monsanto Co.), such earnings forecasts must be "appropriately prepared," "extensively reviewed," "honest," "reasonable," and made by the people "most qualified" to make them. [202, p. 14]

Third, when an earnings forecast proves wrong, the price of a stock can literally collapse. Institutions, in particular, have become especially sensitive to little wiggles in corporate quarterly earnings.

Fourth, the suggestion that CPA firms might be called upon to validate earnings forecasts has stirred up much furor. Some who oppose CPA involvement feel that CPAs are skilled in documenting the current financial condition of a firm but lack training in forecasting techniques. Others argue that, if a CPA certifies a forecast, he might be biased when the time comes to certify actual performance.

Fifth, the myopia of focusing on one number—earnings per share

—can be bad for both the company and the investor. Joel Stern [170], of the Chase Manhattan Bank, has, for example, documented how the earnings per share criterion often leads to *bad* long-run financial decisions. And forecasting should attempt to answer "if" questions. *"If* sales increase, and *if* credit terms are extended, and *if . . ."* The results of such forecasts, however, are seldom *one number!* Instead, companies usually make "optimistic," "best guess," and "pessimistic" forecast boundaries. Forcing managers to make more precise projections, some contend, erroneously represents forecasting as an exact science.

The foregoing criticisms of publicized company earnings forecasts would be moot if managers could not forecast accurately. The evidence is, however, that they can. Information compiled by Douglas Carmichael, director of technical research for the American Institute of Certified Public Accountants, and by Donald Chapin indicates that required earnings forecasts in Britain are consistently on the conservative side. The indications are, in fact, that the "name of the game" in Britain is to please the public by exceeding your forecast each year by 10 percent. [203, p. 14]

Several recent and rigorous studies have sparked a heated debate over the accuracy of company earnings forecasts and the usefulness of interim earnings data in predicting annual earnings. David Green and Joel Segall [64] ignited the powder keg by showing that there was little difference between executive forecasts and naive extrapolations. These findings were openly challenged by Philip Brown and Victor Niederhoffer. [17]

When the smoke settled, after an exchange of articles such as "Brickbats and Straw Men" [65] and "Return of Strawman" [66], the generally accepted conclusion was that "managers' forecasts are substantially 'better' than those produced from naive models." [27, p. 498] Thus, it is both logical and experimentally verified that corporations, which have more relevant information than do outsiders and can, to some degree, control their performance, can do a superior job of forecasting earnings.

Predicting Stock Prices from Earnings Forecasts

The major conclusions on this issue are summarized below:

1. The goal of security analysis is to select stocks likely to have above-average total returns—yield plus price appreciation.

2. Price is theoretically related to future earnings.
3. An accurate knowledge of future earnings changes would allow one to select stocks with above-average returns.
4. The common practice of predicting future earnings from historical earnings trends is apparently worthless.
5. In an accounting sense, earnings are hard to define, difficult to forecast, and subject to various accounting interpretations which complicate intra- and interindustry comparisons.
6. Corporate insiders can do the best job of making earnings forecasts because they have the best available information and because, to some degree, they can make their forecasts come true.
7. If earnings data are widely disseminated, stock prices will reflect such information.
8. While the SEC does not require earnings forecasts, it does impose guidelines and sanctions over the quality of such forecasts and the dissemination of the earnings forecasts that companies elect to publicize.
9. If accurate earnings forecasts are disseminated to all investors, their differential value to any single investor is nil.
10. Investment analysis directed solely at predicting a company's earnings in effect focuses attention on an area overshadowed by the larger forces of public reaction to other company-related information, the firm's industry, and market-related information.

11

Other Company-Related Information

Reasoned investment selection comes from knowing what information is, and is not, already reflected in the prices of various investment instruments in different markets. The most popular instruments are common stocks listed on the NYSE or the AMEX. Of the four levels of information—the overall market, the basic industry, the industry subgroup, and the company—most investors concentrate on company-related information. Yet, such information explains only a portion of a stock's price movement. How useful is company-related information? It might be the *most* useful kind of information if we could predict it accurately.

On the one hand, some people argue that the specificity of company-related information should make it the most predictable. On the other hand, skeptics note that constant scrutiny of company-related information by thousands of investors destroys its value to any one individual. This chapter summarizes the scientific evidence on company-related information other than earnings—dividends, stock splits, new listings, professional opinions, secondary distributions, and, most important, insider trading. Taken together, this research allows us to classify such information as being either useful, misleading, or useless.

Under the fair-game theory, when astute investors have equal access to all information, none of them can reliably expect to outperform the market. In looking for clues from company-related information, one can only expect above-average performance by illegal access to information not available to other investors, or by superior analysis of available information. It is the latter area—producing private knowledge from public information—that merits our concern.

The concept of "information," or "news," is synonymous with *surprise* or *change*. If a company's earnings have grown at 5 percent per year for the past four years, and if all forecasts predict continued 5 percent growth, there is little information in an announcement that merely confirms this expectation. Surprises provide information! Hence, the real "information" in an announcement is the degree to which it deviates from expectations.

Dividends

Research by James Walter [180], at the Wharton School, has shown the undeniable impact of dividend policies on common stock prices. Such analysis of dividend information bears on two important issues:

1. Should you buy a high- or a low-dividend stock?
2. Can dividend announcements be used to select stocks with above-average returns?

High- versus Low-Payout Stocks. The rate of return from an investment depends on two factors—capital appreciation and income, as from dividends. Many investors are blinded by visions of grandeur about the expected capital appreciation of their investments. To such investors, dividend income is something for widows or orphans. If you have a tendency to disregard dividends, you should consider the following quotation from Richard Brealey's book *Security Prices in a Competitive Market.*

If in 1926 a tax-exempt investor had purchased an equal amount of all New York Stock Exchange equities, and if he had reinvested all subsequent dividends he would have found that by the end of 40 years his capital had multiplied 35 times [after Fisher and Lorie [50]]. If he had been improvident and squandered all his dividends on bacchanalian pleasures, the value of his portfolio would have increased by a factor of only six. This example is presented not as a warning against prodigality but to demonstrate that the cumulative effect of dividend receipts can be very large. [14, p. 4]

A company can do two things with its earnings. It can distribute them to stockholders as dividends, or it can retain and reinvest them, plowing them back into the company. Retained earnings have an advantage, since they represent an automatic reinvestment of money that, if distributed to stockholders, would be taxed *before* it could be reinvested. Further, once earnings are distributed to stockholders, they cannot be reinvested without an underwriting or brokerage commission.

The portion of a company's total earnings that is distributed as dividends is called the "dividend payout ratio." Typically, a rapidly growing company, such as McDonald's, will retain all or most of its earnings to finance expansion. Similarly, companies with sufficient plant and equipment to meet the demand of their customers need little to finance expansion and can distribute a large portion of their income as dividends.

The importance of the dividend payout ratio lies in the differential between the timing and the rate of taxes on dividends versus capital gains. Dividends are taxed currently as part of income, while long-term capital gains (assets held more than six months) are subject to taxation only upon sale of the appreciated asset and at rates which are generally half of those on income. As a result, for the average investor, *a dollar of dividends after taxes is worth less than a dollar of capital gains.*

We could, therefore, reasonably assume that low-dividend-payout stocks are relatively more attractive for any investor subject to taxes. It follows, then, that the price of low-dividend stocks includes a premium for this advantage. This conclusion—that low-dividend stocks are worth more—runs counter to one of the age-old tenets of fundamental security analysis. Authors such as Graham and Dodd have held that the market's pricing mechanisms are overwhelmingly in favor of liberal dividends. [61]

Surprisingly, though, the factual evidence concludes that there is no substantial difference in the value that the market places on dividends versus capital gains. The market seems to have struck a balance between the traditional belief that liberal dividends are revered and the logic that, because of differential taxation, they should be discounted.

This means that you pay roughly the same price for $1 of future dividends that you pay for $1 of future capital gains. But, since your dividends are taxed at a higher rate, they are worth proportionately less. Hence, in the market's apparent confusion over the relative valuation of capital gains and dividends, and the resultant parity, there appears to be a slight unadjusted *penalty for owning high-dividend stocks.* We can conclude, in the words of Brealey, that "almost any taxed investor will derive a somewhat lower net rate of return from high-payout stocks." [14, p. 20]

Dividend Announcements. We have seen that changes in stock prices are explained largely by expectations about future earnings. Therefore, it is likely that dividend announcements will also affect stock prices, as they also portend a firm's future prosperity or lack of it.

Several researchers have examined the rationale underlying dividend decisions. These studies reveal how firms decide on the amount of earnings to be distributed as dividends versus the amount to be retained by the company. For a variety of reasons, the paramount factor in this decision is the amount of earnings that management feels "should" be distributed. To the astonishment of many people, it appears that notions of the "appropriate," or "target," dividend so dominate this decision that retained funds are viewed as a leftover. If these leftover funds are not sufficient to finance expansion, most firms will either borrow money or defer the expenditure rather than tamper with the dividend level they feel their stockholders expect.

As one analyzes dividend decisions further, it appears that the target dividend is guided by management's desire to establish a pattern of stable dividend growth. This reluctance to change prevails in regard to both dividend increases and decreases, with dividend reduction typically viewed as a last resort. On the other hand, the hesitancy to increase a dividend is attributed to the fear that a higher-level dividend implies a commitment to *continue* at that level. Paul Darling [36] has supported this conclusion by showing that the level of dividends paid between 1930 and 1955 could not be explained by variations in earnings, but instead corresponded to management's optimism about the future.

Here, then, is an important focal point in considering the usefulness of dividend announcements. Studies that have relied on interviews with corporate management [102], and others that have studied dividend histories [43], conclude that firms do not make dividend changes without considerable assessment of the future. Decreases take place largely because firms have little choice other than to cut the payout. Increases, in addition to reflecting high current earnings, reflect management's optimism that the new dividend level can be sustained. It follows, then, that if dividend changes reflect management's opinion about the future, and if managers can correctly assess the future, dividend *changes* should serve as barometers of a firm's future prosperity.

This possibility raises two questions. The first, and most obvious, is whether or not dividend changes portend the future. If they do, the next question is whether or not the market *already knows* that prosperity or difficulty lies ahead, and has fully adjusted the stock's price by the time the dividend news is available.

Joseph Murphy [127] sought a definitive answer to these questions by studying the relationship between dividend changes and the subsequent earnings of 244 companies between 1950 and 1965. While the association between dividend changes and subsequent earnings was not as strong as one would like, Murphy did find a positive relationship. So, while dividend changes do not portend the future exactly, they do tend to reflect management's correct assessment of future earnings.

A more direct study of the relationship between dividend announcements and both subsequent earnings and price changes was made by Richardson Pettit [140], at the Wharton School. Pettit studied the impact of dividend announcements on the subsequent earnings and price performance of 625 companies over four and one-half years. He found that dividend announcements were closely associated with subsequent price performance, and concluded that "dividend announcements convey substantial information to market participants that causes them to revalue their shares."

He also noted that the effect was generally proportionate to the amount of the dividend change. In terms of the market's efficiency, Pettit concluded that the "market's judgment concerning the information implicit in the [dividend] announcement is reflected almost completely as of the end of the announcement month." [140, p. 38] We conclude, therefore, that *news of a dividend change does contain useful information that is not already reflected in the price of the stock.*

Stock Splits

A stock split is a management decision to increase (often double) the number of shares of stock outstanding. For instance, in a two-for-one stock split the price of each new share should be worth exactly half the price of each old share. After a split, each shareholder's ownership value, and that of all shareholders, remains the same. The investor's pieces of paper represent precisely the same proportion of ownership as before. In the words of A. Wilfred May, one of Wall Street's elder statesmen, "A pie does not grow through its slicing!" [116, p. 5]

Some people contend that the lower price per share brought about by a stock split will stimulate investment demand by "broadening the market" for the company's shares. There is really no merit to this contention unless one speaks of those investors who could not afford to buy a *single* share at the former price. But, the argument runs, investors like to buy stock in round lots, and a split lowers the price of a 100-share purchase. Some people favor splits because they expect lower commission rates from round-lot purchases. However, while commissions on some trades are lower after a split, on other trades they are higher. And on average, the lower share prices resulting from stock splits cause slightly *higher* commissions for the same dollar amount of trading.

Even though there is no theoretical reason to expect above-average returns following stock splits, as expressions of progress or optimism, splits might be self-fulfilling predictions. In the stock market, if enough people believe something will happen, their actions can make it happen. May criticized this blindly fatalistic reasoning in an article entitled "Current Popular Delusions about the Stock Split and Stock Dividend." May called stock splits a "speculative Frankenstein ending in stockholder disillusionment." [116, p. 5]

C. Austin Barker has published articles on stock splits in the *Harvard Business Review*. In his first study, Barker concluded that, "contrary to the general belief, stock splits do not automatically produce a lasting price gain." [6, p. 101] His second study found that "split-ups alone produced no lasting real gains in market price for widely held, nationally listed stocks, whether the split-up is effected in a normal market or in an outstanding bull market." [7, p. 551]

Other studies of splits have shown essentially the same thing. Research by R. C. Rieke [145] showed that companies announcing stock splits generally experienced a price improvement in the months *preceding* the announcement of the split. But by the time news of a pending split has been announced to the public, no significant price movement remains. The brokerage firm of Hardy and Co. analyzed the impact of the additional number of shares resulting from the stock split on subsequent stock price performance. As we would expect, this study also concluded that splits provided no useful information (see [145]).

An extensive study of stock splits by Eugene Fama et al. [44] monitored the behavior of 940 stocks for the 30 months that preceded and followed stock splits. The relative performance (that is, with market comovement removed) of these stocks is shown in Figure 11–1.

Split information is generally not available until immediately before the split occurs (designated by "0" on the horizontal scale). Note that the relative price growth *stops* when the split activity occurs. This information indicates that splits are a *consequence* of rising stock prices and not their *cause*. Those who rely on news of impending splits should note that, for two and one-half years after the split, *the relative price remained within one percentage point of the split price.* Not surprisingly, Fama et al. reported that "there seems to be no way to use a split to increase one's expected return." [44, pp. 20–21]

FIGURE 11–1

Relative Pre- and Post-Split Performance of 940 Stocks

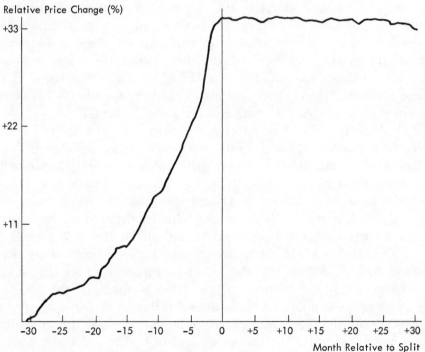

Source: Fama, Fisher, Jensen, and Roll [44] and Brealey [14].

Another study of stock splits was reported by Hausman, West, and Largay in 1971. [72] In this study Hausman et al. carefully synthesized the most recent research on stock splits and then, through their own research, reconciled some of the differences that had appeared.

Our results clearly indicate that buying stocks on (or after) the date on which a split has been publicly announced does not lead to systematic price appreciation greater than the appreciation that might be expected from underlying factors such as corporate earnings and the industry-by-industry outlook for stock price movements. [72, p. 76]

People who believe that news of an impending stock split is useful could reason that, while the underlying value of the company is unchanged, the decision to split reflects management optimism about the future prosperity of the company. However, the research summarized here shows that the market efficiently discounts any such effect. The conclusion is that *news about stock splits is apparently useless.*

New Listings

In this section we examine the usefulness of knowing that a company has decided to list its stock on the New York Stock Exchange. To be eligible for NYSE listing, a company must have a minimum of $2.5 million in pretax earnings, $14 million in net tangible assets, and $14 million in publicly held common stock representing at least 800,000 shares spread among 1,800 round-lot shareholders.

Needless to say, not all companies can meet these criteria. Also, in any one year the number of new listings is relatively small. In 1970, 68 new companies were admitted to NYSE trading, but the figure has averaged much less since then. One could reason that the decision to list on the NYSE represents a pinnacle of performance. Following this train of thought, news that a company has applied for listing might indicate an above-average opportunity.

Several researchers [2, 57, 119, 120, 121, 178] have examined the pre- and post-listing behavior of stocks on the NYSE. The consistent pattern that has emerged may be summarized as follows:

1. When measured from a time three to six months before the application date to the application date, these stocks performed significantly better than the market. Such price advances were doubtless a factor in the subsequent decision to list the securities.

2.   During the time span covering the application date, the approval date, and the listing date, these stocks continued to have some significantly better-than-average price appreciation.
3.   When the period measured was one day, one month, or one, three, or five years from the listing date, the rate of return for these stocks was, on average, below that for the general market.

We conclude from these studies that *stocks which have recently moved their trading to the NYSE do not, on average, represent a likely source of above-average returns.*

Professional Opinions

Stock prices change because people change their opinions. We know of one investor who confided that he had developed a technique for selecting undervalued securities. But his problem was that the market did not have the benefit of his careful analysis. Because "the market did not know any better," his favored securities remained undervalued.

At the other extreme, it is reasonable to expect that the publicized opinion of a respected professional could cause dramatic price changes, regardless of the underlying rationale. Walter Winchell's "Mr. and Mrs. America and all the ships at sea" radio tips caused such landslide reactions that he was restrained from giving further on-the-air recommendations.

Stock market opinions can become self-fulfilling predictions. When people believe "GM is going up," their actions will drive it up, and vice versa. If so, it might be a useful investment strategy to respond quickly to the opinions of widely circulated advisory services. Also, of course, one should not dismiss the possibility that advisory services are correct in their analyses, so that the market will subsequently adjust to the advisory services' correct assessment of a stock's value.

Researchers have long been intrigued by the possibility that advisory services can forecast. As long ago as 1933, Alfred Cowles studied the forecasting ability of 16 financial services, 20 insurance companies, and 25 financial publications. Cowles concluded that the 16 financial services were 1.43 percent worse than average, the 20 insurance companies 1.20 percent worse, while the 25 financial publications failed by 4 percent per annum. [28]

Several modern studies have measured the market's response to published investment advice. In 1958, Robert Ferber, at the University of Illinois, studied the price movements related to recommendations of four major advisory services. After removing market and industry comovements, Ferber found that "in the very short run, stock market service recommendations tend to influence the prices of approximately two thirds of the stocks in the direction indicated." [46, p. 94] By the end of the first week after publication, the average profit attainable from this information was 1.1 percent.

However, Ferber found no evidence of a longer-run impact after this very short-run adjustment. He also concluded that the short-run price adjustments were *caused* by the recommendation, and not *predicted* by them. He based this conclusion on "the failure of the recommended stocks . . . to outpace the market . . . in the week or two immediately preceding the recommendation." [46, p. 94]

The cornerstone study on professional opinions was that evaluating the Value Line rankings for performance, presented at the University of Chicago by Fischer Black [10]. Value Line, a leading investment advisory service, rates some 1,550 stocks for near-term performance, among other things. Black reported that "the one-year rankings are based on growth in earnings, price momentum, and the price-earnings ratio of each stock relative to the market and to historical standards for that stock."

The research reported so far has shown that each of these factors is effective in stock selection. By applying such information methodically, Black concluded, Value Line was able to "provide consistently superior performance even after transaction costs."

Studies by Ruff [150] and Stoffels [172] confirm the general conclusion that professional recommendations accurately foretell future price changes and that there is a measurable short-term price adjustment to reflect the "news." Other evidence, submitted by Cheney [18] and Colker [23], indicates that stocks recommended by advisory services and brokerage houses tend to outperform representative market averages over the following year.

We conclude, therefore, that *widely distributed professional opinions can somewhat presage short-term and (to a lesser degree) long-term relative price changes.*

Secondary Distributions

When the size of a stock offering might swamp the exchange's auction process, it may be organized as a *secondary distribution* and sold by underwriters and brokers using a prospectus. The sellers are typically institutional investors or the trusts or families of the company's founders. The reasons for such sales are as varied as the reasons for any sale. But the fact that these sellers consist of knowledgeable investors, who are sometimes presumed to have superior information, and the fact that *they* are selling, is viewed by many as a portent of bad times.

A detailed study has been made of 345 secondary distributions by Myron Scholes [152], at the University of Chicago. The short-term effect of a secondary offering is shown in Figure 11–2. With market comovement removed, the performance of these 345 stocks did fall off with the distribution.

The size of this percentage drop is obviously not large. Even a

FIGURE 11–2

Relative Pre- and Post-Secondary-Distribution Performance of 345 Stocks

Relative Price Change (%)

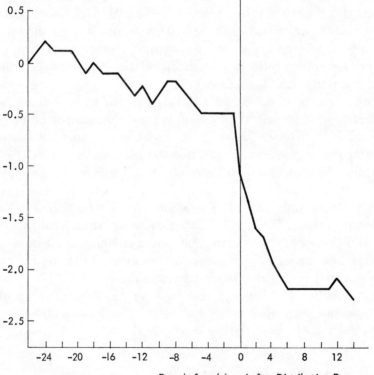

Days before (–) and after Distribution Day,
Which Is Designated by "0."

Source: Scholes [152] and Brealey [14].

FIGURE 11–3

Relative Performance of 1,207 Stocks before and after Distribution

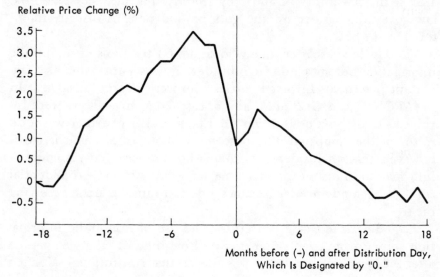

Relative Price Change (%)

Months before (–) and after Distribution Day,
Which Is Designated by "0."

Source: Scholes [152] and Brealey [14].

small percentage decline, however, over a two-month period still slices off that portion of a 10 percent or 12 percent hoped-for annual rate of return. On the other hand, if you already own such a stock and decide to sell it, the sales commissions will about equal the post-distribution price dip, leaving you with approximately the same asset value.

To study the long-term effect of secondary offerings, Scholes traced the monthly performance of 1,207 stocks for 18 months preceding and following such sales. These longer-term results are shown in Figure 11–3. *It is apparent that secondary distributions occur after fairly good performance, which they then effectively negate.*

Insider Trading

Certain insiders are required to report their security dealings to the SEC. These include exchange specialists, substantial owners, directors, and corporate officers. Notably excluded from SEC monitoring are relatives of these insiders, various employees, and banks that might have access to the same confidential information. The fact is that monitoring the stock transactions of every insider's friends and relatives would be inconceivably difficult. So, to protect against the possibility of abuse by secretly informed outsiders, the law governing insider trading goes beyond persons directly monitored by the SEC.

The law holds that anyone who trades on the basis of nonpublic information becomes a de facto insider. Two lawsuits which set important precedents involved parties who were clearly "insiders." In the *SEC* v. *Texas Gulf Sulphur Co.* case, company officers were involved. In *SEC* v. *Cady, Roberts & Co.*, a broker's partner was a director of the company. The outcome of both cases made it clear, however, that an insider is *anyone* who has access to confidential information. This means that a person who is given a confidential tip by a bona fide insider becomes a de facto insider upon receiving the tip.

A landmark test case concerning the use of nonpublic information sprang from events that occurred on June 21, 1966. Sometime after 2:00 P.M. on that day, it was alleged that institutional salesmen from Merrill Lynch began advising certain privileged institutional clients that Douglas Aircraft would soon report disappointing earnings. This information had come to Merrill Lynch in confidence on June 20 in connection with a proposed underwriting. The hearing examiner later concluded that 12 firms sold a total of 154,000 shares for more than $13.3 million on the basis of those tips and prior to public disclosure of the poor earnings.

In a landmark decision, SEC hearing examiner Warren E. Blair used the term *tippee* to refer to persons who, through a corporate insider, become aware of confidential information. He held that it was the responsibility of *anyone* receiving "material inside information" from insiders either to disclose the information publicly or to refrain from trading on it.

Recognizing this enlargement of corporate insiders to include tippees, the SEC spent more than a year reviewing Blair's decision. In July 1971, it reaffirmed that people who act on a tip violate the law if they have reason to know that the information was not made public. To make its position even stronger, the SEC ruled that people who use information that *innocently* comes into their possession are in violation of the law if they have reason to know that the information was intended to be confidential.

The SEC decision on the responsibilities of tippees clears the air on a vital point—*all parties to transactions must have access to the same material facts.* If you buy or sell securities knowing something that the other party to the transaction cannot know, you are in violation of federal law. If your broker gives you some inside information, and you act on it, you are *both* in violation of federal law.

It is doubtful that the significance of the preceding point can be overemphasized. This rule obligates all publicly owned companies to insure that disclosed changes in material facts are widely disseminated. If information is disclosed to one analyst, it must be made *equally* available to all analysts. It is unlawful for anyone to profit from material facts unless they are publicly accessable. This means that *all investment research must be restricted to the gathering and analysis of public facts also available to you.*

The law notwithstanding, when you decide to buy a share of stock, two groups of people already have access to confidential information. The management of the company knows, or certainly should know, more about that company than you do. Similarly, when your order reaches the floor of a stock exchange, the specialist in the stock you want to buy has nonpublic information on pending buy and sell orders at specific prices. Thus, two important questions are:

1. Do either management insiders or specialists use their privileged information for extra profit?
2. Do any of their actions give *us* useful information?

Management Insiders

Of all people, management insiders are in the best position to interpret company-related information. These insiders also have access to confidential information. This does not mean, however, that insiders use either their ability to analyze public information, or their access to private information, for personal profit. There are two deterrents to such insider profiteering. First, there is the moral obligation of corporate officers to meet their fiduciary responsibilities. Second, certain SEC restrictions (against short-term gains, for example) constrain insiders who might otherwise neglect their moral and fiduciary obligations.

Several researchers (see [39, 186]) have studied whether management insiders have better-than-average foresight in their investment decisions. If insiders make the right decision regarding their company's stock more often than do outsiders, they could be using their general understanding of the company and/or inside information for personal profit. This research shows that transactions by management insiders do provide above-average returns, meaning that they can, on average, forecast the future price of their stock better than the market.

Donald Rogoff [147] studied the relationship between the number of insider trades and subsequent stock performance in his doctoral dissertation at Michigan State University. Rogoff defined a buying consensus as existing when buyers exceeded sellers by at least two in a given month. For example, if, in a given month, one insider sold, but three bought, there was an insider buying consensus that month. Using this measure on 98 stocks between 1957 and 1960, Rogoff found that in 108 cases of insider buying consensus the stock outperformed the market during the next six months and that the stock underperformed the market in only 54 cases. Of 210 instances with an insider selling consensus, 112 preceded relative declines, while 98 preceded relative gains.

In a study of insider activity during 1963–64, James Lorie and Victor Niederhoffer [108], at the University of Chicago, found stock market performance almost identical to that reported by Rogoff after insider buying consensus—36 advances versus 19 declines. Lorie and Niederhoffer, however, found a stronger tendency than did Rogoff for insider sales to precede declines: of the 124 selling consensus cases, 81 preceded declines and 43 preceded advances. In sum, this clearly reflects insider foresight.

Shannon Pratt and C. W. DeVere [142] took the issue of insider trading a step further and studied the profitability of 52,000 insider transactions between 1960 and 1966. They defined an insider consensus as three or more buys or sells and none of the other. The relative performance following such insider activity is shown in Figure 11–4. Notice that one year after a consensus of insider sales, those stocks had an average return of 9.6 percent. This is a respectable rate of return and reflects the general market uptrend during the period covered by the study. The results following insider buying, however, are almost too good to be true. Stocks bought by three or more insiders during one month appreciated 27.1 percent after a year had passed. Further, there was an obvious long-run difference between the performance of the two groups.

The important question is whether *we* can use the actions of management insiders as indicators. Insider transactions of publicly

FIGURE 11-4

Performance of Stocks Experiencing Unusual Insider Activity—No Lag

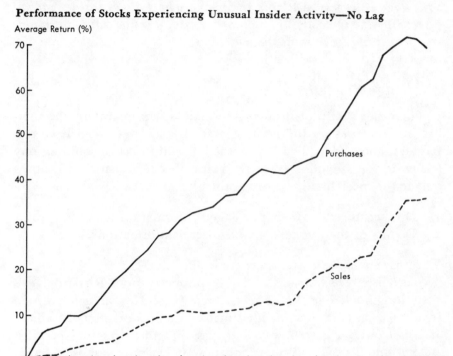

Source: Pratt and DeVere [142] and Brealey [14].

traded stocks are reported to the SEC. After a clerical and printing delay of about one month, a complete record of these transactions is available in the *Official Summary of Security Transactions and Holdings*. Studies of the usefulness of these published reports have provided encouraging results.

Pratt and DeVere found that imitating insiders' behavior one or two months after the record of their actions was published still allowed one to achieve above-average performance. Robert Hamanda [69] studied the relationship between insider trading volume and market-level changes. His findings suggest that insider opinion is a leading indicator of which direction the market will take.

Thus we can conclude that management insiders have special ability and/or inside information which makes them better-than-average investors in their own stock. What is surprising is that *this advantage is largely available to anyone who follows inside trading by reading the Official Summary of Security Transactions and Holdings—or listening to someone who does.*

Exchange Specialists

The other group of insiders—specialists who maintain the markets in securities on the floor of a stock exchange—also have differential knowledge. They know the size and prices of standing buy and sell orders. Under exchange rules, this information is known only to the specialist. So we can again ask:

1. Do specialists use their privileged information for extra profit?
2. Do any of their actions give *us* useful information?

The answers to these questions are again "Yes!"

Specialists received much adverse publicity from Richard Ney's bestselling book *The Wall Street Jungle* [128]. Ney, an actor turned investment adviser, documented many instances of specialist abuse. It is not our purpose however, to pass judgment on the specialist system, but instead to understand how it bears on our investment decisions.

The tendency for a stock's price to cluster at particular levels is termed *resistance* or *support* by stock market technicians (cf. Edwards and Magee [40]). In economics, the same phenomenon is known as the "Taussig Penumbra," honoring the renowned Harvard University professor F. W. Taussig, who introduced the concept in 1921. [175] There are two versions of this clustering phenomenon: congestion and reflection. Congestion implies that a stock's price remains within a particular range for an inordinately large number of transactions. Reflection implies that price levels exist from which a price change in one direction is much more likely than a price change in the other direction.

A reflection barrier above the stock's current price is called a "resistance level." Upon reaching this level, the stock's price would be deemed more likely to turn down than to move up further. A barrier below the current price is called a "support level."

Do stock prices get congested between support and resistance levels? In 1962, M. F. M. Osborne brought his training as an astronomer to bear on this issue. He studied the fractional portion of closing prices for a sample of NYSE stocks. Osborne reported "a pronounced tendency for prices to cluster on whole numbers, halves, quarters, and odd one-eighths in descending preference." [**139**, p. 287] This means that stock prices are more likely to trade at whole numbers than at a particular fraction. Such clustering is *not* consistent with the random-walk model.

Osborne probed the issue further. He studied what he called the "partially reflecting barrier" aspect of resistance and support. He hypothesized that if stock prices moved within reflecting barriers, then their highs and lows would tend to cluster near such barriers. For example, if a stock's price is reflected back down as it rises to whole number levels, we should find the number of daily highs ending in $7/8$ fractions significantly greater than would be expected on a chance basis. Similarly, if prices are reflected back up as they sink to whole numbers, we should find too many daily lows with $1/8$ fractions.

Osborne found this distribution of prices to be the case. He interpreted these findings as evidence of price congestion between support and resistance barriers. Whole number, and even half-number, price levels acted as partially impenetrable barriers. Thus, many stocks had daily highs of $7/8$ or $3/8$ because they were unable to reach the "barrier" price level. Conversely, an inordinate number of lows was observed at price levels just above integers and halves—at $1/8$ and $5/8$. Thus, as stock prices move either up or down toward whole or half numbers, there is a tendency for price *reversal* or, in a sense, for resistance or support.

In 1964, Victor Niederhoffer, then a promising young honors student in Harvard's Department of Economics, elaborated on this work in his bachelor's thesis [**129**]. The portion of Niederhoffer's thesis dealing with stock price clustering—which later drew academic attention (see [**130, 131, 132**])—confirmed Osborne's results for a much larger sample of stocks. These early studies provided evidence that, for the fractional price movements of concern to a specialist, *all is not random.*

These fractional price irregularities are the telltale signs of specialists' trading patterns—like the footprints of foxes in the snow leading to and from the hen house. These "tracks" constitute residual evidence of the feast "inside." These statements were tested statistically and verified in research conducted by one of the authors. [**68**]

Findings for 784 major stocks, classified by price range, are summarized in Table 11–1. These results clearly support the reflections-at-whole-numbers hypothesis. For example, look at the stocks in the $30–$39 average price range—132 stocks had *more* intraday lows than highs at the 1/8 fraction. Only 6 stocks in this price range had *fewer* intraday lows at 1/8 than highs. In the same way, the 7/8 fraction tends to act as a daily high point. In the $30–$39 price range, for 3 stocks this was not so—but for 135 stocks, it was!

Table 11–1

Comparison of Intraday Lows and Highs at 1/8 and 7/8 Fractional Prices for Stocks Classified by Average Price Range

Average Price Range	More lows at 1/8	More highs at 1/8	More lows at 7/8	More highs at 7/8
0–9	60	59	60	57
10–19	90	43	28	108
20–29	102	17	8	112
30–39	132	6	3	135
40–49	108	6	2	113
50–59	70	2	0	73
60–69	40	0	0	40
70–79	23	0	0	23
80–99	12	1	0	13
100–999	9	1	0	9
Total	646	135	101	683

The specialist system is a curious anomaly. Evolving legal theory holds that *all* parties to a stock transaction must have equal access to information. Yet, the exchanges allow specialists, who trade with the public for their own accounts, to have private material information. Their "book," or list of pending buy and sell orders, can be and apparently is used for personal profit.

The exchanges seem to equate the need to maintain fair and orderly markets with allowing specialists an unfair competitive advantage over the public. Unquestionably, the market-making mechanism must smooth out temporarily unbalanced buy or sell orders. But the system for accomplishing this has many inherent flaws that should be eliminated in the evolving central market. In the meantime, stock prices tend to get pushed up and down between whole-number, resistance and support levels. We conclude that *you can use this knowledge to slightly improve your decisions on purchase and sale points.*

Conclusions

Our examination of company-related information has led to several surprising conclusions.

1. The market is often caught off guard by announcements of unexpectedly high or low earnings. After such news, it takes several weeks for the price of a stock to "catch up" to the new information. Hence, above-average investment decisions can be made following such unanticipated announcements.

2. Contrary to the thinking of many seasoned market professionals, high-dividend-payout stocks provide the taxpaying investor with a somewhat lower rate of return than do low-payout stocks of comparable risk.

3. Dividend changes do mirror management's largely correct assessment of the firm's future prosperity, presumably because corporations do not alter their dividends casually.

4. To the chagrin of many advocates, stock splits and new NYSE listings typically signal the *end* of relative price growth and not its continuation.

5. Professional opinions and secondary distributions do cause small, short-term price movements.

6. Perhaps most important, management insiders do have extra insight into their company's future. Insider net buying or selling provides a useful guideline to follow, even after such activity is publicly reported.

7. Exchange specialists cause predictable patterns of fractional price movements.

Thus, we conclude that an investor who stays on top of earnings and dividend announcements and who uses professional advice and monitors insider activity can attain above-average returns.

12

Industry-Related
Information

The importance of industry-level effects on a company's stock price cannot be doubted. Recall that King's research traced 49 percent, on average, of a stock's price movement to its narrowly defined industry (for example, copper producers, mobile home manufacturers, supermarket chains, and so on). The firms in any industry are all influenced by such factors as overall demand for their product, suppliers' prices, government regulation, nationwide unions, international competition, new technology, and the like. We therefore find similar corporate performance—and hence similar stock market performance—in response to these common industry-related factors.

Defining Industries

To seek useful industry-related information and then to discover how to apply it, we must first define what an industry is. It is a *group of organizations supplying a market with substitutable products.* Thus, firms get lumped into the same industry category by providing comparable products (or comparable services, if one chooses to make this distinction).

Notice that this definition includes the public sector of the economy. We said "organizations," not "corporations," so that local governments or nonprofit hospitals or real estate partnerships each constitute an industry. However, outside investors have no ownership opportunities in such cases. Even a monopoly is included in this

114

definition. The "group" of organizations then has just one member.

The word *market* can be used to mean a certain geographic area, such as the distribution region of a water company or the reach of a TV station. This would narrow down the list of industry members. However, most products—wheat, for example—can be transported, and enjoy national or international markets. Also, the word *market* can expand the number of members in an industry because it allows divisions of a single company to be included separately. Thus, a single firm can be in many separate regional markets or, as is the case for conglomerates, in many unrelated products. It is therefore difficult to say what *single* industry some large firms are in.

Industry classification has other subtle problems too. The most difficult is defining *"substitutable."* Take energy, for example. In today's autos, energy comes from gasoline of specified octane and lead content. Electricity is no substitute. Neither is home heating oil, although it and gasoline are made from the same barrel of crude oil. For household heating, electricity and oil *are* substitutes, and coal and natural gas also compete for this market. Substitutability often has a time dimension too. In 10 or 20 years, electric energy might be a substitute in auto transportation and solar energy might be a significant factor in home heating. Such substitutions will occur, if economical, but they take time.

The Statistical Policy Division of the Office of Management and Budget has attacked this classification thicket and produced a thick book of its own. It is called the *Standard Industrial Classification Manual.* [168] The manual defines industries and assigns each a number called an SIC code. This system allows for broadly defined industries and more narrowly defined ones.

For example, Manufacturing is called Division D. (Others are Division A—Agriculture, forestry, and fishing; Division B—Mining; Division C—Construction; and so on.) Within Manufacturing, there is, for example, Major Group 24, which is defined as "Lumber and Wood Products, except Furniture." Such Major Groups are commonly called *two-digit industries.* These are then subdivided into three-digit and four-digit industries having increasingly narrow definitions. Continuing our example, we find that 243 is "Millwork, Veneer, Plywood, and Structural Wood Members." And within that industry there is, for example, 2434—Wood Kitchen Cabinets." Such a narrow industry would, of course, have much of its performance determined by common economic factors.

Research has confirmed that the more narrowly defined an industry is and the more completely a company belongs to that industry, the stronger is the company's industry comovement. As Table 8–1 showed, "Retail Stores" as an industry explained 8 percent of that group's stock price movements. But which retailing *subgroup* a firm belonged to (for example, grocery chains, department stores, specialty shops, and so on) accounted for another 42 percent of the typical firm's stock price movements. Also, no common factor *other than industry group* explained as large a fraction of stock market behavior.

Industry Analysis

The reason for industry analysis is that choosing among industries is typically more important than choosing among companies in the *same* industry.[1] This is especially true for homogeneous industries—ones that sell relatively undifferentiated products like oil, steel, bulk chemicals, banking services, and air transport. In a nutshell, next year should you be in steel or airlines? Or maybe it's drug stocks. Worried investors swallow a lot of aspirin!

Fortunately, studies of particular industries abound. Brokerage firms, investment services, and industry trade associations bulge with such statistics. Unfortunately, most Wall Street analysts specializing in industries try to decide which of their companies are "buys." The more important issue is whether or not to buy *anything* in a given industry. Figure 12–1 shows this by graphing the long-term stock market performance of various industries. Clearly, *being in the right industry produces superior results.*

Picking the Right Industry

Knowing that picking the right industry is useful, how can you do it? Like picking the right company within an industry, it's difficult. The largely efficient capital market constantly reflects the combined expectations of millions of thinking, resourceful investors. So one must look beyond what the market *already expects.* Gen-

---

[1] A comprehensive text on industry analysis—spanning 27 industries—is Sumner N. Levine, editor in chief, *Financial Analyst's Handbook* (Homewood, Ill.: Dow Jones-Irwin, 1975) , Part 2.

FIGURE 12–1

Comparative Industry Performance (percent change in 25 selected industry indexes, 1958–1974)

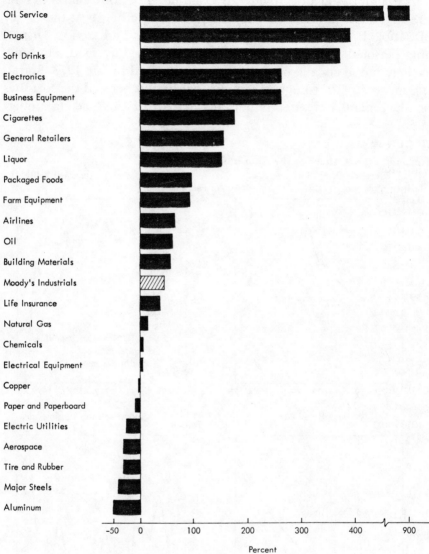

Source: Moody's Stock Survey.

erally, this means forecasting which industries are likely to have exceptional earnings changes.

Automobiles again provide an example. The four charts of Figure 12-2 show how the auto industry, like any other, is at the mercy of national and international economic events and trends. Disposable personal income—from which consumers buy food, clothing, shelter, and so on, and occasionally cars—peaked in late 1973. Spiraling fuel costs altered new-car buying habits and boosted the fortunes of the generally smaller imported cars. All of this had an under-

FIGURE 12-2

Economic Trends Affecting the Auto Industry

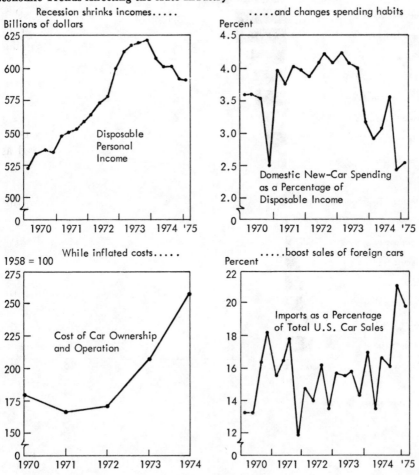

Source: Data, U.S. Department of Commerce, Data Resources, Inc., and Ford Motor Co.; chart, *Business Week*, July 28, 1975.

standably adverse impact on auto sales, profits, prospects, and stock prices.

The study of such economic events and trends is the crux of industry analysis. For as sure as all firms in an industry are affected similarly by them, they affect different industries differently. When grain prices rise, it's good for farmers, tractor makers, and the rural banks, but it's bad for cattlemen, bread bakers, and the urban banks. One industry's gain is often another's loss.

Long-term interest rates provide another example. The housing industry fluctuates violently on this single factor alone. Other industries, such as consumer-loan firms, are more influenced by short-term interest rate swings. Jewelry is affected by gold prices, steel by a coal strike, export earnings by dollar fluctuations, and on it goes. *If you can predict any such economic trends, there almost certainly is an industry vehicle by which you can profit from your knowledge.*

Industry Profitability

Forbes magazine provides an excellent annual summary of industry profitability. This ranking for a recent year is reproduced as Table 12–1. (In later years, *Forbes* used an expanded list of industries less well suited to this discussion.)

Table 12–1 shows dramatic differences in the long-term profitability of different industries. The best five-year rate of return on shareholder's equity was 17.2 percent a year for consumer goods: health care. The least profitable industry was transportation: airlines, at only 4.8 percent.

Interestingly, consumer products *tend* to rank higher than industrial products. Also, fast-growth industries *tend* to do better than slow growers. On the other hand, heavy-capital industries *tend* to rate lower, as do price-sensitive products, such as distribution: supermarkets and steel. Finally, price-regulated industries also *tend* toward the bottom of the heap. Let's look at the airlines industry as an example of that point.

An Example Industry—Airlines

The ten domestic trunk lines form a homogeneous industry: they use the same type of equipment (basically, Boeing, Lockheed, and

TABLE 12–1

Long-Term Profitability and Growth of Major Industries (five-year average)

Company	Profitability		Growth	
	Return on Equity	Return on Total Capital	Sales	Earnings per Share
Consumer goods: health care........	17.2%	15.1%	12.5%	9.9%
Consumer goods: personal..........	14.5	13.3	9.8	7.3
Financial........................	14.3	7.3	11.6	6.0
Lesiure and education.............	13.9	10.2	11.5	9.6
Construction and drilling...........	13.1	8.2	14.1	10.2
Consumer goods: food and drink.....	12.9	9.5	9.0	5.9
Distribution: retailers..............	12.8	9.7	11.4	5.9
Banks...........................	12.6	10.9	16.5	9.9
Utilities: natural gas...............	12.6	6.9	9.7	5.5
Consumer goods: household.........	12.2	9.2	10.8	5.4
Distribution: wholesalers...........	12.1	10.0	11.1	8.8
Nonferrous metals.................	11.8	8.7	9.1	2.1
Electronics.......................	11.7	10.0	11.2	4.8
Insurance........................	11.7	11.6	12.8	12.1
Information processing.............	11.4	8.8	11.6	9.1
Multicompanies: conglomerates......	11.2	7.7	14.2	4.8
Utilities: electric and telephone......	11.1	5.8	9.3	4.2
Automotive......................	11.0	8.6	8.6	2.4
Energy..........................	11.0	8.2	9.9	4.7
Industrial equipment...............	11.0	7.8	10.7	1.9
Aerospace and defense.............	10.9	7.7	6.4	1.6
Building materials.................	10.7	8.8	10.5	3.2
Chemicals.......................	10.5	7.8	7.8	1.9
Distribution: supermarkets..........	10.4	7.9	11.2	2.6
Consumer goods: apparel...........	9.6	7.2	10.7	1.7
Multicompanies: multiindustry.......	9.5	7.9	6.5	4.3
Forest products and packaging.......	9.4	7.1	10.2	2.9
Steel............................	6.1	5.1	6.0	−4.5
Transportation: surface.............	5.4	4.7	8.7	1.0
Transportation: airlines.............	4.8	3.1	12.7	−18.8
Industry medians.................	11.4	8.2	10.7	4.8

Source: *Forbes*, January 1, 1974, p. 112.

McDonnell Douglas jets) ; they have the same staff structure (pilots, stewardesses, ticketing and maintenance crews, and so on) ; they have similar capital structures (lots of debt and long leases) ; they compete for the same overall market (business and pleasure inter-city travel) ; and they are subject to the same government regulatory agency—the Civil Aeronautics Board (CAB) . So their stock market performance *should* be largely similar.

Value Line, a leading investment advisory publication, groups the companies it follows by industry. This is especially relevant and useful, as Figure 12–3 shows. Notice that all domestic trunk lines have annual profitability patterns that are *very similar* to the industry average. Even their level of risk is remarkably consistent. (The "risk index" is each stock's *beta,* a concept discussed in Chapter 15.)

The airline industry and its profit profile were investigated by Howard Conklin. [24] He sought to correlate major CAB policy changes with airline earnings. Conklin noted that "in 1961, the domestic airline industry as a whole reported the first deficit for any calendar year since 1948."

Conklin then observed that, beginning in late 1961, under a newly appointed CAB head, "many positive and progressive actions [were] taken by the CAB." This helped produce profits showing "a dynamic five-year upward swing of major proportions."

"In July of 1965, the CAB announced that the trunk lines were earning the allowable 10.5 percent return on invested capital. The CAB recommended fare reductions and improvements in service to prevent excessive profits. . . . These negative decisions by the CAB started a decline in earnings which . . . lasted for five years" and produced an industry deficit by the first half of 1970.

Then, in late 1970, another new CAB chairman was quoted by *Fortune* as saying, "We simply have to work out their [the airlines'] problems. If we can't, there will be bankruptcies." What followed? Airline profitability was restored. But it peaked and then eroded again with the energy crunch and stagflation.

Have airline stock prices paralleled this regulation-influenced profit profile? Indeed they have. From the market low of 1962, airline stocks more than doubled and doubled again within five years. Then they plunged 60 percent by 1970, when earnings vanished. By 1972, they doubled from this low, only to be halved or worse in 1973–74. They were up again by half or more in 1975.

Changes in Industry Earnings

Stock prices, even for industries, are strongly influenced by earnings changes. The profits of airlines are affected by government regulation of prices, services, routes, and schedules. When airline earnings almost vanished again, in the second quarter of 1975 (see Table 12–2), talk began in Washington about reducing industry regulation. In the meantime, airlines and all other industries should

FIGURE 12–3

Percent Annual Return on Shareholder's Equity

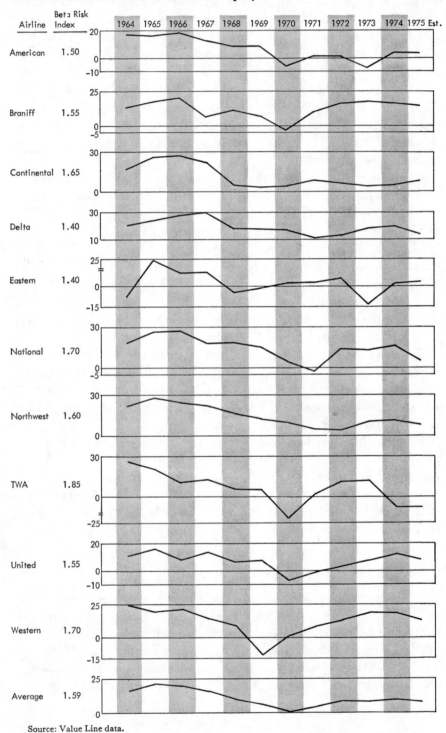

Source: Value Line data.

TABLE 12-2

Second-Quarter Standouts—1975 (percent change in earnings, second quarter, 1975, versus second quarter, 1974)

Best		*Worst*	
Oil service and supply	+60%	Real estate and housing	−82%
Specialty machinery	+56	Airlines	−79
Nonbank financial	+36	Retailing (nonfood)	−56
General machinery	+21	Metals and mining	−54
Food	+19	Railroads	−49

All-industry average was −15 percent.

Source: *Business Week*, August 18, 1975, p. 53.

be continually scrutinized for *exceptional changes in earnings,* such as those listed in Table 12–2.

Of course, *predicting* such exceptional earnings changes is the real trick and the key to industry analysis. The courageous forecasts of one firm are shown in Table 12–3. Note the exceptional spurts in earnings that are forecast for autos and airlines.

TABLE 12-3

Percent Change in Earnings versus Prior Year (actual and estimated percentages for selected industries)

	1974 (%)	1975 (est. %)	1976 (est. %)	1977 (est. %)
High Growth:				
Cosmetics	− 3.1	+ 9.4	+ 30.1	+ 8.3
Office equipment	+ 28.5	− 4.7	+ 39.0	+16.1
Computers	+ 12.4	+ 3.2	+ 16.5	+13.3
Drugs	+ 13.7	+11.8	+ 18.2	+11.2
Restaurants	+ 7.8	+13.1	+ 31.0	+16.8
Moderate Growth:				
Hotel-motel	− 23.6	+ 8.6	+ 45.9	+14.3
Savings and loan	− 12.4	+13.5	+ 30.5	+17.2
Brewers	− 7.0	− 7.7	+ 28.9	+22.7
Crude oil	+ 54.1	−22.1	+ 6.1	+ 3.2
Cyclical:				
Autos	− 64.3	−31.9	+234.5	+ 7.1
Aluminum	+ 79.4	−36.8	+ 46.0	+11.6
Bituminous coal	+240.3	+62.9	− 19.3	+12.4
Copper	+ 14.5	−60.0	+ 97.4	+12.7
Chemicals	+ 31.1	−21.1	+ 42.4	+ 2.0
Paper	+ 52.9	−32.7	+ 51.7	+ 8.3
Steel	+ 94.1	−32.0	+ 35.5	+ 5.8
Airlines	+ 49.5	−85.1	+613.9	+ 4.2
Semiconductors	+ 17.0	−37.5	+ 56.6	+14.6

Source: Data Resources, Inc., estimates per *The Wall Street Journal*, October 22, 1975.

Cyclical Industries

During the different parts of an economic cycle, demand stays more uniform for some products than it does for others. People must eat. Thus, food stocks are often called "defensive." They tend to resist drops in sales and profits (and therefore stock prices) during recessions. By contrast, consumer durables—such as cars, appliances, and, to some extent, apparel—experience sales drops greater than those of the overall economy. Knowledge of such consistent, long-lasting relationships of industries to economic cycles can be useful in translating economic forecasts into investment decisions.

Another helpful concept is leading versus lagging industries. Often, some economic variable (s) or a particular industry will tend to signal changes in another industry. For example, permits for housing construction are an early indicator of lumber demand. If the demand for residential lumber goes up, can the demand for plumbing fixtures lag far behind? And following this comes changed demand for floor and wall coverings and furniture. On the other hand, when new residential construction drops, demand tends to climb for do-it-yourself fix-up supplies.

Integrating Company-Related and Industry-Related Information

You can't buy an industry. However, by holding the stocks of several of its representative firms, you will closely mirror the industry's overall performance. Nonetheless, after you have picked the right industry, the job of company selection cannot be avoided. How do you integrate company-related and industry-related information?

The answer is to view company performance and management policies in the context of the industry's structure and external environment. By "structure," economists mean such characteristics as sales concentration, the nature of demand, plant size and location, labor intensity, and the relative sizes of certain critical cost areas, such as advertising, research and development, transportation, and raw materials.

The *price* of raw materials, on the other hand, is a factor in the industry's "external environment." There is little a firm can do about a price rise if it needs a particular material to make its product. Other external factors are the availability of raw materials (including capital) , the fiscal health of customers, unilateral actions by national labor unions, and government tax, environmental, and regulatory policy.

Against this industry background, you can compare a particular firm's profitability (as measured by return on equity) , market share (as measured by relative sales or sales in product lines) , and the growth rate and stability of both sales and earnings. Then note the historical relationship of the firm's P/E to the industry's P/E. This kind of relative-to-the-industry screening, based on facts contributing to a stock's fundamental value, can be used to classify those stocks likely to outperform—or underperform—the industry.

Conclusion

We expect that industry analysis will increase in importance in investors' decision making. Almost any prediction of change, due to changing economic events and trends, can be translated into a tendency for some industry or other to move in a particular way. *It is fertile ground for performance improvement.*

13

Market-Related Information

Following our examination of company-related and industry-related information in the preceding chapters, we review market-related information in this chapter. Specifically, we will examine the usefulness of information about economic forecasts, seasonality, market timing, new issues, odd-lot transactions, short sales, and market volatility.

Taking into account the research examined thus far, you might conclude that common stocks constitute a "generally" efficient capital market. A perfectly efficient market would *always* price stocks to reflect all available information. Yet, some creditable research shows that this is not completely so.

Paul Samuelson, the Nobel prize–winning economist, was the first author to offer the efficient market explanation for what researchers had generally observed. In his classic 1965 paper, "Proof That Properly Anticipated Prices Fluctuate Randomly," Samuelson [151] provided the theory for this efficient market school of thought. His contention was reinforced by Benoit Mandelbrot's results [112, 113]. Thus, the perfectly efficient capital market became a benchmark against which researchers interpreted their findings.

In December 1969, Eugene Fama, of the University of Chicago, presented a paper to the 28th annual meeting of the American Finance Association. Only in one area—where insiders have access to information that others do not have—did Fama find instances that investors possess *useful* information. Even so, Fama stated that "there is no evidence that deviations from . . . the efficient market's

126

model permeate down any further through the investment community. For the purposes of most investors, the efficient market's model seems a good first (and second) approximation to reality." [45, p. 416]

Here, then, is the way academic researchers have come to see the stock market. *It is impossible for you, or the skilled professional, to utilize most publicly available information to select stocks likely to outperform comparably risky stocks chosen on a purely random basis!*

These findings run counter to most people's intuition. But our investment intuition has been derived from market folklore that, until recently, was never subjected to scientific inquiry. Still, many investors prefer to believe that *their* intuitive analysis or judgment can outdo the market's. They are reluctant to discard such beliefs despite overwhelming, respectable evidence. To those who believe in such a stock market Santa Claus:

> 'Twas the night before Christmas,
> And all through the land
> The investors were sleeping,
> Their heads in the sand.
> Then from journals obscure
> There arose such a clatter,
> As academics asked,
> "Does analysis matter?"

Economic Forecasts

The answer is a qualified "yes"—analysis *can* matter. But too much analysis overlooks the major issues of common stock investing —the decision to be in or out of the market and the decision to deploy funds in (or to avoid) certain industries. A relatively new and promising branch of economics, called econometrics, seeks to forecast market-related information via mathematical models programmed into computers. In fact, in 1969 the first Nobel prize ever given for economic science went to Ragmar Frish of Norway and Jan Tinbergen of the Netherlands for their work in econometrics. Since that time the most popular and widely followed econometric models have provided ever-improving results. Thus we conclude that *great value can be gained from above-average economic forecasting.*

It is helpful to classify economic or econometric forecasts into four categories:

1. Econometric forecasts.
2. Monetarist forecasts.
3. Consumer confidence indexes.
4. Leading indicator analysis.

Econometric Forecasts

Information from econometric forecasts can be invaluable in helping establish an investment policy that *anticipates forthcoming changes in econometric conditions.* This budding and even more sophisticated science produces detailed forecasts of each key economic subsector. For example, automobile sales are forecast from an equation that combines data from forecasts of after-tax income, prices, unemployment, consumer spending, and interest rates. Government spending and tax policies plus money supply forecasts are incorporated in these models. The best known forecasts—those of the Wharton Econometric Forecasting Associates, Data Resources, and Chase Econometrics—are *not* overlooked by astute investors.

Monetarist Forecasts

The monetarist view has been expressed by Milton Friedman [51] and Beryl Sprinkel [166, 167]. Two Princeton researchers, Kenneth Homa and Dwight Jaffee [73], showed that, if you could predict the money supply, which is a key determinant of interest rates, you could outperform the market. But to use this knowledge, you still need news on what the Federal Reserve Board will do about money supply in the next quarter. Reasoning that changes in the money supply were largely dictated by the decisions of Federal Reserve chairman Arthur Burns, Homa and Jaffee tried to model Dr. Burns to predict *his* behavior. This approach and other less inventive ones are yet to be perfected.

Nonetheless, monetarists watch the money supply like hawks. Now you may think that the U.S. money supply consists of that green paper in your wallet. It doesn't. The money supply actually comes in three flavors: M_1, or cash plus demand deposits at commercial banks; M_2, which adds in savings account deposits; and a facetious M_3, which was coined by Adam Smith [163] in *Supermoney*. M_3 is the nicely appreciated stock certificates of supergrowth companies. Unfortunately, today it seems to be a devalued currency.

Can money supply data be used to forecast the stock market's direction? Allan Rudolph [149] demonstrated that they *could.* And it is widely assumed in professional circles that they can. Indeed, when *Investing* magazine surveyed money managers and economists as to their favorite indicators, the money supply headed the list. [196] (Other favorites were the market breadth index, the consumer sentiment index of the University of Michigan, corporate profits, and the 90-day Treasury bill rate.)

The validity of money supply data as a market predictor was addressed by *Fortune* magazine. No serious student of the market doubts that stock price movements and money supply changes are correlated (see Figure 13–1). The question is, Which one *leads?* Citing research by Michael Rozeff [148], assistant professor at the University of Iowa, *Fortune* concluded that *the stock market leads money supply changes,* hence "it is hard to believe that any individual investors are using the available data to beat the market." [195]

FIGURE 13–1

Comparison of Stock Price Movements and Money Supply Changes

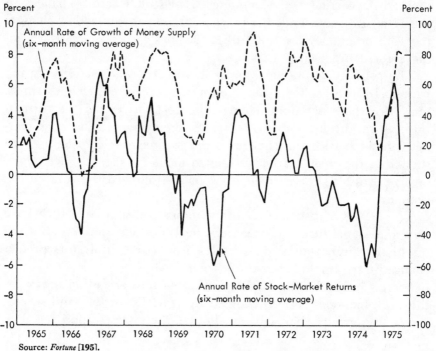

Source: *Fortune* [195].

Consumer Confidence Indexes

The consumer confidence cult of indicator watchers reasons as follows. The consumer component of the economy is larger than the other sources of demand: the government, business capital expenditures, inventory buildups, and net exports. Therefore, if we merely *ask* consumers about their confidence in the economy and their spending plans, most of our forecasting problem will be solved. Indeed, the most widely followed survey, that of the University of Michigan, was the number three favorite indicator in the *Investing* poll already cited. The survey is described by its creator, Professor George Katona, in his book *Psychological Economics.* [85] *Consumer confidence data accurately foretold the severe bear markets of 1970 and 1973–74.*

Leading Indicator Analysis

Another group of forecasters relies on statistics prepared by the National Bureau of Economic Research (NBER). Each month, the NBER updates a host of economic statistics and reports this information in the *Business Conditions Digest,* a monthly publication of the U.S. Department of Commerce. Based on whether changes in these statistics have tended to precede, accompany, or follow changes in past economic cycles, the NBER classifies each of them as a leading, coincident, or lagging indicator.

The NBER maintains records of our economic activity dating back to 1871. Since then, our economy has reversed itself 43 times. On 36 of those occasions, changes in stock prices led the turn in business conditions. On two occasions, the change in the stock market coincided with the change in the business cycle. And, as if to show that the stock market refuses to move consistently over time, on five occasions the turn in stock prices followed the turn in the economy.

The NBER statistics cover other indicators, some of which have *tended* to signal turns in the general health of our economy. But the question of importance to us is: Do any NBER indicators predict changes in the level of the *stock market?*

Success in combining NBER indicators into a leading index for the stock market has been claimed by Jesse Levin [96] and several forecasting groups that will not divulge their secret approach. Unfortunately, their failure to quantify either the size or lead time of moves prevents subjecting their claims to rigorous analysis.

Another successful publicized effort to combine published economic statistics into a stock market forecasting method has been made by Professors Baumol, Malkiel, and Quandt, at Princeton University. Such forecasts were based on a combination of seven economic variables. These include: forecast consumption (from the University of Michigan's consumer sentiment index) ; anticipated investment (as measured by new orders for durable goods) ; government expenditures (as reflected by new defense obligations) ; the interest rate on AAA corporate bonds; anticipated labor disruptions (as portended by data on expiring labor contracts) ; anticipated unemployment; and projected consumer prices. When Baumol et al. tested a predictive scheme based on these inputs, they found that their return was roughly half again as much as that from a buy-and-hold strategy. [158]

Commenting on the usefulness of economic indicators that have tended to lead price movements, Richard Brealey stated:

> The strong upward trend in stock prices   . has imposed a heavy penalty on those who have erred in attempting to predict cyclical movements [from leading indicator analysis] and . . . although the investor may well feel that the broad nature of stock market cycles and the relationships to other economic series will persist in the future, it is difficult to believe that they will endure in detail. [13, p. 35]

Seasonality

The demand for soft drinks, air conditioners, and agricultural machinery is seasonal, based on the weather. Does it follow, therefore, that companies making these products also have seasonal stock price fluctuations?

Julius Shiskin [159], at the University of Chicago, conducted an exhaustive study of seasonal price movements. He found that any effects were so weak that their influence was negligible at best. Furthermore, the weak seasonal patterns he did detect tended to shift over time and could not be used to develop a profitable stock market strategy. It seems that Mark Twain was correct when he observed that "October is one of the peculiarly dangerous months to speculate in stocks. The others are July, January, September, April, November, May, March, June, December, August, and February."

We have already recited some research verifying shifts in commodity prices based on the growing season. But these shifts amount to compensation for the costs of physically storing these goods. They do not have a useful corollary in the stock market.

People, not nature, are to blame for another type of seasonality—the election season. *Political economy*, the British term for economics, certainly doesn't mean inexpensive campaigning. Rather, it reflects the intertwined relationship of politics and the economy. During presidential election years we might expect a stronger and more positive relationship between politics and the economy. It turns out that stock prices have, in fact, done well during election years. *Stocks have gone up during 14 of the 19 presidential election years of this century. And seven of the last eight election years produced a rising market.*

A shorter season, also statistically intriguing, is the tax season. Because of tax and calendar considerations, stocks are often sold for losses near year-end, and much income (as from interest and dividends) is received at the beginning of the next year. Perhaps because of this down-up, one-two punch, January has proven to be an especially strong indicator of the market's upcoming trend. *The market trend in January has forecast the year-long trend about three quarters of the time in recent decades.*

A final seasonal effect might occur during the rather short cycle of a single week. Frank Cross, [32] after studying the movements of the Standard & Poor's Composite Stock Index across 844 pairs of Fridays and following Mondays, reported an interesting phenomenon. As we would expect, a rising market on Friday was followed by a rising market on Monday about half the time. But surprisingly, a down Friday was followed by a down Monday about *three quarters* of the time. Apparently, troublesome economic news that surfaces on Friday, often gets worse over the weekend or on Monday.

Market Timing

In the nearly 12 years from early 1964 to late 1975, the stock market went nowhere. The Dow Jones Industrial Average began and ended this period at approximately 800. In the meantime, it sailed up near 1,000 a few times and soared past 1,000 once. It also sank down near 600 twice and dived through that low-water mark once. Dividends were the reward for holding, but capital gains, on average, were not.

By the end of the period, the very names that were synonyms for stock market growth—Avon, IBM, Polaroid, and Xerox—sold at fractions of their earlier prices. Outside of stocks, little else did.

With such a volatile history, there is much incentive to try to *time* stock market purchases. In other words, who wouldn't want to buy low and sell high *and then buy low again only to sell high again!* So let us see what market timing is, whether it's being tried, and whether it works.

Market timing is the opposite of the buy-and-hold philosophy. Market timing means significantly shifting the portion or composition of common stocks in your portfolio, based on an up or a down market forecast. If you think stocks will go up, you invest fully (or even on "margin" by borrowing capital). Pessimism would dictate pulling out of the market to some extent or shifting to lower-risk stocks. Some might completely retrench and invest in Treasury bills or even sell stocks short.

Despite the allure of market timing, many investors stay fully invested—even in the face of an economic recession. The bullish bias of brokerage houses is to recommend buys in any market climate. Large institutions, such as bank trust departments, also tend to shun market timing, because of both their gargantuan size and some inclination toward a philosophy of "one decision stocks" or "holding quality forever." According to conventional wisdom, when trying timing, "giant investing institutions [are] almost helplessly musclebound. . . . But, if the largest managers could take only limited advantage of . . . [fluctuating] stock prices, the situation has been tailor-made for small, independent investment advisors to display their flexibility." [203]

As time passes, the need to try market timing is being reevaluated, even by the giants. Carl Hathaway of Morgan Guaranty Trust, which manages the country's largest mostly-stock, money pool— some $20 billion—was recently quoted in *Money* magazine as saying, "We're paying a lot more attention to timing the fluctuations in the market." [199]

In 1975, William Sharpe [156] analytically evaluated various timing strategies, such as selling stocks at one year's high and holding Treasury bills until the next year's low and then repurchasing stocks. Sharpe showed that with such perfect foresight, rates of return were improved by about 10 percent or more annually over a buy-and-hold strategy, depending on the period studied. Sharpe then considered less-than-perfect predictive accuracy and added transactions costs. His conclusion was that *"a manager who attempts to time the market must be right roughly three times out of four, merely to match the overall performance of those competitors who don't."* [italics added]

New Issues

The function of the new issues market is to channel investment capital into promising new companies. The creation of a new issue involves three steps: origination, underwriting, and distribution. Origination involves the negotiations between investment banking firms and the issuing corporation to determine price, assure legalities, and so forth. Underwriting refers to the purchase or guaranteed sale of the issue by participating investment banking firms. Finally, distribution involves the sale of the shares to the public.

In these transactions, the underwriter has the "two-hat" role of trying to obtain the *highest* offering price for the issuing company while, at the same time, insuring that the offering price will be *low* enough to be successfully sold. If the offering is priced above what the market is willing to pay, the underwriter guaranteeing sale at the offering price can sustain large losses. Thus, one could reason that, to play it safe, new issues are underpriced.

Such underpricing was alleged in a 1963 SEC study and later refuted by Professor George Stigler [171] at the University of Chicago. In a pointed article criticizing the SEC, Stigler contrasted the performance of new issues for periods both before and after such issues were required to meet SEC registration requirements. His investigation found no evidence of underpricing before or after SEC registration requirements were imposed. In fact, Stigler showed that *the relative long-term performance of new issues was consistently below that of the market.* Brealey has presented Stigler's findings in a quickly readable format that has been reproduced in Table 13–1. Note the remarkable consistency with which the subsequent prices of new issues tend to decline.

In an apparently contradictory study of the postoffering behavior of seasoned new issues between 1953 and 1963, Irwin Friend et al.

reported "no evidence of any penalty or premium associated with new issues." [54, p. 492] Still another contradictory study by Frank Reilly and Kenneth Hatfield, at the University of Kansas, traced the relative appreciation of 53 new issues between 1963 and 1965 and came up with impressive results. Whether referring to a span ending a week, a month, or a year after the new issue, "all tests showed superior short-run and long-run results for the investor in new stock issues." [144, p. 80]

Results paralleling those of Reilly and Hatfield were reported by Dennis Logue in his doctoral dissertation at Cornell University in 1971. Logue studied 250 new issues marketed between 1965 and 1969

TABLE 13-1

Price Changes of 135 Newly Issued Stocks Relative to Market

Year of Issue	Number of Years after Issue (by percent)				
	1	2	3	4	5
1923	− 7	−15	−22	−38	−33
1924	− 2	−24	−31	−34	−49
1925	−15	−33	−45	−58	−67
1926	−10	−18	−23	−37	−33
1927	−15	−31	−40	−27	+ 3
1928	−28	−50	−59	−55	−43
1949	− 7	−12	−13	−13	−35
1950	−16	−24	−47	−42	−53
1951	−16	−21	−24	−20	−25
1952	−12	−26	−29	−30	−30
1953	−12	−21	−25	−30	− 6
1954	−47	−51	−44	−52	−58
1955	−28	−35	−18	−22	−17
Average	−18	−32	−38	−40	−38

Source: After Stigler [171] and Brealey [14].

and reported that "on average, the risk-adjusted rates of return of new issues bought at the offerings were significantly greater than they should be in an efficient market no matter if the holding period is two weeks, three months, or one year." [106]

Still different results were reported by J. G. McDonald and A. K. Fisher [118], at Stanford University. They tallied the postoffering performance of 142 unseasoned new issues during 1969 and 1970. Their findings showed extremely large (plus 28.5 percent) returns, adjusted for market effects, for initial subscribers one week after the offering. From the end of the first week to the end of the first year, 51 weeks later, the mean adjusted return was minus 18.1 percent.

McDonald and Fisher also showed that the size of the price change in the first week was unrelated to future performance.

Hence, research on the performance of new issues is contradictory. On the one hand, Logue concludes that the significantly better post-offering rates of return indicate that "underwriters, in general, underprice new issues." On the other hand, Brealey concludes that "the inferior long-run rate of return from new issues implies too much capital rather than too little has been committed to these businesses." [14, p. 107]

One explanation for these apparently contradictory results is that unseasoned new-issue performance is itself an indicator of investor optimism or pessimism. If investor optimism is running high, new issues are likely to outperform even those high-risk stocks that they should be measured against. This would explain their better-than-average performance in past bull markets. Conversely, if investor pessimism predominates, the unseasoned new-issue market is likely to be vulnerable and may overreact. Studies of new-issue performance during bear markets also confirm our generalization. In fact, in the 1973–74 debacle, the volume of new issues slowed to a trickle. And almost without exception, they declined in price.

In summary, all studies agree that, if an investor has an opportunity to participate in a popular new issue, he is likely to enjoy above-average short-term gains. Whether this short-term price appreciation is attributable to market adjustments in the wake of the underwriter's conservative pricing, or results from the aggressive selling that accompanies a new issue, is immaterial.

In the long run, new issues, like any investment, demand careful scrutiny. The best recommendation is to base entering the new-issue market on your current assessment of economic and market optimism. *Above-average returns, in exchange for above-average risks, are available in optimistic markets. Conversely, during a bear market, new issues are not the place to invest.*

Odd-Lot Transactions

Suppose you were asked to rank various classes of investors in terms of their "closeness" to important information. You would probably begin such a list with management insiders, closely followed by market professionals. The last entry on such a list would probably be the small amateur investor. Given such a list, there is a temptation to attribute above-average rates of return to the informed, presumably skillful, investors, and, conversely, to attribute below-average returns to the relatively unskilled and uninformed amateurs. Intuitively, this makes sense.

The *odd-lot theory* is based on the assumption that odd-lot trading (transactions involving less than 100 shares) reflects the sentiments of small, presumably amateur, investors. Further, this theory holds that these odd-lot investors are consistently below-average performers.

This raises three questions:

1. Do odd-lot investors behave differently from round-lot investors?
2. Do odd-lot investors perform differently from round-lot investors?
3. Do aggregate odd-lot statistics forecast market movements?

Odd-Lot versus Round-Lot Investor Behavior. The odd-lot market is relatively small in size—only a few percent of NYSE volume. Moreover, in recent years odd-lot customers have consistently sold more shares than they have purchased. These figures do not say anything about the relative performance of the odd-lot and round-lot groups, only that they differ widely in size and in the trend of their activity.

Odd-Lot versus Round-Lot Market Performance. D. J. Klein [92], at Michigan State University, compared the rates of return from the 20 most-sold and most-bought odd-lot stocks. Regardless of the period measured, the odd-lotters' purchases yielded a lower rate of return than did the stocks they sold. This conclusion was subsequently confirmed by Stanley Kaish [81]. While the studies of aggregate performance differences have not been as numerous or as definitive as one would like, and there is some countervailing evidence of no differences (see [14, p. 134]), we can conclude that odd-lot investors are relatively unsuccessful in both the timing and the selection of investments.

Odd-Lot Trading Rules. There is widespread belief that useful trading rules can be developed from odd-lot statistics. (Odd-lot short-interest trading rules are discussed later.) Some strategies based on odd-lot statistics (see [87, 88]) have shown outstanding performance. The problem is that they have been "fine-tuned" on historical data. Indeed, *if* the future is like the past, they should prove extremely useful. But, without some *reason* why odd-lot sale/purchase ratios *should* continue to work, we are skeptical.

Short Sales

Another contrary-opinion approach to stock selection and market timing is based on short-sale statistics. Short sales are made by people who expect the market to go down. In a regular securities transaction, you buy first and sell later. In a short sale, you sell first and buy later.

To sell short, you borrow stock through your broker and sell it at the current market price. The proceeds of the sale are then held as collateral for the loan of the stock. When you want to close the short position, you must replace the borrowed stock. This is done by buying an equivalent number of shares at that time's market price. For example, if you short stock at $50, and you can later cover the short by buying the stock at $40, you would have a $10 per share profit (before you deduct expenses or replace any dividend income).

Market technicians know that, *eventually,* each short position must be closed out with a purchase.[1] Hence, they reason, a large short interest represents potential demand serving as a downside cushion. Conversely, followers of this system reason that a drop in outstanding short sales means less latent demand and makes the market weak.

To assess the usefulness of short-sale data, we address five basic questions:

1. Do short sellers consistently attain above-average performance?
2. Can short-sale data be used to predict the movements of the overall market?
3. Can short-sale data be used to predict the movements of individual stocks?
4. Do short sales by exchange insiders predict the market?
5. Do short sales by odd-lotters predict the market (in reverse)?

Performance of Short Sellers

The word *trader* implies a short-term, in-and-out speculator. It appropriately describes most short sellers. SEC statistics show that most short positions are held for only about two weeks. In view of

---

[1] Short sales "against the box" are not replaced by market purchases but rather by stock already owned. The term *against the box* means against stock held in a safe-deposit "box." For a full description of this trading strategy, and when it might be used, see Cohen and Zinbarg [21].

the general long-range upward trend of stock prices and the difficulties inherent in predicting such short-term movements, one would expect short sellers to do *worse than average*. This would be so *unless* they tend to sell short before declines.

Thomas Mayor [117], after studying the short-interest transactions in 14 popular stocks, concluded that short sellers, on average, had absolutely no market timing ability and, as a result, incurred large losses. We conclude from this evidence that stocks should not be shorted unhedged against a generally upward market trend unless one is extremely confident that a price decline is imminent. The poor performance of short-interest speculators does not, however, rule out the possibility that their behavior serves as a market predictor.

Short-Sale Market Indicators

One measure of this behavior is the ratio of outstanding shorts to the average daily trading volume, as published by *Barron's*. Studies (see [14, 70, 153, 154]) of the short-interest ratio and the market reveal a slight relationship—as predicted by proponents of the short-interest indicators. It is difficult, however, to apply such information profitably to trading strategies.

A successful application of the short-interest ratio was illustrated by Cohen and Zinbarg [21]. Buy and sell signals were generated when the ratio moved above or below a statistically predetermined level. However, the buy and sell signals were very sensitive to even slight changes in the "signal points." Moreover, without a clear cause-and-effect relationship, one should be cautious, as Cohen and Zinbarg remind us, about inferring that these bands will be useful for individual stocks, or will be as useful in the future as they were in the past.

Short-Sale Stock Indicators

To test the use of short-interest statistics for predicting individual stock movements, Randall Smith [164] studied portfolios selected according to the short-interest theory. He found that the portfolios contained many volatile stocks. This is easily explained by the proclivity of the short-interest trader for quick action. Indeed, Smith found that the stocks selected by using short-interest statistics as a guide had widely fluctuating profits and losses. But the overall performance of these stocks merely equaled that for randomly chosen stocks with similar risk.

Short Sales by Exchange Insiders

Another use of short-sale statistics is to note *who* is short. Members of major stock exchanges, because they do not encounter the commissions faced by outsiders, are much more likely to sell short than are outsiders. They are also knowledgeable professionals, in the business of taking risks, and in some cases they are recipients of useful short-term supply and demand information obtained in the course of doing their jobs. So if *they* are shorting, it might be wise to follow their lead. Figure 13–2 generally confirms that *exchange insiders are knowledgeable short sellers.*

FIGURE 13–2

Short Sales by Exchange Insiders

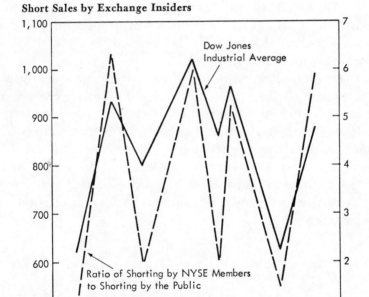

Source: Data, William X. Scheinman, Wiesenberger Services; chart, *Business Week*, July 28, 1975, p. 54.

Odd-Lot Short Sales

Many people who consider both odd-lot transactions and short sales to be plausible indicators reason that together—odd-lot short sales—they provide an even more useful indicator. The logic is that small investors are usually not short sellers. When they do move to the short side, they must feel *strongly* that the market is going down. On the assumption that the little guy is always wrong, this small-investor pessimism is taken as a sure sign of a market bottom.

TABLE 13-2

Relation between Levels of Odd-Lot Short-Sales Ratio and Changes in Market Index over Subsequent Month, 1960–1969

Odd-Lot Short-Sales Ratio (in percent)	Number of Occurrences	Percentage of Occasions That Market Rose	Average Market Change (by percent)
0.0–1.0	1,222	56.1	0.2
1.0–2.0	652	71.0	1.1
2.0–3.0	181	63.0	0.4
3.0–4.0	65	67.7	1.8
4.0–5.0	43	72.1	2.3
5.0–6.0	35	88.6	3.3
Greater than 6.0	50	96.0	6.1

Source: Kisor and Niederhoffer [91].

Odd-lot investors *do,* with remarkable consistency, sell short at market lows. Manown Kisor and Victor Niederhoffer [91] demonstrated this by looking at levels of odd-lot short sales compared with the subsequent month's market performance during 1960 to 1969. Their results are reproduced in Table 13–2. More recently, swelling odd-lot short sales also signaled the end of the bear markets of 1970 and 1973–74. These results mean that *odd-lot investors who sell short have consistently misjudged the market.*

Market Volatility

"The stock market will fluctuate." This tautology is among the first bits of wisdom a market novice learns. Or, as one potential buyer said to the seller, "Why argue? We're only haggling over price. On everything else we agree!"

Just how much the market fluctuates, however, is a source of surprise in a world of 5 percent *annual* interest on savings accounts. Stocks can easily bounce that much in a single day. Indeed, the New York Stock Exchange's ten largest risers and fallers typically move by 10 percent to 20 percent each day. Warrants and stock options and the smaller stocks listed on the American Stock Exchange or over the counter tend to be even more volatile. The breadth of this condition was confirmed by Frank Reilly [143], who showed that the indexes for the smaller exchanges fluctuate even more than do those for the NYSE.

Beyond this, Steven Leuthold [203] has reported in the *Wall Street Journal* that the volatility of the overall market has been increasing. He measured the frequency of *daily* 2 percent or greater changes in the Dow Jones and other market indexes. From 1897 to 1974, such volatility occurred on about 3 percent of the trading days. But in 1973 the figure was nearly 6 percent, and in 1974 it was *16 percent*. There was also some tendency for the volatile days to be down days as well.

Monthly market volatility was studied by Franco Modigliani and Gerald Pogue [123], of M.I.T. and CUNY respectively. They composed a portfolio of approximately 100 securities, each having equal weight. Then month-by-month rates of return were calculated for the period from January 1945 to June 1970. Modigliani and Pogue reported that "the arithmetic average return for the 306-month period is 0.91 percent per month. The standard deviation about this average is 4.45 percent per month." Thus, the market sometimes rises, or falls, by as much as 5 percent per month. In January 1976, it rose by over 14 percent.

Conclusion

Part Two was meant to aid your understanding of the stock market. To summarize it quickly, stock prices appear to generate alluring, hopefully predictable, patterns. So far as is known, however, they don't—except for:

1. A modest tendency for long-term relative strength or weakness to persist.
2. Short-term, fractional moves of negligible usefulness to commission-paying, taxable investors.

These rude facts led to formulation of a random-walk description of stock prices. While alarmingly accurate, this concept says nothing about what *causes* stock price changes. We know with certainty that a stock's price equals its P/E ratio times its annual earnings. Unfortunately, neither earnings nor P/Es are especially predictable, except for the case of *accelerating* earnings. In this "largely efficient" market, we have looked for clues in the three major influences on stock prices: *company-related, industry-related, and market-related information.*

Fortunately, some clues were found. Price/earnings ratios are an important barometer of value and expected growth. Dividend changes also provide useful news, as do announcements of *unexpected* earnings. Sound professional opinions, insider trading, and certain short-sale data again provide useful information. Industry-level impacts are surprisingly important. And market timing keyed to economic forecasts, might be useful.

Now it is time to apply this objective knowledge produced by modern research to your personal investing. For example, while the last three chapters discussed company-, industry-, and market-related information, for decision making you should reverse this order of consideration and apply the "top-down" strategies developed in Part Three.

part three

Personal Investing Strategies

14

Beyond the Random Walk

Few people like to be considered *average*. Yet, half must be below average and half above average in anything. But if you ask a group to confess who among them is a below-average driver, you will be greeted with deafening silence. Next, ask the group who among them is a worse-than-average money manager, and again there will be few confessors. Even being average seems too undistinguished to admit.

In the stock market, being average is a reasonable objective for most people. Over the long haul, common stocks have provided a nearly 10 percent compound annual rate of return (excluding commissions and taxes). This is better than bonds, savings, and most tangible commodities have done. And common stocks traded on national exchanges are widely quoted, readily salable, and comparatively free of fraud or inadequate disclosure.

Furthermore, if you consciously decide to seek average performance, modern research confirms a very easy way to achieve it: buy stocks regularly, spread your holdings into many issues and industries, and hold them for long periods, such as until retirement. In this chapter, we will justify this simple investment policy and the assertion that it will produce average results—*which is better than half of those who try harder will do*. We will also introduce ways to beat the market averages, which are then discussed more fully in the remaining chapters.

147

What's Average?

In spite of notions like the random walk and an efficient capital market, some people's stocks perform better than others. Yet, when many people "play the game," some *must* win. Being the winner does not necessarily imply that the investment selection process was responsible for the winning results. For example, if all mutual funds were to select their stocks in a completely random fashion, one of them would still outperform all others. Investors hear much about so-and-so's "expert performance." But how much of the performance

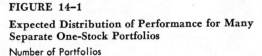

FIGURE 14–1

Expected Distribution of Performance for Many Separate One-Stock Portfolios

Number of Portfolios

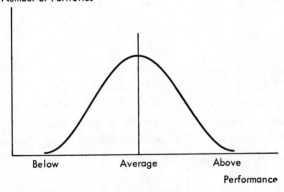

is luck, as in roulette, and how much is attributable to skill? A knowledge of what's average and what the variations from average are holds the answer.

What results would you expect if thousands of investors randomly selected exactly one stock chosen from some eligible list, such as NYSE stocks? You would expect them to have different results, say, after one year. In total, they would provide the market's average, but some investors would, by chance, do better than others. Such differences can be represented by a bell-shaped, or *normal,* curve. The performance results one would expect from purely random selection of many one-stock portfolios are shown in Figure 14–1.

Understanding what is expected to happen from purely random selection provides an important benchmark. Such "no skill" selection can then be compared with the investment results actually obtained by "skilled professionals." As Figure 14–1 shows, random selection produces a cluster of results around some average. Purely by chance, some portfolios will perform very well. Others, by chance, should provide poor results.

How to Be Average

Suppose now that our thousands of investors were to buy *two-stock* portfolios, again using random selection. We would expect the average performance of the two-stock investors to again equal the

FIGURE 14–2

Performance Outcomes from Random Selection of One-Stock and Two-Stock Portfolios

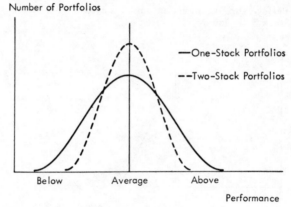

Number of Portfolios

—One-Stock Portfolios

--Two-Stock Portfolios

Below   Average   Above

Performance

market average, but their results should *cluster more around that average.* Fewer two-stock portfolios would end up with the extreme returns exhibited by some one-stock portfolios. This result is shown in Figure 14–2.

What causes the comparative performance depicted in Figure 14–2? These results—the same average performance, but with less variation for the two-stock investors—do not result from more accurately forecasting the market. While the investors in this case could not beat the market average, they successfully defended themselves against variations from the average by *diversification* (discussed more fully in Chapter 17). Carried further, holding *many* stocks tends more and more to approach the market average.

How to Avoid Being Average

Suppose, for comparison, our investors do *not* diversify their investments by using random selection. Imagine the investor who buys only computer-related companies and thus puts "all his eggs in one industry basket." Another investor might "understand" the oil industry or "like" airlines. He might also diversify *less* than he would if he used random selection. In these cases, his portfolio contains a high degree of industry risk. His performance would be characterized by wider variations from the average than would be the case with randomly selected, and more diversified, portfolios. This riskier policy is shown in Figure 14–3.

FIGURE 14–3

Performance Comparison for Random versus Risky Stock Selection

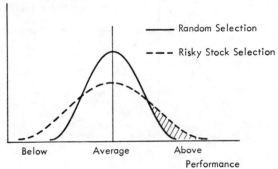

The bell-shaped curve drawn with the solid line in Figure 14–3 again represents the results from many random portfolios. The dashed line shows the more widely varying investment results of *less* diversified, riskier portfolios. These do not "hug" the vertical line of average performance as much as does random selection. This is so because risky portfolios are more subject to wide swings in performance, as we discuss more fully in the next two chapters.

Notice that many investors perform *better* than they would have performed if they had relied on random selection. This is shown in the shaded area on the right side of Figure 14–3. Unfortunately, by selecting risky stocks or by diversifying inadequately, many investors also obtain results that are *worse* than those obtained by random selection. The gamble for high returns carries the concomitant risk of high losses. And in this case, the risky investor's average performance is shown as no better or worse than random performance. Rather, it is more widely varying, and hence riskier, around that average.

Do Institutions Only Do Average?

Before settling on an objective of "only" doing average (or before deciding to be above average), you might wonder whether large investment institutions only do average. The answer is: they don't *settle* for average, and few admit that being average is their objective, but as a group institutions only do average. This momentous assertion deserves proof, and proof abounds. Initially, only mutual funds, among all institutions, had to disclose their performance. Now, bank trust departments, pension funds, and insurance companies are all under more scrutiny.

The first comprehensive study of the mutual fund industry was released as the now-classic Wharton School *Study of Mutual Funds*, prepared under the supervision of Professor Irwin Friend. The startling conclusion of this study was that, on the average, mutual fund performance "did not differ appreciably from what would have been achieved by an unmanaged portfolio consisting of the same proportion of common stocks, preferred stocks, corporate bonds, government securities, and other assets as the composite portfolios of the funds." [52]

Importantly, the 1963 Wharton study does not deny the possibility of making money with mutual fund shares. In fact, it says that they do *average*. And they do play a role, which we discuss in Chapter 20.

In 1965, Friend and Douglas Vickers, then also at Wharton, published another study of portfolio performance. They compared the common stock portfolios of 50 mutual funds with 50 randomly selected common stock portfolios over a six-year period. (Mutual fund performance data were again more readily available and therefore more subject to such scrutiny.)

Friend and Vickers reported "for the six-year period as a whole, from the end of 1957 through 1963, the random portfolios experienced a slightly higher average return than the mutual funds." [53, p. 398] Friend and Vickers concluded that "there is still no evidence—either in our new or old tests, or in the tests so far carried out by others—that mutual fund performance is any better than that realizable by random or mechanical selection of stock issues." [53, p. 412] These results prompted Friend and Vickers to remark that their results "raise interesting questions about the apparent inability of professional investment management on the average to outperform the market." [53, p. 413]

Summary, on Average

Most people expect to do better than average. Only half will. For those who decide that average is good enough, there is an easy strategy: buy regularly, diversify, and hold. The statistical odds are that your performance will cluster closely around the market's average. In doing this, you rely on the random walk—that stock prices move unpredictably and that one stock is likely to be as good as another.

Friend's studies, and numerous more recent ones that include banks and other institutions, confirm that in doing average you will not be alone. The average institution also does *average*. This almost must be so because institutions are a large part of the market itself.

The moral is to know the odds of the game. Chances are that you will move with the market. And the market's odds, in the long run, are stacked in your favor, unlike Las Vegas, state lotteries, or New York's Off Track Betting system. You can exaggerate this market movement, either up or down, by investing in the "swinging" (literally) stocks. But the hardest thing to remember when you win is that winning should not automatically be attributed to genius. *Using random selection, the market has provided an average of almost 10 percent in annual rate of return.*

Beyond the Random Walk

Investors should know the odds and pick the "game" they want to play. The famous economist John Maynard Keynes noted that "the game of professional investment is intolerably boring and over-exacting to anyone who is entirely exempt from the gambling instinct; whilst he who has it must pay to this propensity the appropriate toll."

If you try to go beyond the random walk—deliberately straying from average, hopefully above—Friend and Vickers' research raises another relevant and crucial issue. They reported that their first year's data revealed mutual fund performance significantly better than the results obtained from their randomly selected portfolios. Did this mean that mutual fund managers did do above average during that period? Could something else explain the results?

It so happened that the variability of the returns for mutual funds was consistently higher than the variability of the randomly generated portfolio returns. The mutual funds were, on average, riskier than the random portfolios. In such a case, we would *expect* the mutual funds to be above average in a year of sharp upward movement for the overall stock market. Could risk differences, asked Friend and Vickers, explain this facet of their findings? More important, this question recognizes that *risk* must be factored into measurements of *performance*.

15

The Role of Risk

Consider for a moment the chance American Telephone and Telegraph—the most widely owned stock—has of either doubling or halving in value in the next year. The risk-reward structure inherent in blue-chip securities is usually more balanced than is that of something like "Fly-by-Night Air Freight, Inc." If Fly-by-Night boomed, it could conceivably double your investment next year or sooner. If things went badly for Fly-by-Night, you could lose substantially in a few months. Some stocks are simply riskier than others. Generally, the potential for extraordinary gain is accompanied by the potential for extraordinary loss.

How to Perform—Maybe

Imagine two hypothetical money managers, one who invests in the stocks of mature companies traded on the New York Stock Exchange and one who invests in the stocks of small, speculative companies. Now, suppose we go back to the mid-1960s and consider the performance achieved by each manager. In the rapidly expanding economy of the mid-1960s, phenomenal successes materialized in some small, unknown firms. Perhaps as important, investors zealously rewarded "growth" with increasingly rich stock price valuations.

As we would expect, during this period price increases in the speculative stocks far outpaced the gains returned by mature blue-chip securities. With 20–20 hindsight, any money manager who invested in speculative stocks during the middle and late 1960s should have had a "performance" record that outpaced those who concentrated on less glamorous securities. Notice, however, that reporting only the *rate of return* is not fair. The issue of performance also involves an assessment of risk.

An Enterprising Story

The preceding example of differing investing philosophies is really not hypothetical. One such speculative mutual fund manager was Fred Carr, whose investment philosophy was to specialize in what he called "emerging growth companies." In fact, his Enterprise Fund "made itself famous by specializing in tiny OTC companies with thin capitalizations that nobody ever heard of, that have a way of roaring up like skyrockets and down like punctured balloons." [**82**, p. 33]

In our rapidly expanding economy, Fred Carr was golden. He bought Kentucky Fried Chicken at an adjusted price of $3.50 and watched it go above $50. He acquired a position in Republic Corporation at $5 and later sold above $60. In fact, Carr's Enterprise Fund was the only mutual fund to rank among the nation's top 25 performers for *six straight years*. In 1967 alone, the value of Enterprise shares jumped 116 percent, followed by another 44 percent gain in 1968. Carr was a "star" in the performance arena.

There was only one thing wrong with this performance. It ended. Fred Carr was playing one of the riskiest "games" a money manager can play. In the latter half of 1969, our red-hot economy slowed down. Carr's "emerging growth companies" led the slowdown. As the hot air burst from his balloons, the value of the Enterprise Fund tumbled. The fund finished 1969 with a performance that failed to match the Dow Jones Industrial Average, as it has since. Did Enterprise Fund really *perform?* The answer clearly involves understanding the role of risk.

What's Risk?

Risk, in short, means the adverse impact of unforeseen events. Several different types of risk are discussed below:

1. Market risk.
2. Business (industry and company) risk.
3. Interest-rate risk.
4. Liquidity risk.
5. Inflation risk.

Further, these basic risks can be magnified by leverage, or the use of borrowed money. Both the type and the amount of risk vary greatly between one investment and another. Yet, whether the investment decision is to hold cash or to gamble with very speculative stocks, it will involve some form of risk.

Market Risk

As we have seen, the fortunes of the overall market have a significant impact on the performance of individual securities. This market effect combines investors' collective judgments on the economy at large. In the short run, this often outweighs the significance of business risk alone. Even a great company makes a poor investment in a bear market.

Business Risk

Not all firms that issue stock reward their investors with profitable performance. Many factors affect the profitability or ultimate solvency of an enterprise. Thus, when an investor purchases a company's securities, he or she undertakes the risks of that industry and company.

There is little business risk in U.S. government bonds or the bonds of broad-based, well-financed, blue-chip corporations like AT&T. It is very doubtful that these institutions will, in the foreseeable future, lack the capacity to pay their obligations. It is important to realize, however, that all profit-seeking enterprises face some degree of business risk.

Business risk stems from a variety of factors, some of which are not under the control of a company's management but can still influence its earning power. Such factors include competition in the industry, changes in demand, and government policies. A firm's future is also dependent on its management's ability to guide the firm successfully in this changing environment. Because every business faces uncertainty with regard to its future earning power, the investor assumes some business risk when he invests in a company.

Interest-Rate Risk

Most investments provide current income, such as bond interest, a cash dividend, or rent. Total return means this income plus any capital gain or loss. The relative desirability of current income varies over time. Fluctuations in the interest rate (the rental charge for money) reflect the changing supply of and demand for this "commodity." Furthermore, the desirability of an investment reflects its adjudged future ability to pay income or provide capital gain.

If interest rates rise, a bond paying a fixed return will be relatively less desirable than other alternatives until its price falls. Thus, bond prices fall as interest rates rise. The value of a current dividend or fixed monthly rental is similarly diminished if alternative investments begin to pay more.

An important related factor is the maturity date of the investment. Short-term bonds will not fluctuate much in price because the fixed-sum loan repayment lies in the not-too-distant future. As long as the repayment is assured (reflecting elements of company or market risk), the bond price will not drift far from the solid anchor of a fixed final payment. Long-term bonds maturing in 20, 30, or even more years, however, can swing substantially in price when interest rates change.

Ownership securities are usually assumed to have an infinite life, as they do under the law. Buildings and other real property typically also have long life. Accordingly, stocks and other investments with an anticipated long life span are subject to substantial interest-rate risks. Stock or real estate price swings are sometimes mitigated by simultaneously changing *expectations* of future income and future value, whereas bonds are much more certain in regard to future income payout and principal repayment. If interest rates rise, say, from increased inflation, then future dividends or rents might be expected to rise as well—thus, the asset's price may not drop at all. Interest-rate risk in stocks may be partially offset by rising expectations about the future.

Liquidity Risk

Liquidity is the degree to which an investment can be quickly converted into cash. Liquidity risk, therefore, is the possibility of sustaining a loss from current value just by the process of converting or "liquidating" the asset into cash. In some investments, there is the extreme risk of not being able to liquidate at any price.

For the average investor, a few hundred shares of an NYSE company can be considered a highly liquid holding. But an institution holding 100,000 shares of even a large company will have a perceptible impact on the market when it desires to sell as, indeed, it also does when it buys. Large institutions sometimes find that a major portion of their holdings cannot be liquidated without significant reduction in value, such as 5 percent, just from the process of liquidation. Investors who hold or buy "letter stock," which carries transfer restrictions, sometimes find practically no market at all when they wish to liquidate.

Inflation Risk

We hear a lot about inflation these days, and its threat to certain investors is indeed serious.[1] It is startling to realize, for example, that the purchasing power of the 1940 dollar had shrunk by 1976 to about 25 cents.

Economists attribute our inflationary spiral to various causes. The champions of industry like to blame "wage push" inflation. They contend that sharp increases in labor costs push prices higher. Conversely, as we might expect, labor union economists blame a "profit push" tendency of big business to raise prices. Still other economists attribute the inflationary malady to "demand pull" resulting from too much money chasing too few goods. As this process continues, demand pulls prices up. Still others contend that the government's deficit spending lifts price levels by boosting consumption pressures faster than the available supply of goods and services. Whatever the cause, inflation means that you are like Alice in Wonderland: "If you want to keep in the same place, you must run. If you want to go someplace else, you must run twice as fast."

Consider the investor who puts $10,000 in a bank at 5 percent interest and plans to spend his principal and $500 of interest income after one year. During inflation, while this investor's money is *earning* 5 percent a year, the purchasing power of the principal and accumulating interest might be *losing* 5 percent a year. In terms of

---

[1] The impact of inflation on real estate investing is analyzed in Chris Mader, *The Dow Jones-Irwin Guide to Real Estate Investing* (Homewood, Ill.: Dow Jones-Irwin, Inc., 1975).

purchasing power, capital has been preserved but not increased. Moreover, income tax is due on the interest income, further reducing the apparent return on investment. So even cash or a savings account is not free of risk.

How Much Risk for You?

An investment manager is likely to ask the following question: "Is your investment objective to ensure the safety of your principal or to aim for capital appreciation?" The investor stereotype connoted by the phrase *widows and orphans* exhorts a prudent money manager to exhibit paramount concern for the safety of the investor's principal. On the other hand, the stereotype described by *wealthy young bachelor* will evoke the opposite response from many money managers. Most of us, however, belong to some in-between category. We want investments which offer both protection of principal and a high potential for capital gain.

It is a fact of life that one must incur risks in order to get the opportunity to make profits. Becoming a better investor requires *using your own risk preferences* to select among available investment alternatives. But how *should* this personal attitude toward risk affect investment choices? What has the blend of modern research on risk and stock price behavior discovered that is useful in decision making?

When one considers the wealth of recent stock market research, perhaps the most far-reaching result has been the explicit integration of risk and uncertainty into the framework of investment analysis. Yet, before reviewing this recent research, we should define further what is meant by risk.

People are continually selecting among alternatives on the basis of risk and their objectives. The classic example of risk-return preferences is to contrast insurance with gambling. When you buy insurance, you avoid the risk of uncertain events. By paying an insurance premium, you accept a loss in the amount of the premium for the certainty of insurance against further loss.

Contrast the purchase of insurance with placing a $10 bet on a long shot at the horse races. The gambler risks the loss of his wager against the slim chance that he will win big. In effect, the insurer has chosen safety while the gambler has chosen risk. And while people don't mind (or even enjoy) a *small risk,* on the big items they usually *insure.*

Similarly, if one selects a career in government civil service, income is almost sure to remain within certain limits. On the other hand, a singer or actor is subject to extremes in compensation. There is a small probability that success will provide a phenomenal salary. But there is also a high chance of little or no pay. The return is highly variable.

Selecting risk in the stock market is somewhat like insuring gambling or selecting among occupations. Some stocks' prices tend to remain relatively stable. Others offer highly uncertain returns. *Risk* is related to the *uncertainty* of the investment's return and the possibility of outcomes adverse to the investor's objectives.

Volatility, Uncertainty, and Risk

When an investor buys or sells a particular stock, his action impacts on the dynamics of demand and supply for that stock. This action can, but does not have to, cause the stock's price to move up or down. As investors' confidence changes, so will stock prices. Thus, the uncertainty of investors at large is reflected in something that can be measured—the volatility of stock price changes. While J. P. Morgan reminded us (when asked what the market will do) that the market will "fluctuate," not all stocks fluctuate to the same degree.

Would you feel "safer" with a stock that typically had weekly price changes of 1 or 2 percent or with one that had wide weekly swings of as much as 10 percent? Intuitively, most investors would feel an extra margin of safety with a stock that experienced relatively stable price movements. Indeed, modern research concludes that stocks that have been volatile in the past will continue to be volatile in the future. This means that *a security analyst can predict which stocks will be volatile—and therefore risky—from an analysis of historical data.*

Beta as a Measure of Risk

One of the most significant findings of modern research has blossomed into the so-called beta revolution. Beta, properly called the "beta coefficient," is a mathematical expression relating a stock's (or a portfolio's) movement relative to the overall market.

Seeded by the ideas in John von Neumann's and Oskar Morgenstern's seminal 1940 book, *The Theory of Games and Economic Behavior* [179], the beta measure of comovement was brought to fruition by Harry Markowitz. Now known as "the father of the beta," Markowitz began his search for a quantifiable measure of risk while a doctoral student in economics at the University of Chicago. After much careful research, he formalized the concept in a 1952 paper [114] and later elaborated on the idea in his now-classic book, *Portfolio Selection: Efficient Diversification of Investments* [115], published in 1959.

While Markowitz's concept attracted little public attention, it generated widespread academic interest. By 1968, the *Financial Analysts Journal* listed a bibliography of 253 articles and papers and 89 books and pamphlets on the subject. Curiously, in spite of Wall Street's frantic search for the newest *news,* the beta *knowledge* was not really noticed by the investment profession until 1971.

To illustrate the suddenness of the beta revolution on Wall Street, Chris Welles began an outstanding article in the September 1971 issue of *Institutional Investor* as follows: " 'If you had told me six months ago that Wall Street would go crazy over something called a beta coefficient,' says a somewhat flabbergasted security analyst, 'I would have said you were totally off your rocker. But, by God, that's what's happened.' " Describing this unexpected revolution, Welles noted that "an obscure statistical term which has lurked quietly and innocuously for 20 years in abstruse, equation-filled scholarly journals, the beta coefficient over the past year, with remarkable force and suddenness, has staged a massive assault on the real world of investing." [181, p. 21]

Unfortunately, like much of the research we have cited, the beta concept is still not understood well enough by investors. On the other hand, nearly all of the professionals who really understand the beta concept also believe in its usefulness.

Without minimizing the significance of the voluminous beta research, it is fair to say that the concept is relatively simple. Beta is simply a measure of how a particular stock (or portfolio) responds to the movement of the market as a whole. By comparing a stock's (or a portfolio's) volatility, say, on a weekly basis, with the volatility of a representative market average, it is possible to quantify how this investment has reacted to overall market fluctuations. *Because such comparative volatility is remarkably stable over time, betas based on past behavior are rather reliable indicators of the future as well.*

The beta calculation assigns a beta equal to 1.0 for the fluctuations of some representative market index. If a stock, or a portfolio, has a beta equal to 2.0, this means that its market-related movements have been double those of the overall market index. For example,

FIGURE 15–1

A Zero Alpha and 1.5 Beta Stocks Performance Relative to the Market

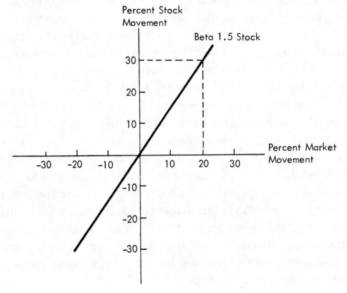

if the market went up 10 percent, a beta = 2.0 stock would tend to go up by 20 percent. Similarly, a stock or portfolio which has a beta of 0.5 has historically been only half as volatile as the overall market. Therefore, beta tells us the degree to which a stock or portfolio has *amplified* or *dampened* the market effect.

Beta theorists ascribe stock price changes to a beta (the market-related movement) and "everything else." The industry and company factors contribute to the "everything else" and are labeled "alpha," that part of price movement not dancing to the tune of the overall market.

Figure 15-1 shows this alpha and beta relationship graphically. On the horizontal axis, we have plotted various possible changes in some overall market index (the Standard & Poor's 500-stock index is often used). The vertical axis shows various possible changes in the particular stock (or portfolio) being analyzed. The straight line represents a stock with a zero alpha and a 1.5 beta. Thus, in a neutral market, this stock would be expected to show no price change. But it amplifies any market movements. In a bull market, say, up 20 percent, this stock should go up 1.5 times as much, or 30 percent—thus seemingly "performing" one and a half times as well as the market. Notice, however, that price drops are also amplified. This stock is simply riskier than the market (beta greater than 1.0), and goes up and down accordingly.

Using Beta for Higher Returns

According to the beta theory, there are two ways to attain above-average performance. One way is to forecast overall market moves and adjust your beta accordingly. That is, you can *double* the market's appreciation with a 2.0 beta in an up market. Risk's double-edged sword, in beta terms, means that this same 2.0 beta investment will give you double the market loss in a down market.

The other way to secure better-than-average performance is to obtain a high alpha. That is, derive your performance from something other than the fact that you have ridden the market's coattails. Unfortunately, while beta—the historical amplification or dampening of market comovement—tends to persist over time, alpha does not! Stocks that have done better than average in the past, even when adjusted for their beta risk level, do not persist as exceptional performers. (Too bad—such a backward glance for high alpha stocks would have been an easy way to beat the market averages!)

In summary, then, beta is a mathematical measure of an investment's historical sensitivity to the overall market. Because such relative volatility tends to persist over time, beta is a reasonable estimate of an investment's *future* sensitivity to overall market movements. Readers should be cautioned, however, not to overrate the wizardry of mathematics and a computer's ability to calculate beta to several decimal places. When asked to comment on the calculation of beta to *two* decimal places, Professor Merton Miller, at the University of Chicago's business school, offered a succinct "Phooey!"

Placed in its proper perspective, the beta coefficient serves two important functions. It can be used:

1. To dissect past performance records to determine the portion that was related to overall market movements.
2. To predict the approximate degree to which a stock or portfolio can be expected to amplify or dampen future market movements.

16

Returns versus Risk

Intuitively, it seems correct that a stock's degree of risk persists over time and is predictable. For example, it seems logical to assume that a well-diversified, conservatively financed, mature company that has exhibited low risk in the past would continue to exhibit low risk in the future. Since this premise has in general been verified, we can study the riskiness or variability of a stock's past price behavior and then predict its future riskiness. But we might also wonder whether risky stocks are better *on average,* to justify the possible bad results of down markets.

Several scholars have studied common stock rates of return versus risk. One outstanding contribution was Shannon Pratt's doctoral dissertation at Indiana University in 1966. He asked, "Is the investor who is willing to assume a greater risk in his investments compensated for such risk by a higher *average* return? Will an investor who continually seeks risky investments be rewarded for such an investment strategy or will he be destroyed by losses?" [141]

To Risk or Not to Risk

To test these questions, Pratt observed what would have happened if stocks were selected purely on the basis of their risk (measured as price volatility over the prior three years). Using as many as 992 stocks and 372 portfolio buy and sell dates, Pratt devised the following experiment. First, he sorted all the stocks on the basis of risk. The least risky stocks were put at the top of the list, while the most risky were put at the bottom. Pratt then divided this list of stocks into five groups, designated "A" through "E." Thus, the stocks in group A constituted the lowest-risk group, and the stocks in group E constituted the highest-risk group.

Pratt then defined five hypothetical investors, who chose among stocks purely on the basis of historical risk. Thus, the most conservative investor would select a portfolio composed of stocks that had been the least risky in the past (group A). Similarly, the investor with the highest-risk posture would select stocks only from group E, which showed the highest variability in the past.

TABLE 16–1

Subsequent Returns Received from Portfolios of Stocks Selected on the Basis of Past Risk

	One-Year Return (in percent)	Three-Year Return, Annual Rate (in percent)
Investor A (low risk)....................	9.8	10.8
Investor B............................	11.0	12.8
Investor C............................	11.2	13.5
Investor D............................	11.2	13.6
Investor E (high risk).................	10.9	13.2

Source: Pratt [141, p. 82].

Table 16–1, which has been abstracted from Pratt's dissertation, shows that the rate of return tended to increase as the investor held portfolios with stocks having higher historical risk. Pratt also confirmed that price volatility (hence risk) does persist over time. But notice Investor E's results. This highest-risk level has *not* been rewarded with higher average returns. In fact, *the mid-risk level looks like the best place to be, considering both return and risk.*

Return and Risk—a Balancing Act

Why incur risk? Risks are undertaken because investors expect to be rewarded accordingly. Even gambling can be explained on the basis of rewarding people for their risks. While the "rewards" derived from Las Vegas generally are not monetarily sufficient, most gamblers would testify that the excitement derived from the casinos is sufficient extra "compensation." Most investors, however, expect to be compensated monetarily for risks that they voluntarily assume. This raises a fundamental question: Are investors compensated according to the risks that they assume?

Conceptually, we should be able to define an entire spectrum of investments on the basis of risk. Consider, for example, the difference between the common stock and the bonds of a particular enterprise. Common stock, the inherently riskier investment, has historically yielded a higher *average* rate of return than have bonds, which are, of course, the inherently safer investment vehicle.

FIGURE 16–1

Relationship between Risk and Expected Return if Expected Return Increases *Proportionately with* Risk

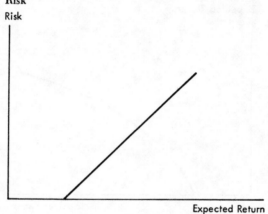

Are investors compensated for risk? Yes! As we would suspect, modern research has shown that investors who are willing to assume higher levels of risk will, in general, and assuming fairly long investment periods, receive higher average returns—up to a point. So we must ask: Are investors compensated *enough* for risk? In addressing this question, researchers are interested in the relationship between incremental returns from extra risk. One *possible* relationship is shown in Figure 16–1. The graph shows that an investment of "no risk" should offer some rate of return. For example, this might reflect a bank savings account or a U.S. government savings bond. In such cases, the investor's outcome is assured with certainty: hence, the definition of "no risk." (Although, as noted, inflation and taxes take their toll.)

If an investor accepts more risk, he expects higher returns. Here, an investor would be willing to move to progressively riskier investments if for each move he was compensated by a *proportionate* increase in his expected return. Hence, the straight-line relationship, with expected return increasing uniformly as the risk level rises.

Some economists have suggested, however, that moving to progressively higher risk beyond some point is *undesirable*. If this is so, a rational investor could be enticed to assume such high risks

FIGURE 16–2

Relationship between Risk and Expected Return if Increases in Risk Are Compensated by *More Than Proportionate* Increases in Expected Returns

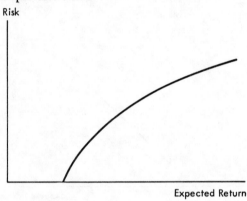

only in the hope of attaining an increasing margin of expected return. If that suggested relationship held true, the risk-return diagram would look like Figure 16–2. As risk increases, larger and larger returns must be available as a necessary incentive for investors.

The actual behavior of investors does not follow either of these "rational" descriptions. Pratt's research showed that, as an investor moved to riskier investments, he generally did receive a higher return. But the expected extra returns were, contrary to intuition, *not commensurate* with the increased amounts of risk. This relationship is shown graphically in Figure 16–3. A miserly additional return resulted from substantially increased risk. (At very high risk, the returns actually decreased.) Looking at the extra return per unit

FIGURE 16-3

Relationship between Risk and Expected
Return Showing That Increases in Risk
Are *Not* Compensated by Proportional
Increases in Expected Return

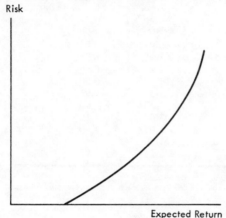

Risk

Expected Return

of additional risk, *it does not appear that investors are fairly compensated for taking high risks.*

Long Shots and Favorites

Why doesn't high-risk investing result in proportionately higher return? The stock market is made by people. People, it turns out, are very poor estimators of long-odds bets. Analysis of the behavior of bettors, at the horse races, for instance, reveals that people overbet the long shots. This proclivity extends broadly throughout human behavior. We favor the underdog. The result in the stock market is that many investors seek high return through high risk. As in other markets, this excessive competition for the long shots lowers the return for all who bet on them.

It is more understandable that *low*-risk investments also return less than mid-risk ones. After all, they are safer. Again this carries over to the race track, for example, where "favorites" are relatively poor bets despite winning fairly often. In bond market investing as well, the highest-grade bonds are also overbet. Meanwhile, lower-grade bonds yield more additional income than would be warranted by their historically moderate risk.

TABLE 16-2

Returns from Stocks Classified by Beta and Holding Period

1948–69		*1956–69*	
Beta†	*Mean Return* (percent)*	*Beta*	*Mean Return* (percent)*
0.45	0.99	0.28	0.95
0.64	1.01	0.51	0.98
0.76	1.25	0.66	1.12
0.85	1.30	0.80	1.18
0.94	1.35	0.91	1.17
1.03	1.37	1.03	1.14
1.12	1.32	1.16	1.10
1.23	1.33	1.30	1.18
1.36	1.39	1.48	1.15
1.67	1.36	1.92	1.10

* Monthly arithmetic mean returns.
† Beta, here, is the average beta for each decile, when all NYSE common stocks were marked by beta.

In the stock market, there is further evidence that the riskiest stocks provide no more, and sometimes actually less, average return over long periods than mid-risk stocks. Irwin Friend and Marshall Blume, at the Wharton School, showed this effect even among stocks of NYSE caliber. [56] Beyond the point of mid-risk (a beta of 1.0), stocks provided little, if any, additional return despite their higher risk. These results are shown in Table 16–2.

Performance Ratings

Performance has been a two-edged sword. First, the traditional approach to seeking a higher-than-average return has been to buy higher-risk stocks. The evidence indicates, however, that speculative stocks subject investors to *undue* risks. Second, most good portfolio "performance," when it occurs, can be traced directly to inherent riskiness. Thus, comparing the returns of high-risk and low-risk portfolios is like comparing apples and oranges. Without measuring risk, there is no common denominator for performance comparison.

Jack Treynor [177], editor of the *Financial Analysts Journal,* was the first to publish a performance measure for mutual funds (or for any portfolio) which included that vital ingredient—risk. He devised a way to compare the distinctive risk "characteristics" of different mutual funds. Prior to his research, investigators noted that rates of return for mutual funds typically show wide variations from year to year. The problem was to devise a stable risk-related measurement that could be included in the measurement of "performance." Treynor approached the problem by showing the remarkable stability of a fund's "characteristic line," which can be used to measure risk.

Suppose we plot the rate-of-return history of two portfolios over the past ten years. The horizontal axis records the rate of return for the *general* market, while the vertical axis records the rate of return for each fund. Notice that the characteristic line representing each of our two funds in Figure 16–4 provides a descriptive picture of that fund's performance.

Drawn in this way, Treynor's characteristic lines allow comparison of these two funds on both their rates of return and their historical market risk over some period. *The slope of Treynor's characteristic*

FIGURE 16–4

Characteristic Lines Representing Different Historical Risk Postures

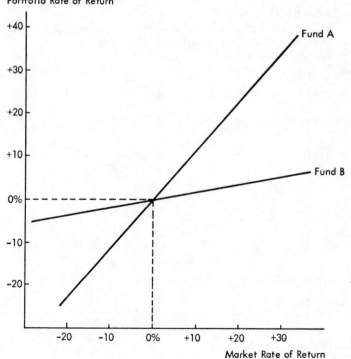

line gives a graphic measure of the fund's volatility in relation to that of the general market. Notice that a steeply sloping characteristic line, such as that of Fund A, means that the historical rate of return for the fund has magnified the general market's rate of return. By contrast, the slope of Fund B's characteristic line is less steep than that of Fund A. Fund B's line indicates a lesser sensitivity to general market fluctuations. Fund B carries a lower component of general market risk.

Treynor observed, "The slope-angle of the characteristic line obviously provides a more refined measure of a fund's volatility than the usual categories of 'balanced fund,' 'stock fund,' or 'growth fund.'" [177, p. 66] Treynor reported further that "the range of volatility observed in actual practice is enormous." He found, for example, that a 1 percent change in the rate of return of the Dow Jones Industrial Average was often accompanied by changes more than twice as large in the rate of return of certain funds.

Besides comparing the historical risk posture of funds, characteristic lines disclose other performance information. Notice that the slopes of the characteristic lines for Fund X and Fund Y in Figure

FIGURE 16–5

Characteristic Lines Representing Identical Historical Risk Postures with Different Average Rates of Return

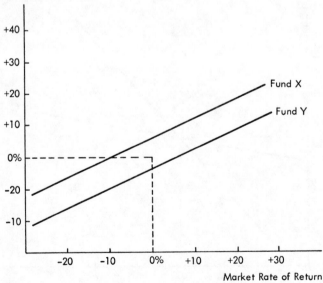

Portfolio Rate of Return

Market Rate of Return

16–5 are identical. The volatility, or risk, of these two funds is the same. Fund X's characteristic line, however, lies *above* the line for Fund Y. This means that Fund X has historically demonstrated consistently higher return than has Fund Y—in good years and bad. Thus, Treynor's characteristic line reflects both distinctive ingredients of a fund's performance history—return *and* risk.

In his now-classic paper, Treynor used this graphic technique to compare the performance of 54 mutual funds. He noted that, over a ten-year period (1954–63), roughly 80 percent of the funds studied maintained a constant posture toward risk. By and large, these funds did *not* shift to more speculative investments when they felt optimistic. Similarly, they did not become more conservative when there was reason to be pessimistic. Such a policy produces portfolio returns in any year that are largely determined by the general market.

The Performance Derby

William Sharpe also set out to dissect the causes underlying the performance of mutual fund portfolios. Sharpe utilized a ratio, similar to the one devised by Treynor, that measured the "reward per unit of variability." This statistic described the reward provided to the investor for assuming risk. Sharpe was able to confirm large differences in how the 34 mutual funds he analyzed rewarded their investors for assuming risk. Further, Sharpe's research showed that "past performance appears to provide a basis for predicting future performance, especially when measured with the Treynor index." [155, p. 131]

Sharpe's reward-to-variability ratio overcomes the problem of the popular "performance derby," which generally reports only on returns. A portfolio of volatile AMEX stocks, for instance, should not be expected to perform the same as a portfolio of stocks drawn from large companies on the NYSE. Volatile stocks have more dramatic upside performance in good markets and correspondingly worse downside performance in weak markets. Nor should the reader be deluded into reasoning that one can reap phenomenal profits on highly speculative stocks merely because "the market goes up more than it goes down." A single bear market undoes a lot of previous "performance." *Remember,* if your four-year record is "up 20 percent, up 40 percent, up 20 percent, down 50 percent," *you're even!*

Naturally, there are differences among the results of various portfolios, such as those of mutual funds. However, the investor tends
to be sold on "performance," with little regard for "risk." Yet,
Sharpe found that 70 percent of the difference in the rate of return
among funds could be explained solely by their different riskiness!

George Douglas [38] in his doctoral dissertation at Yale University provided additional support for this finding. The same
results were also reported by Fred Arditti [4]. In effect, each of these
scholars was confirming that, up to a point, the higher the risk, the
higher the *average* return. Of course, any particular high-risk portfolio might do very well or very poorly—that's what *risk* means.
The long-term *average* return of mid-risk portfolios should, however, exceed the average return of low-risk portfolios.

Through all of this research the recurrent question arose: Are
investors compensated *enough* for risk? Upon close inspection, one
gets the rather uneasy feeling that returns are *not commensurate*
with increasing levels of risk. Brealey, for one, concluded (although
with less than complete statistical certainty) that rate-of-return
"premiums received on high-risk stocks have tended, in retrospect,
to be inadequate." [13, p. 54] (This provides a role for the risk-
lowering hedge strategies we discuss in Chapter 21.)

Conclusions for Investors

The goal of investors is to maximize rate of return *for some level
of risk*. Evidence supports the conclusion that increased risk (at least
among higher-quality stocks listed on national exchanges) generally
does produce increased average return. Happily, the risk level of a
stock is highly predictable—it corresponds to its price volatility in
the recent past. Unfortunately, however, it also appears that high-
risk securities do not proportionately compensate the investor for
his extra risk. And very high-risk stocks may actually provide lower
average returns.

This research does not mean that investors seeking high rates of
return may not, on occasion, find them. In fact, higher-risk, more
volatile stocks tend to produce higher *average* returns and *wider
variations* (up and down) from this average. Thus, on occasion,
risky stocks provide extraordinary returns. The results for the low-
risk group are seldom as dramatic.

Stated simply, it is easy to find risky stocks which, with luck, will do better than average. But the "performance" that results is overwhelmingly the direct result only of risks taken—risks possibly unjustified by hoped-for extra return. It takes little investment skill to produce "performance" in bull markets when picking high-risk securities is the only technique used. Therefore, *true performance measurement must consider risk.*

17

Diversification

Broadly speaking, there are two categories of investors—those who prefer to concentrate their holdings, and those who prefer to diversify them. Investors who concentrate their assets in relatively few investments typically reason that they can better focus attention on a limited group of stocks. Conversely, other investors reason that picking better-than-average investments is tough. So they typically diversify their holdings over many stocks and industries. This insures getting close to the market's average rate of return, plus whatever their security analysis skill can yield.

The "If All Your Eggs Are in One Basket, You Can Watch Them" Investor

If concentration is the gospel of some professional money managers, Gerald Tsai was the apostle of this gospel when it was at its height. Tsai (pronounced sigh!), who was born in Shanghai, came to the United States in 1947 to attend Wesleyan University in Middletown, Connecticut. He later transferred to Boston University, and after graduation he worked briefly in the research department of Bache & Co. Tsai then moved to Boston's Fidelity Management and Research Company, where, in 1958, he was placed in charge of the Fidelity Capital Fund. The subsequent "performance" of the fund was phenomenal. Tsai's credo was *concentration!*

During this era, Tsai received much publicity from the press as

Wall Street's "Wonder Boy." He was even thought by some to possess mystical powers of the Orient which allowed him to glimpse the future of high-flying growth stocks. By the mid-1960s, this aura and an irrational climate caused waves of enthusiasm and a frantic rush to acquire whatever Gerald Tsai was acquiring. By generating such demand for the stocks he selected, Tsai's "genius for picking stocks" became somewhat self-fulfilling and appeared impeccable.

The journalistic license of news media augmented the mystique. For example, *Newsweek* described Tsai as "something of a mystery man" who "radiates total cool," and remarked with awe on his "black, impassive gaze." In 1966, he left Fidelity to start his own mutual fund. With his reputation and philosophy of investment concentration, he hoped to attract $30 million of initial investment. Instead, on *the first day* of his Manhattan Fund, underwriters provided Tsai with *$270* million of public money, at what proved to be the market's high.

Tsai's modus operandi during his years at Fidelity has been summarized as follows:

Tsai's specialty was the big glamour stocks such as Xerox and Polaroid which generally had been considered too speculative for anyone but private traders. At a time when broad diversification was the prevailing philosophy, Tsai concentrated his portfolio in a small handful of these glamour issues. Though all responsible money managers bought on fundamentals, Tsai freely admitted that he traded by the charts. He would establish positions with dramatic snatches of tens of thousands of shares. Then, watching the technical progress of his holdings very carefully, he would dump his positions with equal suddenness. . . . His annual turnover generally exceeded 100 percent, an almost scandalous level, then unparalleled among other institutions. [82, p. 84]

When Tsai initiated the Manhattan Fund, he quite naturally intended to run it with the same modus operandi he had used at Fidelity.

Tsai began 1968 with $500 million in a group of 40 stocks which looked like a typical Tsai portfolio for any time in the previous ten years: lots of data processing (Control Data, IBM); electronics (Collins Radio, General Instrument, Itek, Raytheon, Teledyne); office equipment (Burroughs, National Cash Register); along with touches of conglomerates (Gulf & Western, Walter Kidde, LTV); some oils, and his long-time loves, Polaroid and Sperry Rand. [82, p. 87]

To aid in the collection of "technical information," Tsai surrounded himself with almost every conceivable gadget.

To facilitate his chartist maneuverings, he built an elaborate trading room with a Trans-jet tape, a Quotron electronic board with the prices of relevant securities, and three-foot-square, giant loose-leaf notebooks filled with Point-and-Figure charts and other technical indicators of all of his holdings. Adjoining the trading room was erected "Information Central," so aswarm with visual displays and panels that slid and rotated about that it resembled some Pentagon war room. Three men were hired to work full time maintaining literally hundreds of averages, ratios, oscillators, and indices. [82, p. 86]

From the material covered thus far, you should be able to make a few observations about the Tsai investment philosophy. First, his investments were concentrated in high-risk glamour stocks. We would expect stocks in this risk category to do very well in up markets and very poorly in down ones. Second, many of the specific stocks he selected could be expected to have large components of industry-based and market-based volatility. They were concentrated in similar industries that were particularly sensitive to the overall market. Hence, Tsai's portfolio should have done extremely well in an expanding economy accompanied by a rising market. But during a general market downturn, we would expect his portfolio to experience a worse-than-average decline—unmitigated by meaningful diversification.

The technique by which Tsai hoped to prevent such downside disaster was his mystical use of charts. Yet, the wealth of evidence summarized earlier dismisses the mechanistic approaches Tsai used for his "Information Central." Such gadgetry amounts to nothing more than an expensive electronic Ouija board.

Scientific research leads us to predict that a philosophy of concentration in volatile stocks would do well in a bull market, subject to periodic disastrous downside performance. But in Tsai's case, by purchasing a significant percentage of the outstanding shares of a few stocks, he pushed their price to the high-water mark, where comparatively little buying demand was left. The inevitable followed:

In 1968, without warning, Jerry Tsai collapsed as the aura of the big glamour stocks, upon which his entire market philosophy was based, abruptly ended. While the Dow Jones Industrial Average was up 5 percent, and many other performance mutual funds were up 30 and 40 percent, Tsai's Manhattan Fund, which he had started to loud fanfare in 1966 after leaving Fidelity, was actually *down* 7 percent, the worst record of any of the 310 funds in the Arthur Lipper survey of mutual fund performance. Superman had been confronted with a giant hulk of kryptonite. . . . the star had fallen. [**82**, pp. 80–81]

When the star fell, he took a lot of innocent investors with him. After ten years of operation, Manhattan Fund shares sold in early 1976 for less than half the amount that initial investors had paid for them. Investors had received only nominal income in the meantime. Anyone feeling sorry for Jerry Tsai need only recall that in August 1968 he sold his fund management company to CNA Financial Corporation and became that company's largest stockholder, with personal worth then valued at approximately $30 million. To settle subsequent litigation, Tsai later agreed to pay back $1 million of this gain. *Sigh!*

The Other Way to Play the Game—Diversify

Many successful investors have adopted the opposite philosophy of diversification. One of the wealthiest investors to espouse a philosophy of diversification was the famous Texas wheeler-dealer Clint Murchison, Sr. After a roaring start in wildcat oil drilling in the 1920s, Murchison started to diversify his holdings. At one point, he was said to control 115 companies spread from Canada to South America. Doubtless, Murchison had an awareness of industrial and national market "comovements" and protected himself against them through diversification. His philosophy of diversification was a simple one: "Money is like manure, when it stacks up it stinks, when you spread it around it makes things grow." [**201**]

The premise underlying diversification is that the overall risk from owning many stocks is less than the risk of holding one or a few stocks. The fewer stocks you hold, the greater your injury if one does poorly. It can be shown mathematically, in fact, that when your investments are spread among several stocks—which are not related to one another—the overall risk will be reduced (see [**151**]). The complication, however, is the "not related to one another" proviso. We have seen that many stocks are interdependent through common industry or economic factors. Herein lies the problem of portfolio analysis.

Modern Investment Management

The job of modern investment management consists of two quite separate parts: security analysis and portfolio analysis. Research shows that security analysis is fraught with many misconceptions that render some of its techniques useless. This does not mean that investors should disassociate themselves from the stock market. And research does suggest that there is merit in the science of *portfolio analysis,* which seeks to predict the collective behavior of *groups* of securities. Therefore, *careful portfolio analysis is one of the most important aspects of modern investment management.*

Portfolio Analysis

Let's examine first, what portfolio analysis is, and second, how the practices of many investors are inconsistent with modern research findings. Later, we will incorporate what should be done into your investment strategy.

Portfolio analysis is the study of the behavior of *groups* of securities, including their combined rate of return and risk. The portfolio analyst attempts to apply the results of individual security analysis to selecting a portfolio with the highest expected return for some level of risk. He considers:

1. The degree of risk that the investor is willing to assume.
2. The nature of the risk.
3. The number and dollar amounts of specific investments which diversify that risk.

The Degree of Risk. We have already examined the riskiness of individual stocks. Historical volatility has been found to be a suitable predictor of future risk. Thus, when considering a stock for inclusion in a portfolio, it is possible to make accurate assumptions about the stock's future volatility and, hence, its inherent riskiness.

The Nature of Risk. It is possible to trace the cause of stock price movements to four components: the market as a whole, basic industry comovements, industry subgroup comovements, and the individual company. Research has shown, for example, that 48 percent of the price movement in oil stocks can be attributed to industry comovements, and that another 37 percent can be attributed to the influence of the overall market. For cosmetic stocks, on the other hand, only 11 percent of price variations can be attributed to either market or industry influences. The degree of diversification obtained from adding a cosmetic stock exceeds that from adding another oil stock, whose fate is closely tied to its industry and the economy. Little diversification is achieved when a portfolio manager selects two stocks which respond in the same way to changes in the economy, or to changes in the industry's outlook. For this reason, *diversification requires the grouping of securities which have a minimum amount of comovement.*

With appropriate diversification, an investor can minimize the risk inherent in any one company's stock, while preserving the rate-of-return expectation for the overall portfolio. Harry Markowitz, wrote:

> In discharging his function of selecting securities to enter the analysis, the analyst should keep in mind the properties of a security which may make it a worthwhile addition to a portfolio. Not only should promising leads with respect to expected return (and risk) be considered, but also the value of low correlations should not be forgotten. [115, p. 115]

Unfortunately, what Markowitz said "should not be forgotten" frequently is. Gerald Tsai and his intertwined collection of stocks ignored portfolio diversification techniques for reducing investors' risk.

The Number and Dollar Amounts of Specific Investments. A third aspect of portfolio analysis is deciding on the number of different securities to hold, as well as the dollar amount to be invested in each particular security. To establish a benchmark for diversification, suppose a portfolio analyst pays no attention to comovement and just groups stocks into portfolios. In this situation, how many stocks would you have to hold to achieve the desirable risk-reducing effects of diversification?

The Research Bombshell

The effect of diversification in reducing risk was studied extensively by Jack Gaumnitz [59] in his doctoral dissertation at Stanford University in 1967. Gaumnitz reported that the further lowering of risk was insignificant once the number of independently chosen securities in the portfolio reached 18. Furthermore, he reported that the returns from randomly generated portfolios tended to be higher

than the returns from representative mutual funds. Gaumnitz concluded that "relatively few securities [are] needed for adequate
diversification and good performance compared to mutual funds."
[**59**, p. 146] Thus, Gaumnitz questioned two reasons why investors
buy mutual funds: diversified risk and professional performance.

In 1968, John Evans [**41**] also studied the effects of diversification
in his doctoral dissertation at the University of Washington. Evans
randomly constructed 2,400 portfolios, which were composed of
from 1 to 60 stocks: his results, which are summarized in Figure
17–1, are most surprising.

FIGURE 17–1

Lowering Risk by Diversification

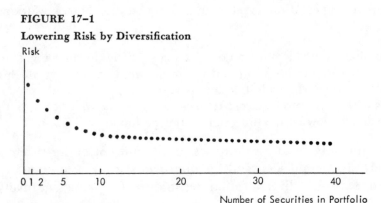

Source: Evans [**41**, pp. 57–58].

Evans' calculations show that a portfolio with only one stock
should have a six-month variation in rate of return of approximately
20.5 percent. The startling part of Evans' research is what happens
when an investor holds equal dollar amounts of two, five, ten, or
more securities.

Notice in Figure 17–1 that the additional reduction in risk is
relatively minor as one moves from a portfolio containing 5 or 10
securities to one containing 20 or even 40 securities. In fact, a portfolio with equal dollar amounts in just five randomly selected stocks
is only slightly riskier than a portfolio invested equally in *all* of
Evans' stocks, which even together are expected to fluctuate 11.9
percent during a six-month period. It is interesting to note, however,
that *international diversification* through other countries' stock markets can cut this latter level of risk about in half. [**165**]

Another Popular Belief Is Disproved

The evidence is clear! Holding more than a small number of un-related stocks has a negligible impact on reducing your portfolio's risk. The importance of portfolio management lies not in the *number* of holdings, but rather in both the nature and the degree of the combined risk of the underlying stocks. Brealey has shown quite dramatically what can happen when one considers both the nature and the degree of risk in portfolio composition. He has reported that a portfolio containing only 11 securities carefully selected for their risk-diversifying characteristics would be less risky than a port-folio of 2,000 securities selected without regard to risk. Modern research shows quite conclusively "that the quality of diversification is more important than the quantity." [13, p. 127]

This research does not mean that large institutions should restrict themselves to a limited number of securities. In fact, the disruptive market influence of large institutional holdings is already serious and would be compounded if institutions concentrated in still fewer securities. Rather, this research shows that there is a risk-reducing advantage to be had from true diversification. The importance of the research lies in its implications for the small investor. The repre-sentative individual can achieve most of the diversification that large portfolios offer.

Investors should realize that diversification, and the concomitant reduction of risk, pays off handsomely as holdings are increasingly diversified among two, three, four, and five unrelated stocks. But the belief that small investors cannot adequately diversify their holdings is a myth. *A typical portfolio with equal dollar amounts in just five stocks, selected for diverse risk characteristics, will have only slightly more risk than would be attained by placing equal dollar amounts in all stocks.*

Do Investors Diversify?

The evidence suggests that investors do *not* diversify. A detailed report on stock ownership patterns appeared in the U.S. Commerce Department's *Survey of Current Business.* [173] The report notes that "a surprisingly high proportion of the portfolios held by indi-viduals was dominated by a very small number of issues; thus, the portfolios were not well diversified. This finding applies to all income groups."

This failure to attain diversification extends beyond common stocks. Too few stockholders balance their holdings by also investing at least part of their funds in bonds, real estate, or other vehicles. This needless riskiness prompted the report's observation that "when the market value of NYSE stock as a whole dropped nearly 40 percent from its high point, millions of investors—including many with moderate means—must have experienced catastrophic losses."

Summary

You, as an intelligent and informed investor, can strike a happy balance between the philosophies of Gerald Tsai and Clint Murchison, Sr. Through proper diversification, you can achieve the same stable investment posture as Murchison, with a small fraction of the money he invested. While you will probably not enjoy Tsai's occasional performance spurts, you will gain insurance against concentration's double-edged sword—volatile ups *and* downs. As few as five nearly equal investments in stocks selected for their offsetting risk characteristics can provide the stability of most mutual funds, which invest hundreds of millions of dollars!

18

Contest Psychology

There is an easy strategy for doing average in the stock market—
buy, diversify, and hold. Yet, surveys of individual behavior show
that few investors actually do this. Even institutions, which are
forced to diversify by regulation and size, find ways of focusing their
holdings, for example, into consumer goods stocks, growth stocks,
low P/E stocks, or gold stocks. It seems that few are willing to settle
for *average*—although historically even average has been attractive.
And clearly, not everyone can be better than average. Thus, a pecu-
liar kind of "contest psychology" pervades the market.

Value Line, a widely distributed investment advisory service, has
sponsored three public stock selection "contests." Although the rules
and the performance analyses of the three contests differ, the results
reveal the investment psychology of the contestants. Because of their
reflection of investor attitudes and because of their challenge to
efficient capital market concepts, these contest results deserve special
discussion.

The First Value Line Contest

According to the 1965 contest's rules, each entrant picked exactly
25 different stocks from a list of 350 specific stocks, which Value
Line had rated "below average" or "lowest" in probable market
performance. Value Line itself entered the contest. But unlike the
other contestants, Value Line picked its portfolio from stocks it

185

ranked highest in probable market performance and then *published its picks.* Value Line's objective in running such a contest was, of course, to demonstrate the accuracy and usefulness of its ranking system.

Six months later, the price appreciation of all portfolios was compared. Of the 18,565 contestants, only 20 outperformed Value Line's selections. This appears to be strong evidence supporting Value Line's ability to forecast the market. Unfortunately, though, it is impossible to say whether Value Line picked stocks well or whether the stocks performed well because they were picked, published, and promoted by Value Line.

John Shelton [**157**], chairman of the Finance Department of UCLA's Graduate School of Business Administration, published a thought-provoking analysis of the contestants' portfolios that gives us much useful insight into our own contest psychology. Shelton noted that "Value Line's good results may have arisen from the phenomena of self-fulfilling predictions. There is no way of knowing." [**157**, p. 267]

The real significance of Shelton's analysis of this contest lies not with "the competition between Value Line and the participants, but . . . with the unstated 'contest' between the total performance of the entrants and the average performance of the universe of stocks from which they made their selections." [**157**, p. 255] This "contest" can be thought of as an experiment to see whether the contestants did better, or worse, than the market average.

Shelton concluded that "the average performance of the contestants was better than could have been expected if . . . stock prices [were] utterly unpredictable." [**157**, pp. 265–66] This much-heralded finding, arrived at by a careful and respected researcher, bolstered Wall Street's rejection of the efficient capital market theory. Shelton's conclusion that investors did a better-than-random job of stock selection was what people wanted to hear.

Unfortunately, Shelton's publicized conclusion was not based on a risk-adjusted measure of performance. His statistical analysis assumed that contestants picked their stocks from the eligible list with equal likelihood. But, as Shelton himself clearly pointed out, the contestants favored certain stocks and neglected others. In fact, 10 percent of the stocks on the Value Line list accounted for 28 percent of the actual selections.

Warren Hausman, a member of Cornell's faculty, then showed

how investors' tendencies to select particular stocks muddied the statistical waters in Shelton's study. Hausman cautioned that Shelton was not necessarily correct in concluding that the average performance of contestants was significantly better than the performance that would have been obtained from random selection. Hausman's more elaborate explanation of contestant behavior led him to conclude that it was "questionable" whether any nonrandom "skill" was demonstrated by the contestants. [71, p. 320]

The Second Value Line Contest

In 1969, Value Line held another contest. This time, the rules allowed contestants to select their 25 stock portfolios from Value Line's entire list, which included 1,258 stocks. The public's response to the second contest, which was indicative of the publicity received by the 1965 contest, was overwhelming. The task of mailing entry forms to possible contestants far exceeded Value Line's estimates. Even with mail snafus, there were 65,000 on-time entrants. A separate contest was held for another 4,000 entrants who did not receive their entry forms before the filing deadline.

With such a large number, Value Line decided not to calculate the performance results for all portfolios. Instead, it provided each contestant with a list of how all 1,258 eligible stocks had performed during the six-month contest. Each entrant was asked to calculate the average return for his contest portfolio. If a contestant's actual portfolio entry exceeded the performance of all eligible stocks by 4 percent, he was instructed to submit a claim for validation and ranking. Unfortunately, this meant that nothing was known about the losers.

The data from the 1969 Value Line contest was analyzed by John Murphy, a financial analyst at American Express Investment Management Company. Murphy's conclusion, as published in the *Financial Analysts Journal,* was that "a large number of portfolio selectors did significantly better than random." [125, p. 99] This is a startling conclusion, especially since nothing is known about the results of people who performed poorly. Notice, too, that Murphy did not (and could not) conclude that the *average* performance of investors showed better-than-random selection. Instead, he only wrote that "a large number of portfolio selectors did significantly better than random."

It is very likely, however, that people entering such a contest would submit undiversified portfolios of favorite stocks and industries. Indeed, this occurred! The contestants' portfolios were not well diversified and were structurally different from the random portfolios assumed by Murphy's performance comparison. Hence, his conclusion says no more than that the contestants' portfolios were less diversified than the random portfolios and showed more widely varying returns.

While many contestants "did better than random," it follows logically that many may have done *worse* than random. The results, in fact, indicate that those contestants who did outperform the market did so merely by adopting high risk!

The Third Value Line Contest

Value Line's third contest spanned the six-month period from August 18, 1972, to February 16, 1973. Again, the procedure was modified. Value Line supplied all contestants—nearly 90,000 this time—with a complete list of the service's rankings of over 1,400 eligible stocks from which each 25-stock portfolio could be chosen. As during the second contest period, the market was again for the birds and, like them, headed south for the winter. During this six-month period, the eligible stocks went down an average of 6.7 percent.

Contest Performance

In the three Value Line contests, substantial cash prizes were offered to those entrants whose portfolios appreciated most during a six-month period. There was, of course, no penalty for loss and hence no risk. It was a *game*. Also, with few prizes for thousands of entrants, only the most extreme performance could win the game.

If one is to "play" such a game cleverly, *one should assume the wildest of risks.* If luck blesses the particular selections made, a prize might be won. If the high risk turns out unfavorably, so what! But, almost certainly, any prudent, sound, or conservative portfolio would be buried somewhere in the middle of the performance game— winning nothing for its creator. Clearly, therefore, the way to win the game is to maximize risk by concentrating your selections in a single volatile industry.

If you hold such a high-risk portfolio, Nature's roulette wheel is more likely to toss you to the very high end (or very low end) of the performance scale. Without wide swings—risk taking—there would be almost no way to reach the top (or bottom) of such a large heap. With great rewards for being on top and no penalty for being on the bottom, this is the only way to play the game!

Murphy's analysis of the 1969 contest verifies that there were an extraordinarily large number of better-than-random portfolios *as measured by rate of return only*. Shelton's data from the first contest showed the same effect. Yet, these results are easily explained by the fact that investors consciously or habitually chose risky portfolios. So, while many people outperformed random selection in the Value Line contests, a large group also did worse than random. Contestants merely chose to diversify less than the requirement of picking 25 different stocks would imply. Deliberately or naturally, they selected high-risk, concentrated portfolios.

Contest Strategy

Many rational entrants looked at each Value Line contest as just that—a contest. The payoff opportunity came from an extremely slim chance for a large prize, coupled with no risk of personal loss for poor performance. In this situation, the best strategy is to pick an extremely risky portfolio, and hope that its widely swinging results will happen to be on the upside.

It is not difficult to select a risky portfolio. One method is to hold only a few issues. Value Line, however, required exactly 25 issues in each contestant's portfolio. This tends to lessen the impact of any single stock's performance. Wit must be matched by wit. Skilled contestants sought to revoke this law of large numbers that tends to stabilize many-stock portfolios. How can this enforced numerical diversification be nullified?

We know that stocks in most industries tend to move together. The risk-reducing effect of diversification comes from the fact that a loss in a stock in one industry can often be offset by gains in another industry. To thwart this risk-stabilizing effect, you can pick 25 stocks from a few closely related industries—or, better yet, from a single industry.

Stock price movements within certain industries, such as metals and oils, are highly correlated. A Value Line contestant's success, or lack of it, is likely to be far more dramatic if he tries to pick a "lucky" industry than if he scatters his 25 stocks among several, often counterbalancing, industries. With such a concentration strategy, risk is high and the impact of diversification is reduced, despite the fact that the contestant is forced to hold 25 separate stocks.

Value Line's contest data reflect precisely this kind of contest psychology. Far from selecting random stocks, contestants picked certain stocks and accented risk. In effect, their results show a statistical pattern corresponding to holding fewer than 25 randomly chosen stocks. Contestants avoided full diversification and encouraged risk. Their portfolios were therefore characterized by wider swings—both up and down—than would be expected from random 25-stock portfolios.

Clearly, this investment strategy is fine for a *contest*, but should investors entertain such a strategy when their personal capital is at stake? In sum, the Value Line contests only confirm that a game is a game. When the chances of winning are slim and there is no real penalty for losing, contestants should naturally gamble for outstanding performance. This is very rational psychology for a contest!

Winning the Investment Contest

It is clear that high risk—concentration in the highly volatile shares of similar companies—offers the only hope of performance exceptional enough to win the Value Line contest. Within this strategy, there are still many possible portfolios from which to choose. Which portfolio has the best chance of being rare in its performance? In addition to being dependent on their industries, almost all stocks are also dependent on the market as a whole. Since all stocks tend to move together, it becomes especially difficult to pick a 25-stock portfolio likely to be significantly different (hopefully, on the upside) from the thousands of other contestants' portfolios.

For the clever contestant who realizes that his chances of winning improve by adopting a wildly different strategy, there is a very logical additional step—selecting an industry that is likely to move *counter* to the general market. For many years, gold-mining stocks have been havens for the bears because of their tendency to go up when the market goes down. Gold stocks represent the one industry whose "market effect" is generally opposite from that of all other groups!

Now we have the perfect strategy for the Value Line contest. First of all, assume a very risky investment posture so as to separate yourself from (hopefully, above) the crowd. This is best done by concentrating your 25 selections in very volatile stocks in a single industry or in closely related industries. Even with this extremely risky posture, your investments and those of the thousands of other contestants will be swept along by the market. You are gambling, in this situation, that you can outdistance the run of the market.

There is another very good gamble. You can concentrate your investments in the "counterindustries" that can be expected to move most *differently* from the parade of all the rest. In short, you can gamble on a gold crisis, on an energy crisis, or on whatever industry is likely to move independently—and differently—from the market at large. Should the market go down (an almost 50–50 bet in any six-month period), most portfolios will go down with it. A portfolio designed for counter-to-the-market speculation should pay off handsomely.

Such contest psychology makes no pretension to superior analysis. The strategy, in fact, assumes that the market is unpredictable! Working from this premise, we have merely developed the most logical *contest* portfolio. The strategy does not require skilled investment selection. It merely says that, if the market declines, our portfolio will stand a good chance of winning by being concentrated in an up industry.

What happened during the 1969 and 1972–73 Value Line contests? The market went down! In the six-month period from November 15, 1968, to May 16, 1969, the average stock in the contest fell 1.51 percent. Not surprisingly, virtually every winning portfolio in the 1969 Value Line contest had "a heavy concentration in extractive industries, particularly gold mining." [125, p. 99]

In the third contest, a period from August 18, 1972, to February 16, 1973, the average stock on the official list fell 6.7 percent. The winning portfolio, reproduced in Table 18–1, is composed entirely of stocks of *oil and gas companies*—an industry that moves homogeneously and somewhat independently of the market, especially during the incipient energy crisis.

Another "scientific" way to play the Value Line contest is to submit portfolios selected entirely on the basis of beta coefficients. You can only be certain that the market will either go up or down (or end up where it started). If the market goes up, a high-beta portfolio should amplify the upward market movement and perform better than a well-diversified portfolio. If you hold such a high-beta portfolio in a down market, you would expect to amplify the drop and have a loss that is much greater than the loss from a well-diversified portfolio. But since there is no penalty for loss in a contest, a wise strategy would be to hold a portfolio with the highest possible beta and hope for an upward market swing. Conversely, if you anticipate that the market might go down, it would be wise to hold an extremely low-beta portfolio.

TABLE 18–1

The Value Line Contest's Winning Portfolio (August 18, 1972, to February 16, 1973)

Amerada Hess	Mapco
Apco Oil	Mesa Petroleum
Ashland Oil	Mountain Fuel Supply
Atlantic Richfield	Murphy Oil
Aztec Oil & Gas	Pacific Petroleums
Belco Petroleum	Phillips Petroleum
Cities Service	Skelly Oil
Clark Oil & Refining	Standard Oil (Indiana)
Continental Oil	Standard Oil (Ohio)
El Paso Natural Gas	Sun Oil
General American Oil of Texas	Superior Oil
Getty Oil	Union Oil of California
Helmerich & Payne	

This approach to the contest was tested by Robert Kaplan and Roman Weil [84], who submitted one very high-beta portfolio and one very low-beta portfolio. Since the market went down during the period, our a priori expectation would be that their low-beta portfolio would rank well in the performance derby and that their high-beta portfolio would be among the worst performers. Illustrating not only the relevance of beta coefficients, but also the importance of setting your portfolio policy in terms of an overall market forecast, the Kaplan-Weil low-beta portfolio ranked in the top 2.3 percent of all portfolios. Their high-beta portfolio, which amplified the down market, placed them in the lowest 0.6 percent of all contest portfolios.

The significance of these results is that if you do not monitor your portfolio in terms of beta and industry concentration, *you might also have a portfolio designed by contest psychology.*

The Parallel to Investment Management

The closing note of this discussion is to draw the parallel between good contest strategy and the behavior of some investment managers. As of June 30, 1970, following a severe market drop, the best-performing mutual fund for the prior 12 months was a fund investing solely in federal government bonds. Investment in these instruments amounts to the gold stock strategy. By investing in government bonds with a safe, steady, modest return, if the market falls out of bed you will be a comparative winner. Investors should remember, however, that such a fund can be expected to provide poor relative performance in up markets—just as the 1970 winner did in the year *after* it received "contest" accolades.

During the next bear market, we saw the same phenomenon. A new instrument—the money market funds—rose to the fore. In 1974, they provided a high, safe, liquid, short-term yield, which during a down market was a delightful result. They grew by leaps and bounds in the period *after* their superior performance, just as the Enterprise Fund, the gold stock funds, and the government bond funds had after their earlier winning years.

The point is that there is a proper investment instrument for each different market environment. And yesterday's market winner may not repeat. The fear is that contest psychology will cause you or your money manager to seek extraordinary performance merely by being *different* or by concentrating in *last year's winner*. But in the real contest, you also face real losses.

In common stock investing, the crux of the matter is knowing when, and when not, to take risks. Commenting on the correlation between risk and performance, Edward Zinbarg, vice president in charge of common stock investments at the Prudential Insurance Company of America, told a seminar sponsored by the New York Society of Security Analysts, "You've all heard the comment, 'Well, big deal. You did very well because you took more risk.' . . . But the fact is, . . . I did take more risk. I was smart enough to take more risk and you weren't." [181, p. 52] Making *your* investment decisions intelligently is the process we address next.

19

Instrument Investing

These concluding chapters synthesize the new knowledge on common stock investing into a practical strategy you can apply with reasonable hope for above-average return. Fortunately, although much research reveals how *not* to invest, some offers clues on *how to invest*.

Investing should be a seven-step cycle, as summarized below and detailed in this chapter.

1. Setting realistic investment *objectives*.
2. Implementing an "insure, invest, spend the rest" *Personal Financial Plan* that guarantees the annual investment amount needed to reach your objectives.
3. Establishing a balanced *portfolio policy* by setting the relative sizes of the core, aggressive, and speculative layers of your capital structure.
4. Deciding on the *instrument mix* (stocks, bonds, mutual funds, options, real estate, and so forth) most likely to achieve your objectives within your portfolio policy constraints.
5. Determining those *industries* most likely to offer the performance sought.
6. Selecting specific *company* securities that meet the criteria established for each layer of your capital structure.
7. *Monitoring* the performance of each investment against the established objectives.

Notice that the first three steps are personal, almost *philosophical,* choices. You determine what you want, the life-style adjustments necessary to get there, and your tolerance for risk and delay along the way. Step 4 is perhaps the most important and the least addressed. Investing books usually focus on a single *instrument,* as this one does on common stocks. But overall results depend heavily on the instrument *mix* you choose—how much in savings, home ownership, stocks, bonds, real estate, gold, commodities, and so on. Then, when you do choose to invest in common stocks, steps 5 through 7 force you to look at industries before companies, and then to track your results.

Setting Objectives

A prerequisite to successful investing is setting realistic objectives. The great Roman orator and philosopher Cicero, who died in 43 B.C., wrote, "It is difficult to set bounds to the price unless you first set bounds to the wish." Today, investors hear so much about "double your money" strategies that many of them lose sight of what can realistically be expected from investing.

To the astonishment of many businessmen, public opinion surveys repeatedly show that "the man on the street" estimates after-tax profits on sales for U.S. corporations at about 30 percent! In reality, these after-tax profit margins have averaged about 5 percent over the last quarter century. Since people grossly overestimate corporate profits, they are also susceptible to overestimating the probable returns from their own investments. As a *Business Week* editorial commented, "Unless this area of public ignorance is corrected, U.S. economic policy [and investment decisions are] . . . likely to be based on a fantastic misconception." [188, p. 88] To prevent such inflated expectations from clouding investment decisions, the first step toward rational investing is setting a reasonable goal.

Implementing Your Personal Financial Plan

Chapter 3 outlined the steps necessary to translate an ill-defined need for future financial security into a specific financial plan. As stated earlier, attaining your goal requires a plan that depends on:

1. The value of your current investments.
2. The amount and timing of your additional investments or withdrawals.
3. The rate of return on your investments.

It is recommended that you try one of the computerized financial planning services offered by an ever-increasing number of banks and counseling firms (see [197]). These analyses are invaluable for projecting your expected year-by-year financial position. Barring this kind of detailed planning, however, you should at least establish a goal and estimate the approximate annual investment required to reach it.

Portfolio Policy

The third step to successful investing is establishing a portfolio policy by setting the relative sizes of the core, aggressive, and speculative layers of your capital structure. The investments in each layer are distinguished by two factors: the anticipated performance (risk/return) and the anticipated holding period. Figure 19-1 illustrates these two factors for speculative investments: high anticipated return (with concomitant high risk) and a relatively short-term anticipated holding period.

FIGURE 19-1

Speculative Layer of Your Capital Structure

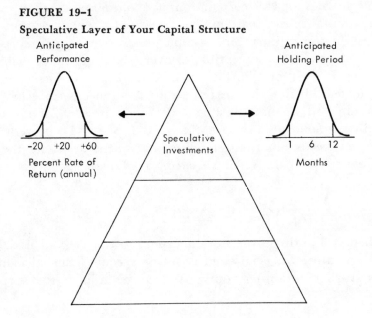

The bell-shaped curve on the left-hand side of Figure 19–1 shows that speculative investments might be *expected to return as much as 20 percent.* In view of the risk, you might also expect the returns to range between −20 percent and +60 percent about 80 percent of the time. Ten percent of these investments might turn out even better, and the other 10 percent even worse. The bell-shaped curve on the right-hand side shows the anticipated holding period of 1 to 12 months.

The distinguishing features of aggressive-level investments are shown in Figure 19–2. They might be expected to return, on average,

FIGURE 19–2

Aggressive Layer of Your Capital Structure

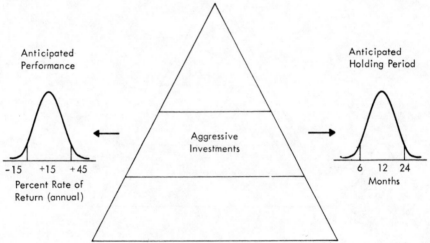

as much as 15 percent annually. Such investments should be less volatile than those in the top layer and, consequently, should be purchased with a longer anticipated holding period in mind.

The bell-shaped curve on the left illustrates that 80 percent of the time the aggressive layer might have returns between −15 percent and +45 percent. On the right, we see that these anticipated total returns are expected to occur in 12 months, though the potential time over which they could take place ranges from 6 to 24 months. Hence, in comparison with speculative investments, aggressive investments are expected to fluctuate less and to be held for a longer period.

The core layer is depicted in Figure 19–3. Investments in this layer are expected to offer an *average return*—about 10 percent per year. Another extremely important requirement of these core investments is that they be good-quality purchases *held for long-term capital accumulation.* Core investments should be carefully selected to protect against downside risk. As shown in Figure 19–3, this layer should seldom provide a total annual rate of return (including dividends) that falls below −10 percent. And, to compensate, it should retain a good upside potential.

FIGURE 19–3

Core Layer of Your Capital Structure

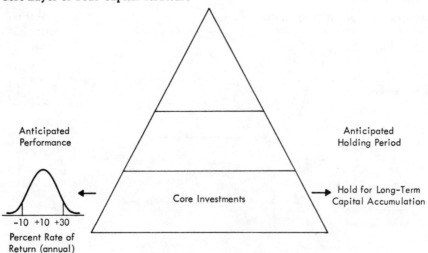

The need to categorize investments that seem to belong *between* these definitions of speculative, aggressive, and core should not blur the conceptual importance of having a profit and time expectation for every investment. The "in-between" classification problem can be handled by the cautious convention that any investment ranking above the guidelines for a particular layer should be included in the higher, more speculative, layer.

Investments that purportedly offer more expected return than is represented by the highest layer should raise a caution flag. Perhaps they *do not belong in a rationally designed investment portfolio.* When such investments do not fit into the speculative level because the possible downside loss is believed to be "nowhere near," let's say, −20 percent, we politely remind the reader that the sunlight of return carries with it the shadow of risk. And people usually underestimate risk.

You should base the relative sizes of the speculative, aggressive, and core layers of your capital structure on two portfolio policy issues:

1. Your certainty about the overall market.
2. Your proclivity for risk.

In investing, knowing the market's future can be profitable no matter what the direction of security prices. In the words of Ralph Waldo Emerson, "This time, like all other times, is a very good one, if we but know what to do with it." Indeed, when we are certain that the market is going down, we can profit just as surely as when we know that it is going up. For this reason, the proportion of your assets in each layer should not depend on the direction in which you think the overall market is heading, but on your *certainty about that forecast!*

The other important ingredient in establishing your portfolio policy and your consequent capital structure is the amount of risk you are willing to take in the hope of securing extra returns. These interrelationships and the resultant capital structures are shown in Figure 19–4.

Many people have *protected growth* as an objective and, most of the time, have only a normal degree of certainty about the investment climate. For such people, the 20–30–50 proportions depicted in the upper left-hand corner of Figure 19–4 might be an appropriate distribution of their investment dollars.

Two things can make us assume a riskier posture. We can, by individual inclination, prefer more risk in the hope of extra gain. Or, if we are more certain about the future, we might also rationally opt for riskier (high-beta) assets.

For example, an individual whose objective is protected growth could, with increased certainty about the future, move to the more speculative 30–40–30 structure shown in the lower left-hand corner of Figure 19–4. Similarly, a speculator with only normal certainty about the future could reasonably allocate investment dollars according to the 30–40–30 proportions shown in the upper right-hand

FIGURE 19–4

Translating Your Certainty and Risk Attitudes into an Appropriate Capital Structure

Preference for Risk

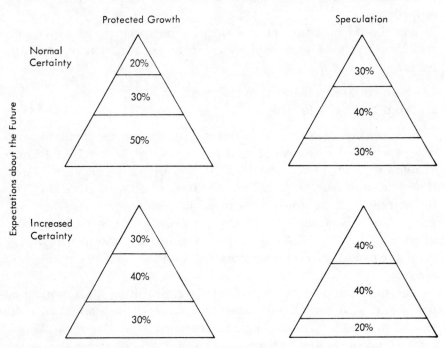

corner. A less frequent case, a more speculative posture combined with increased certainty about the future, could justify the 40–40–20 triangle shown in the lower right-hand corner.

Instrument Mix

Deciding on the *instrument mix* is the fourth step—and the pivot point—of our recommended seven-step investing cycle. It moves you from setting objectives, plans, and policies toward making actual investments. Successful investing demands that you reorient your thinking to the broad spectrum of investment instruments and select those best suited to your personal needs at a given point in time. In addition to *common stocks,* our focus so far, you can use convertible bonds, shares of mutual funds, and options as ways to participate in the stock market.

Many alternatives are also available within other instrument

categories. *Bonds,* for example, include tax-free municipals, speculative discount bonds, triple A corporates, a host of government
issues, and so forth. In *real estate,* there are residential properties,
shopping centers, office buildings, and other ways to invest. *Gold*
appeals to some, and so on.

It has been said that, with so many options available on today's
automobiles, it would be possible to produce cars all year without
making two exactly the same. The same statistical phenomenon
applies to the possible components of a portfolio. Suppose you decide to own only five different types of instruments and consider
only 16 alternatives for each; you then have over a million different
portfolios to choose from. We want to emphasize that there are many
available alternatives from which to choose the *combination of instruments best suited to your specific objectives.*

One result that occurs again and again is that owning "good
stocks" at the wrong time causes disappointing losses. Hence, the instrument mix you choose is crucial. There is more than common
stock to be considered.

If a careful choice of instrument mix precedes your selection of
common stocks, you might avoid being in "good" stocks when the
odds are that even "bad" bonds would be a better *instrument* in the
forthcoming market. In the words of Professor James Lorie, the
acclaimed author-professor of finance at the University of Chicago,
*"The most important investment decision is not the selection of par-
ticular stocks, but the choice of an investment strategy—the selection
of the kinds and types of assets in their relative proportions in a
diversified portfolio."* [**189,** p. 111; italics added]

Figure 19–5 summarizes *guidelines* that can be used to select investment instruments and strategies that will provide the types of
risk-reward expectations and holding periods we have discussed. It is
important to remember also that, at a given point in time, your
expectations may be different for different time horizons. You could,
for example, be neutral about the market's near-term prospects, but
optimistic about its medium- and long-term prospects. If, for example, your near-term market forecast could be classified as "extremely optimistic," the appropriate instruments might be calls,
warrants, new issues, and so on.

The lower level of Figure 19–5 requires special explanation.
Remember that core investments are good-quality assets held for
long-term capital accumulation. The assets in this layer are *not*

FIGURE 19–5

Selection of Investment Instruments Based on Market Forecasts

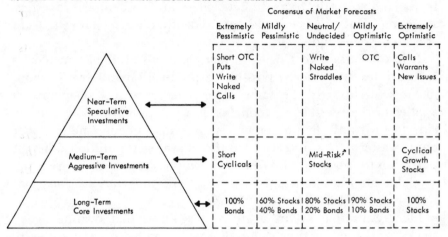

Consensus of Market Forecasts

	Extremely Pessimistic	Mildly Pessimistic	Neutral/ Undecided	Mildly Optimistic	Extremely Optimistic
Near-Term Speculative Investments	Short OTC Puts Write Naked Calls		Write Naked Straddles	OTC	Calls Warrants New Issues
Medium-Term Aggressive Investments	Short Cyclicals		Mid-Risk? Stocks		Cyclical Growth Stocks
Long-Term Core Investments	100% Bonds	60% Stocks 40% Bonds	80% Stocks 20% Bonds	90% Stocks 10% Bonds	100% Stocks

trading vehicles which you have purchased in the hope of catching the market moving in the right direction. But there is a problem with the "hold quality stocks forever" approach.

Consider, for example, the individuals who held "quality" stocks through the 1969–74 bear markets. By 1975, some of these "quality" stocks were still worth approximately half of their early 1969 values. Unfortunate investors who held steadfastly to their convictions or, even worse, bought more of these stocks on the way down, found themselves in a position where they needed a *doubling in the value of a "conservative" investment to get back where they were six years before!*

To prevent such losses one should, when his or her market forecast so dictates, *alter the mix of investment instruments even in the core layer.* For example, it is irrational to hold stocks as a core investment if you are pessimistic about long-term stock market performance. An *approximate guide* for putting together the appropriate mix of stocks and bonds—which are only two of many possible instruments—appears in the lower level of Figure 19–5. These numbers should not be rigidly construed. What is rigid is the principle that rational investing demands that you prevent or curtail losses.

Unfortunately, most Wall Street research comes from analysts who follow *stocks.* These analysts frequently become so enamored with the stock they recommended at $40 that they consider it a better buy at $30, and a still better buy at $25. Maybe it is, but the important point is to look at the forest before you look at the trees. If the forest burns, all the trees go with it. Stated another way, *set your portfolio policy and your instrument mix before you pick stocks.* And caution yourself to remember that many Wall Street analysts publish buy recommendations in every market!

Industry Analysis

One conclusion we can draw from recent research is that *it is more important (and easier) to be in the "right" industry than in the "right" stock.* This has been confirmed by research as well as by the most recent Value Line investment contest. Of the almost 90,000 portfolios entered in that contest, those with the best performance did not reflect the skillful selection of the "right" stocks. As expected, the winning portfolios reflected the skillful selection of the "right" industry.

Much progress is being made in industry forecasting techniques. The most modern and fruitful approach is to attempt to translate various economic, fiscal, and attitude forecasts into predictions of key industry variables. The problem faced by modern industry analysts thus becomes one of translating the forecasts of general economic variables into forecasts of interest in a particular industry. A generalized economic forecast might, for example, estimate future raw materials costs, wage rates, consumer spending power, credit availability, and so forth. In an industry, such as automobile manufacturing, a security analyst is concerned with more specific industry-related information, such as unit sales and price levels of automobiles. By sophisticated methods, researchers are now forecasting specific industry variables, such as automobile demand and prices. In turn, these can be used to forecast company-level information related to stock performance, such as earnings and probable growth.

Company Analysis

Earlier chapters have examined in detail the contributors to return and risk. Our conclusion was that the potential for extraordinary gain is accompanied by the risk of extraordinary loss. The fortune cookie philosophy of "temptation resisted is pleasure lost" does not hold in the area of investments. The "sure thing" just does not exist. Even the seemingly riskless insured savings accounts of banks and savings institutions have the subtle risk of being eroded by inflation.

The important point to remember about risk is not that it can somehow be erased, but that it can, through proper diversification, be controlled. The beta concept measures a stock's market-related risk. As discussed, beta takes note that most stock prices move rela-

FIGURE 19–6

Comparative Volatility of Selected Investments

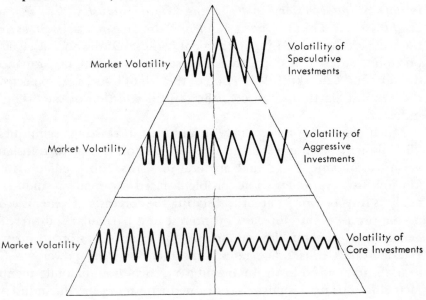

tive to those of the overall market, and stocks with high or low betas can suit different portfolio policies. The beta measurement reflects a stock's (or a portfolio's) sensitivity to the overall market, which is designated as having a beta of 1.0.

When selecting investments for the speculative layer of your capital structure, you *seek* high-beta stocks, which are expected to amplify the movements of the overall market. Conversely, for the core layer you might seek vehicles with a combined beta value below that of the market so as to dampen its impact. This concept is shown graphically in Figure 19–6.

In doing company analysis, it is wise to focus on companies whose stocks behave *most differently* from the market and their industry. Otherwise, accurate company analysis will be overwhelmed by these stronger forces. Also, such "different" companies are themselves the most analyzable—there is something distinctive about them to evaluate. And they often provide the most interesting risk/return possibilities.

Monitoring Performance

Will Rogers' investment advice was, "Take your savings and buy some good stock and hold it till it goes up, then sell it. If it don't go up, don't buy it." We all hope that our investments will increase in value. One of the most difficult things about rational investing, however, is knowing when we have been wrong. The need to know this underscores the importance of setting risk and reward limits on each investment.

Suppose, for example, that you buy a stock for the aggressive layer. For a stock in this category you expect, by definition of the layer, to realize a profit of about 15 percent in approximately 12 months. You also expect that investments selected for this layer will probably confine 80 percent of their return fluctuations within a range of from −15 percent to +45 percent. With these expectations established when you buy the stock, you know when you have been *wrong*. You can, of course, be wrong in two ways. The stock might fall more than 15 percent, or, more happily, it might go up more than 45 percent. The big question is what to do when you realize you were *wrong*.

When an investment's performance has *exceeded* your expectation, there are two schools of thought about what you should do. One school reasons that you have so surpassed your expectation that you should be content with the gain and liquidate the position. The opposing school of thought holds that you should always let your profits run. The latter position is essentially the philosophy of Gerald M. Loeb, author of *The Battle for Investment Survival.* [104] (also see [105])

Basically, Loeb espouses an investment philosophy whereby an investor places 10 percent of his assets in a single listed security that is speculative, yet liquid. He advises the investor to set a short-term objective. If the objective is not realized, he encourages him to move to a more suitable investment. In this way, Loeb contends, the investor can move quickly out of situations that do not work out as planned and, in so doing, can gain by "losing less" in bad situations.

The opposing point of view advocates *dollar-cost averaging,* which takes the position that "if it was a good buy at 40, it is twice as good a buy at 20." The problem with both of these approaches is that there have been times when each would have been wrong. The answer lies *not* in developing hard-and-fast rules, but in knowing when to sell and when to hold.

One important point about the research studies that justify the rationale of buy-and-hold investment strategies is that such studies contrast buying and holding stocks in a particular risk category. Expressed metaphorically, these studies contrast the performance of people who buy and hold apples with that of people who continually trade their apples *for seemingly "better" apples.* Such apple-for-apple traders feel intuitively that they can select better apples or, more appropriately, better stocks. Yet, the wealth of evidence supporting the efficient capital market theory questions the profitability of trading a stock in one risk category for another with the same degree and kinds of risk.[1]

We know from recent research that, when you restrict yourself to a particular type of investment, say, speculative stocks, it is unlikely that trading investments *within that category* can improve your long-run results over those obtainable from a buy-and-hold strategy. This seemingly dour conclusion tells us what must be done to develop a successful investing strategy. Quite simply, you need to avoid downside losses and be in the right instrument at the right time. This means that you must move out of bad investments before losses become serious. But, except for tax reasons, *it is pointless to sell one investment merely to buy another with almost identical risk and comovement characteristics.*

To implement such a strategy, you must establish an explicit performance expectation and an anticipated holding period for *each* investment. By setting your expectations when the investment is made, you can monitor performance relative to your expectations and cut off significant losses. But remember, the *only rational reason to switch an investment is to invest in something in a "different" category*—something that, in addition to being the best in its

---

[1] Realizing capital losses for tax purposes may justify a switch to a similar investment, however.

category, is going to rise, bob and float, or sink differently in the waves of the overall market.

Conclusion

One of the most startling conclusions of the new stock market knowledge is that selecting individual stocks is *not* your most important investment decision. This almost revolutionary conclusion first emphasizes *objectives and a plan, then portfolio policy, an instrument mix, and industry factors.* Unfortunately, however, the current ritual continues to focus on "picking stocks." Yet, in a largely efficient market, can one consistently discern undervalued securities?

Furthermore, analysis which concentrates on company-level information, such as forecasting earnings, can be overshadowed by investors' attitudes toward the company's industry and the market in general. Similarly, information on a stock's risk, as measured by the stock's historical price volatility, affects portfolio composition and hence institutional demand for that stock.

The energy myopically focused on company analysis—and the need to rechannel this analysis—is brought into clear focus by the research supporting the efficient capital market theory. This theory holds that when a large number of buyers and sellers with access to the same information actively compete, the market will become economically efficient. In such a market, *a stock's price, at any point in time, is a risk-adjusted measure of its true value and fully reflects all available information.*

While some investors may be unaware of the efficient capital market theory, the experience of most investment professionals, as well as the bulk of statistical research, supports its conclusion. In practice, many investors are becoming increasingly skeptical about any analysis which countermands the message of the market itself by saying that a stock's price is currently too high or too low.

Practically speaking, when many people study the same company, two things happen. First, its price at any moment is an accurate, risk-adjusted measure of value that reflects the composite opinion of numerous analysts. Second, it is very difficult for any one analyst to be consistently better than the best opinion of all other analysts and investors. James Lorie and Mary Hamilton recently noted the failure of most company analysis "to determine or even consider whether

the price of the stock already reflects the substance of the analysis."
[**109**, p. 100]

Among investors and analysts alike, there is a great temptation to
project opinion and hope into decision making. In the environment
of a largely efficient stock market, the proper approach to investing
involves the seven-step sequence described in this chapter. This
philosophy—which we call "instrument investing"—focuses on those
elements of common stock investing that you can control and that
account for the major part of your performance. Additional instruments related to common stock are discussed next.

20

Mutual Funds

In 1940, mutual funds managed less than $500 million of investors' assets. By 1975, in the relatively short span of 35 years, mutual fund assets had increased nearly 100-fold, to almost $50 billion spread among some 12 million shareholder accounts. Yet, in the last five years, for the first time in history, mutual funds experienced net redemptions—more customers' money going out than flowing in.

Mutual funds seem to be an easy way for the small, or even the large, investor to own securities. By pooling investors' assets into one diversified portfolio, mutual funds relieve their shareholders of responsibility for investment monitoring and decision making. Moreover, brokerage commissions paid by mutual funds on their large block transactions are proportionately less than those charged for small, individual orders. In addition, mutual funds simplify personal tax reporting by giving each shareholder an annual statement consolidating the investment results of many transactions involving different securities. Mutual funds are a *good* idea. This chapter explains how to use them.

Owning Your Share of American Business

During the 1960s, stock ownership grew in vogue. The psychology of growth was pervasive, and brokers were persuasive. As the public became convinced of the merit of owning stocks, mutual funds capitalized on this feeling, as well as helping to create it. Unhappily, because of bear markets in 1966, 1969–70, and 1973–74, over the last decade mutual funds generally did not afford good returns relative to their risks and to other investment alternatives.

Mutual funds are an often recommended way for the "little investor" to own stocks. Through a mutual fund, separate investors share a common portfolio and can tap the professional management and protective diversification that large size can buy. Mutual funds, however, are not restricted to stocks—many seek income through bonds and other instruments, sometimes balanced by stocks. Also, special-purpose funds exist for investing in a particular objective (growth), a specialized instrument (tax-exempt bonds), a philosophy (smaller growth stocks), an industry (financial services), a science (oceanography), a moral philosophy (peace), leverage (in income or capital gain), real property (real estate investment trusts), venture capital (closed-end and private placement funds), and so forth.

It is likely that Mr. Sai ("Small Average Investor," pronounced "Sigh," not Tsai!) is presold on investment in the great American stock market. It is true that a low-expense, diversified fund can effectively provide Mr. Sai with the general rate of return attainable from stocks, minus a modest overhead cost for participation. Mutual funds offer certain pivotal advantages—diversification, professional investment management, and lower commissions due to larger trades— over the do-it-yourself method.

Mutual funds also provide liquidity—fund shares can be sold at any time. *Open-end* funds redeem shares directly and at their net asset value. *Closed-end* fund shares are traded from one shareholder to another, and not with the fund, nor necessarily at their net asset value.

Numerous research studies by unbiased investigators conclude, however, that professional money management, despite a myriad of techniques and research, has usually been unable to provide above-average investment results. In fact, some evidence identifies such management as a source of expense rather than profit. Furthermore, we have seen that diversification, which *is* desirable in reducing risk while maintaining expected return, is easily achieved even in moderate-sized portfolios. The funds' advantage of lower commission costs is to some extent tempered by the fact that funds typically buy and sell more frequently than do individual investors. So, on three counts—expert management, diversified holdings, and reduced commission charges—mutual funds may overstate their advantages to prospective shareholders.

How, then, *do* mutual funds help their clients? Clearly, mutual funds do provide a vehicle that enables small investors to benefit from the general level of investment returns attainable from the securities markets. They also provide reasonably efficient administration of smaller accounts, and they generally avoid the risks of rash investments. Therefore, mutual funds make a reasonable core holding—an investment for the long term. But there are costs, which we discuss below. We also show how to minimize those costs. Finally, this chapter reviews historical fund performance and discusses several special types of funds that you might want to consider.

The Sales Load

The sales load is the first, largest, and most unnecessary cost you encounter with mutual funds. It is a special commission charge that the investor pays in order to buy a fund's shares. Not all funds charge a sales load, but most do. Suppose, for example, that you wish to invest $1,000 in a mutual fund. After consulting with your broker or your mutual fund salesman regarding the selection of a fund, you would mail him a check for $1,000. In turn, he remits this sum to the fund—less his sales commission.

Most of the largest mutual funds charge a sales load in order to induce a broker or mutual fund salesman to sign up investors. A fund distributor, acting as a wholesaler, typically takes a portion of this sales commission. The maximum sales charge (usually charged for investments under $5,000) is shown in Table 20–1 for some of the largest mutual funds, which manage the majority of all fund assets.

Notice that most large funds charge about an 8.5 percent sales load, though some funds have no sales load at all. Hence, for our hypothetical $1,000 purchase, the typical commission charge is $85. Therefore, only $915 of the original $1,000 finds its way into the fund. Thus, restated as a percentage of the actual investment, the sales load is actually $85 on a $915 investment, or 9.3 percent.

Some mutual funds are sold under periodic investment plans.

TABLE 20-1

Assets and Maximum Sales Charge for 50 Large, Common Stock Mutual Funds

Mutual Fund	Assets in Millions (6/30/75)	Maximum Sales Charge
Affiliated Fund	$1,541	7.25%
American Mutual Fund	323	8.5
Anchor Growth Fund	249	8.75
Babson Investment Fund	207	none
Broad Street Investing Corp.	335	8.5
Channing Growth Fund	181	8.5
Chemical Fund	985	8.5
Decatur Income Fund	238	8.5
Delaware Fund	355	8.5
Dividend Shares	306	8.5
Dreyfus Fund	1,579	8.75
Dreyfus Leverage Fund	261	8.75
Enterprise Fund	224	8.5
Fidelity Capital Fund	350	8.5
Fidelity Fund	643	8.5
Fidelity Trend Fund	648	8.5
Financial Industrial Fund	247	none
Fundamental Investors	675	8.75
Hamilton Funds Series H–DA	475	8.5
IDS New Dimensions Fund	260	8.0
The Investment Company of America	1,345	8.5
Investors Stock Fund	2,188	8.0
Investors Variable Payment Fund	693	8.0
ISI Trust Fund	292	8.5
Ivest Fund	227	8.5
The Johnston Mutual Fund	304	none
Keystone Custodian K–2 (Growth Fund)	217	8.75
Keystone Custodian S–4 (Lower Priced)	439	8.75
Massachusetts Investors Growth Stock Fund	1,058	7.25
Massachusetts Investors Trust	1,527	7.25
MIF Fund	232	7.5
National Investors Corp.	766	8.5
National Securities Stock Fund	260	8.5
New Perspective Fund	188	8.5
The One William Street Fund	254	none
Oppenheimer Fund	448	8.5
Pioneer Fund	304	8.5
T. Rowe Price Growth Stock Fund	1,215	none
Rowe Price New Era	267	none
Rowe Price New Horizons Fund	369	none
Puritan Fund	730	8.5
Putnam Growth Fund	680	8.5
Putnam Investors Fund	503	8.5
Technology Fund	461	8.5
United Accumulative Fund	679	8.75
United Income Fund	676	8.75
United Science Fund	262	8.75
USLIFE Common Stock Fund	277	8.5
Washington Mutual Investors	305	8.5
Windsor Fund	455	8.5

Source: *Forbes*, August 15, 1975.

Sales loads on these so-called front-end load plans exceed the average charge during the first few years. Such commissions can run *up to 20 percent*.

Investors should realize that this cost is unnecessary because not all mutual funds have sales loads. It is somewhat incredible that sales load funds persist in the face of alternative "no-load" funds, which are sold via mail or direct advertisement, with no salesman and no commission. In the absence of commissions and personal selling, the investor must sell himself on the merits of the fund. But, as *Fortune* magazine has noted: "Numerous studies have made it clear that the performance of no-loads is as good as that of load funds, and there is really no reason for an investor to pay the standard 9.3 percent sales charge." [194]

In recent years, the no-load funds have attracted increasing numbers of investors—those who decided to sell themselves. During the three years from 1968 through 1970, no-load shareholder accounts more than tripled. Since then, both types of mutual funds have been less in favor, although no-load funds have expanded while load funds have shrunk. Over the full decade 1964–74, the no-load funds moved from only 4.3 percent to nearly 13 percent of total fund assets.

Yet, investors as a whole are still not adequately aware of no-load mutual funds. In 1970, the Investment Company Institute, a mutual fund trade association, analyzed investor familiarity with no-loads. Of families who had heard of mutual funds in general, only 17 percent of those with income under $12,500 had heard of no-loads. Even among families with income over $20,000, only 40 percent of those aware of mutual funds also knew about no-loads. Today, most sales are still of load funds, reflecting the fact that mutual funds are *sold* more than *bought*. An education job remains to be done. (Congratulations, you are now in the sophisticated minority.)

Commissions on Fund Transactions

Portfolio turnover is the proportion of total assets switched from one security to another in a given period of time. Mutual fund managements turn over their portfolios much more rapidly than do individual investors—often three times as fast. Many market professionals believe that seeking high performance calls for such higher-than-average turnover. But turnover is a second cost of owning mutual funds, even though large institutions now incur lower transactions costs than do small investors—in mid-1975, 0.62 percent of the value of the trade to buy or sell, on average, for institutions versus 1.69 percent for individuals. [206]

The very livelihood of investment advisers depends on the belief that, through diligent analysis, one can outperform the market. The efficient capital market theory, on the other hand, holds this belief to be highly suspect. Efficient markets continually digest information on actively traded securities and adjust prices accordingly. Only action taken on the basis of inside information, which is illegal, or good luck, which is unpredictable, can outperform efficient markets.

The existence of high turnover among institutional investors raises two fundamental questions:

1. What causes it?
2. Does it improve performance?

Obviously, the high turnover recorded by mutual funds cannot be traced to a single determinant. We might facetiously hypothesize that turnover is the way a fund manager corrects his mistakes. After all, it is proportionately cheaper for large transactions than for small ones. Or, we might suppose that all that electronic gadgetry and up-to-the-second information makes a money manager's trigger finger itchy. It is amusing to note that the increase in mutual fund turnover coincided not only with the performance craze of the latter 1960s, but also with the availability of instant computerized data, dispensed by desk-top, push-button display units.

On the more critical issue of the performance impact of turnover, rofessor Irwin Friend and his colleagues at the Wharton School, after intensive study of long-term mutual fund performance, reported that "no consistent relationship was found between [portfolio turnover] . . . and investment performance properly adjusted or risk." [55, p. 21] While they found some evidence that in 1964–68 higher trading activity was associated with better performance, the reverse was true in 1960–64 and 1968–69. Another study, which examined data from the 1953–58 period, also found turnover and performance to be unrelated. [52] Research by Hoff Stauffer, Jr., and Robert Vogel [169], at Wesleyan University, examined this relationship and reported some tendency for performance to be inversely related to turnover. Hence, *no comprehensive evidence shows that high portfolio turnover aids mutual fund performance.* Apparently, it just adds to the cost, so a low- or moderate-turnover fund seems preferable.

Management Fees

Mutual funds pay fees to their management companies for rendering certain services, primarily investment decisions. The management fee is a third cost of owning mutual funds. This fee is stipulated in an investment advisory contract between the fund and its management company. Each fund must furnish potential or existing investors with a prospectus or an annual report disclosing the size of the fund's management fee, among other things. This fee is often one half of 1 percent of assets annually. One should therefore be convinced of the merit of paying any fund management fees higher than this norm.

Administrative Expenses

A fourth cost of owning mutual fund shares is a charge for certain administrative expenses borne by the fund and thus by its shareholders. Typically, the annual amount of this cost ranges from 0.25 percent to 0.5 percent of the fund's assets. Although varying from fund to fund, certain legal, accounting, directors', clerical, printing, and office expenses are covered by the charge. Smaller funds tend to have proportionately higher expense ratios, so, on the basis of this cost category, a larger fund is usually preferable.

The Tax Take

A fifth and final cost to fundholders is the tax take. Mutual funds themselves do not pay taxes. They are allowed to flow through to their shareholders the taxes due on any *realized* income and capital gains. The fundholders then pay income and capital gains taxes at their appropriate individual rates.

The sale of a stock in which the fund has a capital gain *realizes* that gain. Thus, fundholders may periodically have to pay taxes, rather than have that capital continue to be invested, untaxed, as with a single common stock. Here again, the answer is to find a low-turnover fund, or one with *past* losses that can shelter future gains, if they materialize.

How to Use Mutual Funds

Despite the sales loads, commissions, management fees, expenses, and possible taxation costs, mutual funds are a good idea. They permit investors, small or large, to participate in the general returns of the securities markets. Professional management, diversification, and lowered commission rates are the selling points. Yet, each of these alleged advantages has probably been overemphasized. What should the investor do? As with any investment instrument, mutual funds should be bought only when they fit into your Personal Financial Plan. For many, they are a suitable, moderate-risk, acceptable-expense vehicle for common stock investing. If so, which fund should you choose?

The past records of mutual funds are widely reported and analyzed. *Forbes* magazine, which publishes its annual survey at midyear, grades fund results for both up and down markets. *Institutional Investor* reports fund rankings and various year-to-date comparisons. Current prices are posted daily in newspaper financial pages. But, as the funds themselves must specify in most advertisements, past performance is no guarantee of the future. Up in good markets and down in bad ones is the rule. Indeed, in the *Forbes* ratings of mid-1971, the *one* fund which ranked A in both up and down markets was Japan Fund, which invests in an entirely different economy. Thus, the type of fund one selects and its investment philosophy are the most important determinants of future performance.

How Have Mutual Funds Performed?

Using a *realistic* measure of performance, William Sharpe reported that, in terms of a reward-to-risk ratio, the odds were "greater than 100 to 1 against the possibility that the average mutual fund did as well as the Dow-Jones portfolio from 1954–1963." [**155,** p. 137] Sharpe traced the cause of this remarkably bad rating to differences between the funds' *gross* and *net* performance. Thus, we see that the costs we have cited do take their toll. In Sharpe's words, "All other things being equal, the smaller a fund's expense ratio, the better the results obtained by stockholders." [**155,** p. 137]

In 1968, Michael Jensen devised a measure for comparing mutual fund performance across "different risk levels and across differing time periods irrespective of general economic and market conditions." Jensen then evaluated the "ability of the portfolio manager or security analyst to increase returns on the portfolio through successful prediction of future security prices. [**78,** p. 389] In seeking evidence of portfolio managers' predictive ability, Jensen studied the performance of 115 open-end mutual funds in the period from 1945–64. His findings are summarized as follows.

The evidence on mutual fund performance . . . indicates not only that these 115 mutual funds were *on average* not able to predict security prices well enough to outperform a buy-the-market-and-hold policy, but also that there is very little evidence that any individual fund was able to do significantly better than that which we expected from mere random chance. It is also important to note that these conclusions hold *even* when we measure the fund returns gross of management expenses (that is, assume their bookkeeping, research, and other expenses except brokerage commissions were obtained free). Thus on average the funds apparently were not quite successful enough in their trading activities to recoup even their brokerage expenses.

The evidence . . . indicate[s] . . . a pressing need on the part of the funds themselves to evaluate much more closely both the costs and the benefits of their research and trading activities in order to provide investors with maximum possible returns for the level of risk undertaken. [**78,** pp. 414–15]

In a more recent study, John O'Brien evaluated the performance of 119 funds during the ten years 1959–68. He reported: "On the basis of the observed results . . . it is concluded that there are no more managers than predicted by chance occurrence either exceeding or failing to exceed the rate of return predicted for them based upon the level of uncertainty they assume." [**136,** p. 102]

Certainly one of the most extensive research studies of the performance of mutual funds and other institutional investors was published in August 1970 by three faculty members of the Wharton School. In this study, Irwin Friend, Marshall Blume, and Jean Crockett reported on the performance of 299 leading funds for the years 1960 through 1968. They reported:

The overall annual rates of return on investment in 136 mutual funds [essentially all the larger, publicly owned funds for which data were available] averaged 10.7 percent for the period January 1960, through June 1968 (9.0 percent for the period January 1960, through March 1964, and 12.8 percent for the period April 1964, through June 1968). Unweighted investment in *all* stocks listed on the Big Board in the same periods would have yielded 12.4 percent (7.0 percent in the first part and 17.8 percent in the second).

* * * * *

When funds were classified by fund size, sales charges, management expenses, portfolio turnover, and investment objectives, no consistent relationship was found between these factors and investment performance properly adjusted for risk. To the extent that a relationship exists between performance and sales charges, the funds with the lowest charges, including the "no-load" funds, appear to perform slightly better than the others. [55, pp. 19–21]

In conclusion, investors should expect about average market performance (or a little less, allowing for costs) from mutual funds, depending on the *type* of fund purchased.

Special Types of Funds

Several special types of mutual funds exist to serve the varying needs of investors. Fund selection should be based on a knowledge of these different vehicles. A fund's stated objective is perhaps its most distinctive aspect. Most common stock funds seek growth, although some seek high current income. Other funds are "balanced" between growth and income, using preferred stock or bond investments for the latter purpose. In the 1970s, REITs, bond funds, and money market funds have successively surged and retreated in popularity. This reflects changing interest rates and investor attitudes especially after the debacle of the "go-go" funds. Perhaps this verifies the saying that "a long-term investor is a short term speculator who lost."

The REITs (real estate investment trusts) have had abominable performance. These portfolios are based on investments in real property, as opposed to common stocks. REITs specializing in short-term mortgage loans have been particularly vulnerable to interest rate swings and builder defaults. Bond funds have fared better, but not great. Often, the principal value has declined, even though current interest payments are reasonably high. The money market funds, too, have cooled off, as short-term interest rates declined in 1975–76 from their historic highs.

Private-placement income funds are another type. These are underwritten funds (closed-end funds sold at one time rather than continuously). Their attraction includes high-income potential through active bond trading to exploit subtle shifts in yields and through participation in securities offered privately. The latter are spared the expense of public registration, and thus usually carry a higher yield or other advantages, such as equity kickers. Also, some funds distribute income monthly. This gives a reassuring feeling to many fundholders. Still another type of income fund specializes in tax free bonds.

Industry funds, in insurance or chemicals, for example, have also been marketed. Here, the advantage of diversification is significantly thwarted, but the chances for extraordinary swings are increased. One further group of funds—the dual funds—deserves explanation, as they offer an unusually attractive opportunity.

Dual Funds

Several dual-purpose mutual funds were marketed in early 1967, and most are now listed on the NYSE. These unusual vehicles had been tried earlier in England and arrived here with great fanfare. None have been introduced since that flurry, however, because their interim performance has been spotty to downright poor. Herein lies the current opportunity.

The dual funds satisfy one of two objectives—growth *or* income. Half of the shares are entitled to receive *all* of the fund's capital gains, while the other half receive *all* income from dividends or interest. In effect, these shares are leveraged in one objective or the other. For example, the capital shares generally rise (or fall) faster than the market. As *Money* magazine headlined, "While mutual funds on average rose about 30 percent in the first seven months of 1975, seven [dual] funds were up 79 percent." [198]

To keep the number of shares evenly matched, these funds are of the closed-end type. As a consequence, they sell for what a buyer will pay and not for net asset value, as do open-end funds. Perhaps because of their unconventional structure or their less-than-satisfactory past achievements, these funds typically sell at handsome discounts.

Unlike most closed-end funds, these shares must rise someday to net asset value. They each have a stated expiration date (ranging from 1979–85) when shares can be redeemed for their underlying value. Table 20–2 shows the discounts from net asset value typically available on the capital shares of these funds. A 25 percent to 50 percent price rise is built into some of the capital shares, *above*

TABLE 20-2

Dual Fund Capital Share Discounts*

	Capital Shares Price	Net Asset Value of Capital Shares	Percent Difference
American DualVest...............	4¼	5.94	−28.5
Gemini.........................	10½	15.42	−31.9
Hemisphere.....................	1¼	0.41	+204.9
Income and Capital..............	5⅛	7.74	−33.8
Leverage........................	7⅝	10.89	−27.7
Pegasus Income & Capital........	6½	5.22	+24.5
Putnam Duo Fund...............	4	6.28	−36.3
Scudder Duo-Vest................	5	7.74	−35.4
Scudder D-V Exchange...........	20	25.22	−20.7

* The table lists the unaudited net asset values of the capital shares of dual-purpose, closed-end investment funds reported by the companies as of the close on Friday, November 28, 1975. It also lists the closing market price or the dealer-to-dealer asked price of each fund's capital shares, with the percentage of difference from the capital shares price.

Source: *Wall Street Journal*, December 1975.

whatever appreciation the portfolio may achieve. (Remember that a 33.3 percent discount, for example, produces a 50 percent rise to reach net asset value.)

Developing a "Better Idea"

In summary, mutual funds offer interesting opportunities. But consider the following surprising and disconcerting facts about fund performance:

1. Historically, there has been little difference between the performance of mutual funds and an equal investment in all NYSE stocks or in a weighted index like the Standard & Poor's average (see Table 20–3).

TABLE 20-3

Institutional Rates of Return*

	1 Year	4 Years	8 Years
Bank Equity.....................	+30.3%	−3.5%	−0.2%
Insurance......................	+33.9	−3.9	−0.6
Advisers.......................	+30.0	−0.4	†
Bank Special Equity.............	+35.0	−5.6	†
Growth Mutuals................	+38.8	−6.0	−2.5
Balanced Mutuals..............	+33.0	−0.3	+2.0
S&P 500......................	+38.1	−0.3	+1.7

* This table lists average annual rates of return for each institutional sector over the one-year, four-year, and eight-year periods ending September 30, 1975.

† Not available.

Source: Frank Russell Co. [**205**].

2. There has been no historical relationship between a fund's performance, properly adjusted for risk, and the size, sales charge, management fee, portfolio turnover, or investment objective of the fund.
3. There has been no evidence of consistently good performance by the same fund in successive periods.

The rational investor should ask himself which would be more beneficial:

1. Performance derived from managed assets with standard sales loads, commissions, management fees, expenses, and taxation.
2. Performance derived from *un*managed assets of comparable risk, but with *no* sales load, *low* commissions from nil turnover, and *low* fees and expenses—plus *deferred* taxation.

Friend et al. noted that unmanaged portfolios with no turnover and consisting of all NYSE stocks provided returns at least equal to those of the average mutual fund. Indeed, *a mutual fund composed merely of a cross section of NYSE stocks* is an interesting concept. Low expenses, including no sales load, minimum turnover, and a modest "management" fee could accompany such a fund. Shareholder benefits, beyond those of investment in the stock market and ultradiversification, would include lowered fees and expenses and the maximum possible tax deferral on accruing capital gains.

No less an independent authority than Paul Samuelson, the Nobel prize-winning economist, has advocated this concept. [200] *Forbes* magazine has tested this concept and has publicized its resultant "Dart Board Fund." To date, the "fund" has outdistanced the average professionally managed fund.

The Economy Fund—a Better Idea

We are beginning to see the advent of such deliberately low-expense, low-turnover, broadly diversified, no-load mutual funds—called *index funds* by some because they attempt to duplicate the performance of some market average, or index. But such a fund might be called *The Economy Fund* to emphasize its low cost and comprehensive holdings.

The Economy Fund advocated here would prove very effective at minimizing the cost factors noted earlier. We have computed the

20-year performance of a hypothetical Economy Fund, compared to the performance of a load and a no-load fund. *Based on the same underlying market performance, it delivers more of the market's potential.*

Let's assume that you bought $1,000 of each type of fund. Let's also assume that the market will provide a 3 percent dividend yield and 7 percent annually in capital gains—a reasonable long-term expectation. Your after-tax results, after 20 years in each fund, are shown below for the three types of funds. These dramatic differences stem from the same market performance. They reflect the impact of the Economy Fund's lowered expenses and deferred taxes.

Average load fund	$3,544
Average no-load fund	$4,060
The Economy Fund	$4,639

Obviously, such a mutual fund should be made available to investors for long-term, buy-and-hold, core investing. Over 20 years—a relevant investment horizon for a middle-aged investor—the Economy Fund significantly outgains those funds burdened with average expenses and, worse yet, average sales loads.

Is such "unmanaged" investing prudent? Two law professors at the University of Chicago, John Langbein and Richard Posner [190], predicted that "courts may one day conclude that it is imprudent for trustees to *fail* to use such vehicles." [italics added]

21

Hedge Strategies

Among Wall Streeters, the game is performance—the weekly, quarterly, or annual casting of rank among their ranks. But we have seen that "return" must be trotted around the ring with its companion horse, "risk." Hedge strategies—which seek to lower risk—contrast with the go-go philosophy that "there is no risk in the past, only results." The credo of some money managers has been "The best way to protect capital is to double it." Yet, this performance mania is alarming in light of research showing that the quest for performance is consistently associated with inordinate risk.

Today, many investors persist in playing only one game—the stock market—in spite of overwhelming evidence favoring diversification into various vehicles. Research confirms that diversification is good. And we have found that stock portfolio diversification is easy to obtain. Several stocks, well chosen for different risk characteristics, can diversify away the major risks not associated with the stock market itself.

However, the risk of the *stock market* is no small matter. Since World War II, there have been 12 significant stock market declines. They averaged seven months in duration and a 21 percent loss in value. And these market losses do not include the vanished opportunity of collecting bank interest or other safe returns.

Investing in the stock market is not the only way to manage money. Real estate, for instance, is an even bigger market than that of NYSE- and AMEX-listed stocks. Commodities, the basic physical goods of our economy, such as wheat, corn, eggs, silver, scrap iron, or lumber, form another investment market. One can invest, or speculate, in such physical goods via commodity futures without ever intending to be the final user of the commodity purchased. These other money management opportunities, and investment possibilities in foreign securities markets, oil and mineral rights, cattle feeding, equipment leasing, art, antiques, jewels, coins, stamps, and so on, demonstrate that the American stock market is only *part* of the money management spectrum, albeit a large part.

The Forgotten Instrument—Convertible Bonds

Convertible bonds, some observers say, have become forgotten instruments. Bonds represent the debts of the organization that issues them. By owning a bond, you become a creditor of that organization. If a bond-issuing company collapses, whatever assets can be liquidated must be used to satisfy debts, including obligations to the company's bondholders. To purchasers of these comparatively low-risk instruments, the issuer promises a regular interest payment and, upon maturity of the bond, repayment of principal.

Bonds reflect the organization that issues them, and are not of

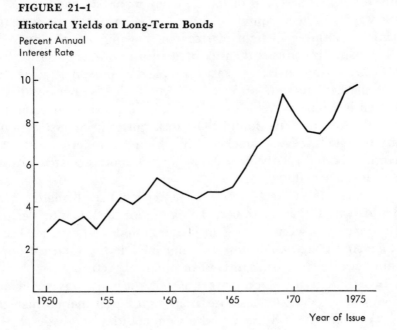

FIGURE 21-1

Historical Yields on Long-Term Bonds

Percent Annual
Interest Rate

uniform quality or yield. *Convertible bonds* carry the additional right to be exchanged for common stock, at a specified price. These bonds, therefore, are less risky for the investor than is direct common stock ownership in the same company.

The potential return from investing in convertible bonds can be attractive. Many astute investors, eschewing lower-yielding savings accounts or the risks of volatile stock markets, have shifted assets into these vehicles. In the 1970s, yields on bonds have been nearly twice as great as the returns several years earlier, as shown in Figure 21–1. Such returns approach the long-term rate of return historically available from the stock market. But how can the lower risk and higher current yield of bonds be had without forsaking the upside potential of common stocks? This is the role of "converts."

What Investors Should Know about "Converts"

Convertible bonds, while not free of risk, are considered more predictable than the corresponding common stocks. Any bond contract has three principal features—*quality, yield,* and *maturity.*

Quality reflects the financial position and prospects of the issuer. The federal government, with seemingly endless taxing authority, is the highest-quality issuer. Major blue-chip corporations also issue bonds of high quality. Excepting railroads, real estate, and retailers, such large corporations have very seldom defaulted on payments.

Yield is the ratio of annual interest to a bond's price. Since a bond's interest payment is fixed, when bond prices fall, their yields go up. For example, suppose a bond originally sold for $1,000 and paid 9 percent interest. If you could now buy this bond for $900, the $90 of annual interest would be 10 percent of the current price. Thus, the *current yield* is 10 percent. *Yield to maturity* is even higher, since a $100 capital gain would also be realized when the $1,000 principal is repaid.

Maturity is the scheduled date of repayment of principal. Some bonds mature in five years, while others do not reach maturity for 30 years or longer. Bonds fluctuate in price as other interest rates or the qualities of the bonds change. Longer-maturity bonds fluctuate more in price since more interest payments are at stake.

There are many types of bonds, each suitable for different kinds of investors. Short-maturity bonds provide greater certainty and an early payback. They generally carry a lower yield as a result. Federal government bonds, because of their quality, also generally yield less. Municipal bonds are exempt from federal income taxes, but New York's problems have clouded this market. Convertible bonds have the right to participate in corporate growth through their convertibility into common stock.

What does research reveal about the profitability of convertible bond investing?

1. Converts have historically returned slightly less than common stocks.
2. Convertible bond yields have recently become almost competitive with the long-term returns of stocks, including price appreciation as well as dividends.
3. Lower-quality bonds yield more than high-quality bonds, even *after* adjustment for risk.
4. The lower the quality, the more helpful it is to diversify.
5. Active and wise bond trading may improve returns—the market is *not* completely efficient.
6. Perhaps most important, many medium-grade and speculative companies whose stocks often appear in individual or institutional portfolios have convertible bonds outstanding with risk-return characteristics surpassing those of the common stock. Returns of 12 percent, 15 percent, or even 20 percent annually, *guaranteed* by the issuer for periods extending to 15 years and longer, can often be found in the convertible bond market.

Convert Investing—An Example

In 1970, Ling-Temco-Vought, Inc. (now LTV), was an out-of-favor former darling. The company had suffered huge losses and had undergone a top management shake-up. While the company has other speculative bonds outstanding, it also has a convert with good current income and potential capital appreciation—provided, of course, that the company meets its obligations.

An investor seeking above-average returns might consider such a speculative investment. For instance, during much of 1974, the approximate price of a $1,000 face value LTV convertible bond maturing in 1977 was $950. This bond is listed in newspapers (NYSE bonds) as LTV cv 7½ of 77. The company is obligated to pay $75 annual interest per bond. In addition, the bond must be repaid in full ($1,000 per bond) on its maturity date in 1977. It is this stream of LTV-guaranteed payments, plus the right to convert the bonds into common stock at $10.50 per share, that cost an investor around $950 during 1974.

The definition of just what constitutes return from a bond is often simplified by computing the bond's "current yield," as published in daily financial newspapers. The annual interest of $75, when divided by the price of $950, results in a 7.9 percent current yield. However, a capital gain is also built into this bond's price, since it must be redeemed for $1,000 in 1977. Therefore, it must go up from $950 to $1,000 by 1977, if the company remains solvent. This represents a capital gain of just over 5 percent in three years, or nearly 2 percent annually. Thus, the investor averages a 2 percent annual capital gain plus the 7.9 percent current yield, or nearly 10 percent in total return.

The kicker with any convert, of course, is that the bond can rise above its face value, given good performance in the underlying common stock. In this case, LTV could be expected to rise and fall with the general market and with the steel industry in particular. Also, there was a prospective turnaround. The converts provided a good mix of moderate risk and possible high return.

The foregoing analysis should not be anything new to investment professionals. Nonetheless, the high level and long duration of some convertible bond returns are likely to surprise most readers. The particular convert cited above may be risky compared to most bonds, but it is less risky than the stock of the respective company.

The recent prices of many converts, some having over $25 million outstanding, were so low as to afford returns to maturity averaging about *12 percent* compounded annually. And their risk was low in comparison to that of the underlying stocks. A diversified portfolio of such medium- to low-quality bonds provides investors with protection against the potential financial misfortune that might befall one or a few such companies. Moreover, either employing leverage or confining selections to a few dozen of the highest-returning bonds permitted *expected returns of 15 to 20 percent compounded annually for a span of nearly 15 years.*

More Hedge Strategies

Still other hedge strategies can be used to achieve good returns at acceptable levels of risk. Some approaches deliberately seek *not* to depend on skillful security selection. One example of this approach was the published success story *Beat the Market.* It revealed the strategy of Sheen T. Kassouf and Edward O. Thorp, whose earlier book, *Beat the Dealer,* had sent Las Vegas twenty-one oddsmakers back to their abacuses and card-shuffling machines.

In *Beat the Market,* Thorp and Kassouf [176] explained the risk-reward structure of a specific type of stock-warrant hedge. This hedge involves holding two related instruments whose *combined* action is deemed desirable or risk lowering. The stock-warrant hedge devised by Kassouf and Thorp involved selling warrants short, close to their expiration, while simultaneously holding a long position in the corresponding stock. A warrant is a right to buy a stock for a specified price. Recognizing that warrants are more volatile than the underlying stock, Thorp and Kassouf experimented with various ratios of short and long positions to alter their combined investment outcome. By hedging a warrant against its stock in this manner, Thorp and Kassouf demonstrated results which were highly predictable, were often *independent* of the stock's price changes, and were nearly always profitable.

Why such a profitable strategy can persist is perhaps explained by a favorite story involving a former student of ours. Upon joining a Wall Street firm, this enlightened newcomer used every available opportunity to ask people he met whether they had read either Brealey's *An Introduction to Risk and Return from Common Stocks* or Thorp and Kassouf's *Beat the Market.* The reply generally involved a lecture that "people on the Street learn from experience." After *eight months* he found *one person*—a partner in his firm— who had read both books. Amusingly, as the partner started to discuss these books, *he nervously arose and closed his office door.* In the sanctity of his office, the partner then advised his young charge that, even though he found the books fascinating, discussions of the "random walk and so forth" tended to alienate "people in the business" and that, in the interest of his career, he should "learn from experience."

Hedging—Another Experience

Once upon a time, a man named Alfred Winslow Jones had a great investment idea. As long as Jones kept the idea to himself, he prospered. Once his idea leaked out, the scheme was destroyed by ubiquitous imitators. There is a hazard in extrapolating such "once upon a time" success stories. Obviously, something that works for a few investors can be destroyed by imitating masses. It does not follow, however, that a technique works merely because someone won't tell you what it is.

When someone has a genuinely good idea on the Street, it is doubtful whether the secret can be kept. Word spreads fast on Wall Street. One day several years ago, a young woman walked out of the Chemical Bank Building. A couple of ardent girl watchers "recommended" the view of her sweater-enveloped 53-inch bust. Within three days, several thousand people—all getting the same tips—were lined ten deep on Wall Street to watch her daily stroll.

Having been forewarned, the parable of Alfred Winslow Jones and his hedging secret continues. Hedge strategies are designed to assure an acceptable return, regardless of the market's future. Basically, this hedge plays one investment against *an unrelated one,* so that if one goes down, the other might still go up. The problem, of course, is to combine investments in such a way that this canceling effect is still profitable.

Jones' strategy, popularized as the hedge fund concept, involved both buying stocks long and selling short. A short sale is selling borrowed stock for repurchase *later.* When an investor sells short, the results are the opposite of those obtained from owning the stock, called "being long." The investor makes a profit if the stock price declines and the shares can be bought cheaper later. Obviously, hedge strategists do not select two *identical* investments for holding both long and short. Instead, hedging is normally practiced by shorting stocks expected to perform worse than average, while holding long stocks expected to perform better than average. In addition, to get more money invested, many hedged portfolios borrow to the limit, achieving leverage that might surprise even Archimedes.

The hedge fund genre was spawned by Jones, who reigned as patriarch of the tribe. His first limited partnership was A. W. Jones and Co., formed in 1952. During the nine years until 1961, Jones compounded his investors' money at a phenomenal 21 percent annual rate. Even so, the public had little knowledge of Jones' achievements on behalf of his wealthy clients. Finally, in its April 1966 issue, *Fortune* published an article entitled "The Jones Nobody Keeps Up With." The article pointed out that, in the long term, Jones had not only outperformed the mutual funds but had also survived the 1962 market collapse virtually unscathed.

What *really* attracted the attention of money managers, however, was mention that under the private, limited partnership form of organization money managers could take as compensation[1] 20 percent of any profits earned on their limited partners' money. To quote Carol Loomis, writing in *Fortune*, "These items of news were enough to create overnight a raft of would-be hedge-fund managers, most of whom were convinced that Jones had discovered the millennium." [193]

In the early years, when he alone was "playing the game," Jones did attain remarkable performance. But in terms of supply and demand, many players make a market efficient. In a nutshell, with everyone trying to outguess everyone else, it is difficult to predict better than the market, which reflects the combined judgment of all who participate in it. Worse still, many hedgers were caught "in their shorts" by the Johnson peace rally of April 1968. In the words of Gilbert Kaplan, "The biggest problem facing the hedge funds is the constant pressure to find good shorts, principally because the host of imitators that Jones has spawned has narrowed down the opportunities." [82, p. 120] An efficient, continually adjusting market makes this Jones-style hedging difficult. The short position too often merely *cancels* the long position, rather than *hedges* it. It thereby fails to preserve return while lowering risk.

Hedging Revisited

The hedge opportunity cited below, unlike the investments of hedge funds, involves two securities of the *same issuer*. Hedge funds which played the stock of one company against a short sale in another were often scissored by these unrelated holdings. Securities with a defined relationship to each other, however, *can* be hedged predictably. One striking hedge opportunity, executed by one of the authors, was available during 1972, using American Telephone and Telegraph securities. Prices for various AT&T securities at the time were approximately:

Common stock . . . . . $42 (then a $2.60 dividend)
Convertible
    preferred . . . . $57 ($4.00 dividend)
Warrant . . . . $8 (right to buy one share at $52)
Bond . . . . $110 (8¾ to 2000)

---
[1] In an income tax sense, this is not "compensation" but the general partner's share of gains or losses.

TABLE 21-1

Capital Gains Results of AT&T Stock-Warrant Hedge*

Final AT&T Price (May 1975)	1975 Value of 100 Warrants	Gain from Short Sale of 100 Warrants	Gain in Value of 100 Common Shares	Total Capital Gain on Combination
$35	$ 0	$ 800	−$ 700	$ 100
40	0	800	− 200	600
45	0	800	300	1,100
50	0	800	800	1,600
52	0	800	1,000	1,800
60	800	0	1,800	1,800
70	1,800	− 1,000	2,800	1,800
80	2,800	− 2,000	3,800	1,800

*Strategy: Buy 100 shares of AT&T common @ $42; sell 100 warrants short @ $8. Total investment = $5,000.

As always, the investment question is, "What should you do with these opportunities?" A stock-warrant hedge strategy of buying 100 AT&T common shares and short-selling 100 AT&T warrants would have the results shown in Table 21-1, if the investment were held until May 15, 1975, when the warrants expired.

A "profit graph" is a diagram of the annual rate of return at various possible prices of the security under consideration. One is drawn in Figure 21-2 for this hedge, including dividends as well as the capital gains noted in Table 21-1.

FIGURE 21-2

Profit Graph for Stock-Warrant Hedge Held to May 1975

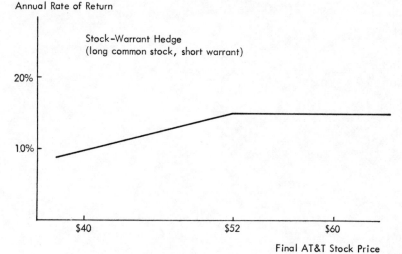

The profit graph for the AT&T stock-warrant hedge is very flat. This means that the rate of return on the hedge is not especially sensitive to the final AT&T stock price. Such a strategy *hedges* one's stake in the stock's price fluctuations. Thus, risk is very low. The stock-warrant hedge, however, offers a significantly higher return than can be expected from the bond or the preferred stock. Moreover, by using leverage, a very handsome return could have been realized. It turned out that AT&T closed at just about $52 per share when the warrants expired—delivering the maximum profit on the hedge.

The Tortoise and the Hare

Hedge strategies require patience while waiting out the relatively predictable movements of appropriate *combinations of securities*. But their annual rate of return can be nicely, if not wildly, rewarding. It's like the old tale of the tortoise and the hare—steady progress is likely to win the race. And by hedging, you moderate the market's risks.

22

Stock Options

Stock options—puts and calls—have become popular, useful investment instruments. Over the last two decades, the volume of option contracts grew slowly until March 1973. Then, regular trading began on a national exchange—the Chicago Board Options Exchange (CBOE). Next, the American Stock Exchange and the Philadelphia-Baltimore-Washington (PBW) Exchange joined in. Option volume grew to over 10 million shares daily by early 1976.

Readers of the *Wall Street Journal* or other financial newspapers are no doubt aware of these options markets. Ironically, while we hear a lot about baseball players' options or real estate options, many investors remain unfamiliar with the analysis of stock options. Their potentially desirable risk-reward profile can play a role in many portfolios.

Put and Call Options

A *put* allows the option holder to *sell,* if he so desires, a specific number of shares of the stock under contract at a fixed price at any time within the contract period. Similarly, a *call* option gives the holder the right to *buy* a specific number of shares at a fixed price at any time within the contract period. The agreed-upon contract price is called the "striking price." The seller, or "writer," of the option must stand ready to make good on his promise to the option buyer. Option contracts are endorsed by an exchange or member firm to assure that the promise is carried out.

Before the establishment of the CBOE, options typically ran for 35 days to one year, with most options running for a little over six months (that is, six months and ten days). This permitted long-term capital gain possibilities by sale of the option itself after a six-month holding period. Options for three-, six-, or nine-month periods, with standard striking prices and expiration dates, are now prevalent.

The strict definition of the word *option* is synonymous with *choice*. In option investing, the choice belongs to the buyer, who can choose to exercise his option at any time during the contract period, and does so only if it is to his advantage. The future right to make such a choice, in the face of uncertainty, is acquired by paying a *premium* to the option writer at the time the contract is established. Conversely, the option seller has no choice. He *must* buy (if he has sold a put) or sell (if he has sold a call) the specified number of shares at the contract price at the election of the option holder.

There are at least two historical reasons why option contracts were not used more prior to the establishment of the CBOE. First, option investing had a rather bad beginning, as will be discussed shortly. Second, options were not widely understood since they were unduly complicated and nonstandard. Kermit Zieg, Jr. [187], showed that before 1970, only 15 percent of the registered representatives surveyed could correctly define various types of options. Another researcher, who was less quantitative, but blunter in his conclusion, stated that "customers' men that understand Puts and Calls are few and far between." [95, p. 46] Indeed, in the 1950s, Herbert Filer, then the dean of option traders, estimated that only one investor in a thousand had "more than a smattering of knowledge of Put and Call options." [47, p. 16]

In the Beginning . . .

The concept of an option agreement has been traced to biblical times. Organized option trading took place as early as the legendary tulip bulb craze in Holland in the 1630s. This was its tainted beginning. As the Dutch became enchanted with tulip bulbs, demand outstripped supply. Prices for the bulbs started a whirlwind rise. Dealers who had to supply a fixed number of tulip bulbs at some future date found that they could insure against this price inflation by purchasing a call option. Thus, if bulb prices continued to rise, the dealers could exercise their call options and obtain bulbs at a known price. If bulb prices fell, they could supply their customers by buying bulbs on the open market. From that time to the present, dealers could *insure* against price uncertainties by holding options. But there was a second motivation for resorting to options.

Enter the Speculator

Speculators soon realized that, as long as tulip bulb prices continued to rise, they could make money by purchasing call options instead of investing directly in bulbs. A speculator could *leverage* his gains, or losses, by buying options. Leverage implies that one small change causes a large change elsewhere. For the relatively small cost of a call, tulip speculators could own an option to buy bulbs at some future date for a fixed price. If prices continued to rise during this period, the speculator could exercise his call, buy bulbs at the predetermined price, and immediately sell them. The profit equaled the price increase less the cost for the call option. The small capital investment for the call could be leveraged into a large capital gain, *if* prices went up.

In the early 1630s, tulip bulb trading became so profitable that virtually everyone in Holland, rich and poor, became involved. In fact, many people left their traditional jobs to join the tulip bulb industry. Everything worked well for all concerned until 1636, when the Dutch found themselves "up to their windmills" in tulip bulbs and the demand stopped! The rest is history—sad history. As prices fell, the economy of Holland faltered. The life savings of a broad spectrum of the Dutch population vanished, and a prolonged economic depression ensued.

For many years, option trading was thought by many to be synonymous with gambling—a word inconsistent with Wall Street's desired image. In fact, legislation proposed after the 1929 stock market crash called for the outright ban of all stock options. Due to the persistent testimony of Herbert Filer, representing the option dealers, puts and calls remained legal. Since then, option trading has grown. Traditionally, most trading was done through firms belonging to the Put and Call Brokers and Dealers Association (PCBDA). Now, nearly all of the volume is handled on organized exchanges using standardized contract terms for these options or "stock futures."

Role of Options

Options are useful to investors because of two properties—their *insurance value* and their *leverage value*. Probably, their more useful function is to insure against risk. Most homes are insured by their owners against the risk of losing them. Yet, in early 1973, how many investors considered insuring their stock portfolios against excessive losses?

There are several theories about how investors can best insure their positions. Nicholas Darvas expressed one view in his early 1960s best-seller *How I Made $2,000,000 in the Stock Market.* [37] He said that an investor should insure profits by automatically selling the stock he owns if its price decreases to an "insurance" level. Under this theory, a "stop-loss" order is placed with the investor's broker so that the stock will be sold if the price drops by some predetermined amount. If the market moves up, the stop-loss price should also be moved up. When the market moves down, the stock is sold out. The theory has appeal for those who believe in price trends.

Options can also be used for this kind of insurance. Buying a put can insure a fixed selling price, confining possible losses to known limits. The various outcomes of such a strategy can be illustrated on profit graphs. For example, suppose a stock is selling at $50, or $5,000 per 100 shares. An investor could choose to buy a six-month put for about a 10 percent premium, or $500 per hundred shares. The profit graph in Figure 22–1 shows the various results of buying 100 shares at $50 combined with a six-month put purchased for $500.

Regardless of the stock's price after six months, the maximum loss is $500. The potential gain is unrestricted. If, after six months, the stock price is below $50, the holder of the put would exercise his option to sell the stock at the option striking price of $50. He would have no loss on the stock sale, but would bear the $500 cost of his option. If the stock were above $50, he would let the put expire because he could sell his stock more favorably in the market. As shown in Figure 22–1, the maximum loss of $500 (plus commissions, of course) occurs if the stock's price does not rise above the striking price. Lesser losses occur if the stock rises, but not enough to recover

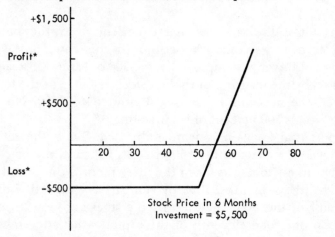

FIGURE 22-1

Profit Graph for Stock Purchase with Put Option*

Stock Price in 6 Months
Investment = $5,500

* Commission omitted.

the $500 put premium. A put option used in this manner acts as an insurance policy to limit financial exposure to an uncertain future.

The second major use of options is for leverage. Here, the option buyer seeks to magnify the rate of return on his capital when stock

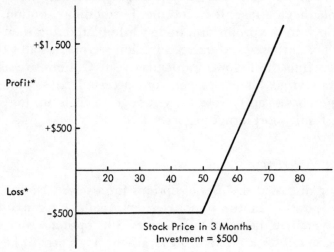

FIGURE 22-2

Profit Graph for Purchase of Call Option*

Stock Price in 3 Months
Investment = $500

* Commission omitted.

prices move favorably. Purchasing a three-month call on our $50 stock might also cost about $500, resulting in the profit graph shown in Figure 22–2.

The result is the same as that experienced by the putholder-stockholder over a six-month period. In this case, however, the leveraged call buyer has employed only $500 of capital instead of the $5,500 used by the insuring putholder-stockholder. For the leveraged call buyer, the maximum loss is still limited to $500. Now, however, this equals 100 percent of his investment!

The potential for gain is again unlimited. Thus, the call buyer has leveraged the effect of the $500 risked. In truth, the price of the stock is not likely to rise as far in the three months of the call option as it might in six months. But, by comparison, the call buyer has gotten most of the play obtained by the stock-and-put "insurance" investor on only one eleventh of the capital—that's leverage!

Tax Implications

Still another feature of option contracts involves their use for tax considerations. Favorable tax strategies are possible in certain instances, but this advantage is less universal than are the insurance and leverage benefits. The advantage is more a property of our tax system than of the option. For instance, puts provide the only means by which an investor can convert a decline in stock prices into a long-term capital gain for tax purposes. Short sales held for any length of time are taxable as income. Furthermore, options can be used to lock in the profits of a trade while postponing their realization for tax purposes, such as reaching long-term tax status or deferring taxes into the following calendar year. Options are also used to generate large, long-term gains on successful risks, while unsuccessful purchases can be sold early enough to chalk up losses in the more desirable short-term category.

Option Writing

Having discussed the uses of options for a buyer, we can investigate the position of the option writer. Again, we can use profit graphs to analyze the possible outcomes. The option writer must be prepared to sell stock (if he wrote a call) or buy stock (if he wrote a put). He must therefore have an assured reserve to make good his promise. A call writer must guarantee his contract either by holding the stock, or sufficient cash to buy the stock on margin, or an option on the stock. Backing an option with cash rather than stock is called writing "naked." Backing an option with another option is called a "spread."

Profit graphs for option writers tend to be, but are not always, the reverse of those for option buyers. Generally, the option writer is seeking a fixed gain while risking a larger loss. But whether risk is taken on the upside or the downside depends on whether cash or

FIGURE 22-3

Profit Graph for Call Writer

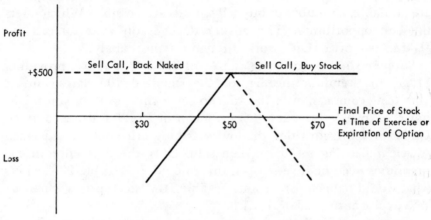

stock is chosen as backing for the option. The writer can also magnify his investment results by leveraging with borrowed money, up to margin-rule limits. Also, the option premium itself can be applied toward the backing reserve. Figure 22-3 contrasts two common ways in which call writers back their contracts—with stock (called "covered option writing") and with cash (naked).

Spreads

One high-risk, potentially high-reward way to play the option market involves spreads—simultaneously buying a call and selling a related one. The "spread" arises from the difference in premiums that you hope to capture by this maneuver. For example, Table 22-1 shows the IBM call prices as of the closing on October 7, 1975, as reported by the CBOE and printed in the *Wall Street Journal.*

TABLE 22-1

IBM Call Option Prices

	October		January		April		Stock
Option and Price	*Vol.*	*Last*	*Vol.*	*Last*	*Vol.*	*Last*	*Close*
IBM 160...................	517	41½	b	b	b	b	201¼
IBM 180...................	1,848	22	710	27	396	31¼	201¼
IBM 200...................	3,095	5	1,440	12⅞	146	18½	201¼
IBM 220...................	1,081	11/16	1,064	5⅜	b	b	201¼

b—no option offered.
Source: *The Wall Street Journal*, October 8, 1975, p. 35.

Since three call expiration dates and four different striking prices are available, a number of buy-sell spreads are possible. Which offers the best opportunity? The answer depends on your forecast for IBM's stock price. Let's work through a typical analysis.

Suppose you sell (or write) an April 200 call at $18½, providing $1,850 in premium income for the standard 100-share contract (omitting commissions). In order to cover this position, you might buy the April 180 call at $31¼, or a cost of $3,125 for one contract. Under SEC margin rules, the lower striking price option is deemed sufficient backing for the option sold. Only the difference in the premiums need be invested—in this case, $1,275. Table 22-2 shows what would happen for various possible IBM stock prices when the calls expire at the end of April.

Notice from Table 22-2 that the total result varies from a loss of $1,275 to a gain of $725 (before commissions and taxes). Thus, the possibilities range from −100 percent to +57 percent on the investment in less than seven months—that's action! If IBM's stock price is above $200 at the end of April, the full profit is made. But if it is

TABLE 22-2

Profit Table for IBM Option Spread

IBM Stock Price at End of April	Value of Option Sold IBM April 200	Gain (loss) from Option Sold	Value of Option Bought IBM April 180	Gain (loss) from Option Bought	Total Results
170.........	$ 0	$1,850	$ 0	($3,125)	($1,275)
180.........	0	1,850	0	(3,125)	(1,275)
190.........	0	1,850	10	(2,125)	(275)
200.........	0	1,850	20	(1,125)	725
210.........	10	850	30	(125)	725
220.........	20	(150)	40	875	725

below $180, the full loss is sustained. With IBM at 201¼ on the day shown, you might try this spread if you thought IBM would hold steady or go up.

Straddles

A "straddle" is an option contract that combines both a put and a call. Each option has the same striking price and expiration date, but they are exercisable separately. Straddles can also be backed naked or with stock, usually held long (backing the call) rather than short (backing the put) .

FIGURE 22–4

Profit Graph for Straddle Writer Backing with Stock

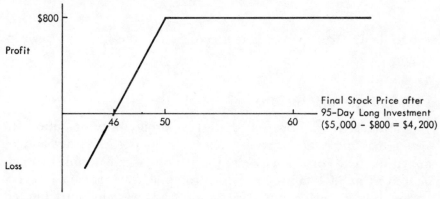

A straddle premium represents the sum of a put premium and a call premium. This package is attractive to option writers. A 95-day straddle on our $50 stock would cost about $800, with the price consisting of a call premium of $500 plus a put premium of about $300. When the straddle is backed with 100 shares of the stock, the profit graph for the straddle writer would appear as shown in Figure 22–4.

The maximum gain for the straddle writer in Figure 22–4 is $800. This is larger than the premium gain from just writing a call. The loss portion of the graph, however, descends twice as steeply as in the profit graph for the call writer, because both the stock and the put subject the writer to losses if the stock declines. The more daring way to back straddles is naked, just as it sounds. The profit graph for

FIGURE 22-5

Profit Graph for Straddle Writer Backing Naked

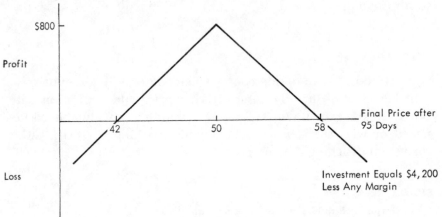

a straddle writer with no offsetting position in the stock is shown in Figure 22-5.

Profitability of Options

The research investigating the actual profitability of option investing has increased in recent years, but it is still scanty and of mixed quality. For a long time, the major piece of published evidence was an SEC staff report which compiled the outcome of every option written during June 1959. That study was obviously limited by not reflecting both up and down markets. It generated about as many misconceptions as it did pregnant understandings.

Papers published in Cootner [25], a doctoral dissertation by Gup [67], popular books by Zieg [187], Filer [47], and Dadekian [35], and computerized simulations by Malkiel and Quandt [111] and Lederman [95] have not produced consistent results. Certain of these studies have flaws of experimental technique or statistical analysis, or their findings lack comprehensiveness. However, the more recent, complete, and technically correct studies have indicated *a substantial investment role for both option buying and option writing in the portfolios of various types of investors.*

Malkiel and Quandt [111], then economists on the faculty at Princeton, tested the various uses of options in computer simulations of 16 different investment strategies. Their conclusions, although stemming from hypothetical rather than historical stock price data, left *no doubt* that a large role for options exists in optimal management of investment portfolios. Depending on one's forecast for securities prices, it appeared quite likely from the results of the simulations that some type and amount of option activity produced the best portfolio outcome from the standpoint of both risk and return. Either the insurance or leverage advantages of options were worth exploiting in many cases.

Some published studies have cited actual returns of 15 percent or higher, at moderate risk, for option writers who properly back their options. [see **58, 134, 135**] Still higher returns and risks have been reported for option buyers who concentrate on more volatile stocks. However, we would expect that, as this market becomes even more efficient through greater public and institutional understanding and participation, the prior levels of return may not persist.

Options Are Here to Stay

Still other investment strategies utilize still other option instruments. Strips and straps are further contractual combinations of puts and calls whose analysis is beyond our purpose here. However, the technique of profit graphs or tables can be applied to understanding their results. Options are useful instruments for insurance, leverage, and tax reasons. They often play a role in a well-constructed portfolio.

The option market has broadened significantly. The traditional weakness in option markets was the need for a customer to deal with put and call option dealers *and* regular brokers. Most brokers could not, themselves, deliver the option "merchandise" a specific customer wanted, such as a three-month call on Xerox. But now the CBOE and other exchanges offer a more efficient market, with standardized, centralized, and publicized options on popular stocks. This has improved the usefulness of option investing.

23

Getting It All Together

It takes time to change the traditional, generally accepted ways of doing things. Bachelier's securities work in 1900 preceded even Einstein in the use of a key scientific equation. And since then, investment research has made quantum jumps in our understanding of common stocks. In the next decade, this new investment knowledge will *revolutionize traditional investment practices.*

Certainly, all knowledge should be reassessed in the light of new theories and evidence. However, many people mistakenly assume that a single exception can invalidate the findings reported here. When hearing such rebuttals, you should remember that the conclusions reported here were derived from the study of many investment portfolios. They are the odds of the overall game. We expect to find exceptions, but *exceptions neither make nor break the rules.*

Knowing the odds is far more important than being misled by stories. A parallel with gambling can confirm this point. A passline bet on a crap table has an expected loss of 1.4 percent of one's "investment." Those are the odds of the game. If you make 1,000 one-dollar bets, you should expect to lose 1.4 percent, or $14. The more you play, the more predictable the results become. Indeed, the average loss on all bets of this type over a given day, month, or year increasingly approaches this percentage.

Still, few will achieve precisely the average result. Some will lose more, while others will win. Legend has it, for example, that a returning GI once won on 27 consecutive craps bets. It makes a

244

great story—but it does not change the odds. And while we anticipate exceptions, there is no reason to expect that *you* will be one of them.

The fragmented capital management and impulse buying that have characterized "investing" during the past decade have too often been based on intuition and stories. Over the next decade, rational investment strategy—based on knowing and applying the scientifically derived odds—can help you achieve well-planned objectives. By getting it all together, we hope that this new knowledge will be your *guide to common stocks.*

Bibliography

References

1. Abelson, Alan. *The 1971 Stock Trader's Almanac*. Old Tappan (N.J.) : The Hirsch Organization, p. 56.

2. Adams, D. F. "The Effect on Stock Price from Listing on the New York Stock Exchange." M.B.A. Thesis, New York University, 1965.

3. Alexander, Sidney S. "Price Movements in Speculative Markets: Trends or Random Walks," *Industrial Management Review*, vol. 2, no. 2 (May 1961), pp. 7–26.

4. Arditti, Fred D. "Risk and the Required Return on Equity," *Journal of Finance*, vol. 22, no. 1 (March 1967), pp. 19–36.

5. Bachelier, Louis. *Théorie de la speculation*. Paris: Gauthier-Villars, 1900. Translation by A. James Boness, reprinted in Paul H. Cootner, ed., *The Random Character of Stock Market Prices*, Cambridge: Massachusetts Institute of Technology Press, 1964, pp. 17–78.

6. Barker, C. Austin. "Effective Stock Splits," *Harvard Business Review*, vol. 34, no. 1 (January–February 1956), pp. 101–6.

7. ———. "Stock Splits in a Bull Market," *Harvard Business Review*, vol. 35, no. 3 (May–June 1957), pp. 72–79.

8. Barney, Walter F. "An Investigation of Parametric Variation in a Moving Average Investment Rule." Unpublished Master's Thesis, Massachusetts Institute of Technology, Cambridge, 1964.

246

9. Bauer, John. "A Diffusion Index as Applied to Price Movements in the Stock Market." Unpublished Master's Thesis, Massachusetts Institute of Technology, Cambridge, 1964.

10. Black, Fischer. "Yes, Virginia, There Is Hope: Tests of the Value Line Ranking System." Center for Research in Security Prices, Graduate School of Business, University of Chicago, May 1971.

11. Blume, Marshall E. "The Assessment of Portfolio Performance— An Application to Portfolio Theory." Unpublished Ph.D. Dissertation, University of Chicago, 1968.

12. Bowyer, John W. *Investment Analysis and Management*. 4th ed. Homewood (Ill.) : Richard D. Irwin, Inc., 1972.

13. Brealey, Richard A. *An Introduction to Risk and Return from Common Stocks*. Cambridge: Massachusetts Institute of Technology Press, 1969.

14. ———. *Security Prices in a Competitive Market*. Cambridge: Massachusetts Institute of Technology Press, 1971.

15. Breen, William. "Low Price-Earnings Ratios and Industry Relatives," *Financial Analysts Journal*, vol. 25, no. 4 (July–August 1969) , pp. 125–27.

16. Brown, Philip, and Ray Ball. "An Empirical Evaluation of Accounting Income Numbers," *Journal of Accounting Research*, vol. 6, no. 3 (Autumn 1968) , pp. 159–78.

17. Brown, Philip, and Victor Niederhoffer. "The Predictive Content of Quarterly Earnings," *Journal of Business*, vol. 41, no. 4 (October 1968) , pp. 488–97.

18. Cheney, H. L. "How Good Are Investment Advisory Services?" *Financial Executive*, vol. 37, no. 11 (November 1969) , pp. 30–35.

19. Cohen, A. W. *The Chartcraft Method of Point and Figure Trading*. Larchmont (N.Y.) : Chartcraft, Inc., 1963.

20. ———. *Technical Indicator Analysis by Point and Figure Technique*. Larchmont (N.Y.) : Chartcraft, Inc., 1963.

21. Cohen, Jerome B., and Edward D. Zinbarg. *Investment Analysis and Portfolio Management*. Homewood (Ill.) : Richard D. Irwin, Inc., 1967.

22. Cohen, Jerome B., Edward D. Zinbarg, and Arthur Zeikel. *Investment Analysis and Portfolio Management*. Homewood (Ill.) : Richard D. Irwin, Inc., 1973.

23. Colker, S. S. "An Analysis of Security Recommendations by Brokerage Houses," *Quarterly Review of Economics and Business*, vol. 3, no. 2 (Summer 1963) , pp. 19–28.

24. Conklin, Howard. "The Airline Industry and Its Profit Profile," *Financial Analysts Journal,* vol. 27, no. 1 (January–February 1971), p. 40.

25. Cootner, Paul H., ed. *The Random Character of Stock Market Prices.* Cambridge: Massachusetts Institute of Technology Press, 1964.

26. ———. "Stock Prices: Random vs. Systematic Changes," *Industrial Management Review,* vol. 3, no. 2 (Spring 1962), pp. 24–45.

27. Copeland, R. M., and R. J. Marioni. "Executives' Forecasts of Earnings per Share vs. Forecasts of Naive Models," *Journal of Business,* vol. 45, no. 4 (October 1972), pp. 497–512.

28. Cowles, Alfred. "Can Stock Market Forecasters Forecast?" *Econometrica,* vol. 1, no. 3 (July 1933), pp. 309–24.

29. ———. "A Revision of Previous Conclusions Regarding Stock Price Behavior," *Econometrica,* vol. 28, no. 4 (October 1960), pp. 909–15.

30. Cowles, Alfred, and Herbert F. Jones. "Some a Posteriori Probabilities in Stock Market Action," *Econometrica,* vol. 5, no. 3 (July 1937), pp. 280–94.

31. Cragg, J. G., and Burton G. Malkiel. "The Consensus and Accuracy of Some Predictions of the Growth of Corporate Earnings," *Journal of Finance,* vol. 23, no. 1 (March 1968), pp. 67–84.

32. Cross, Frank. "The Behavior of Stock Prices on Fridays and Mondays," *Financial Analysts Journal,* vol. 29, no. 6 (November–December 1973), p. 67.

33. Crowell, Richard. "Earnings Expectations, Security Valuation, and the Cost of Equity Capital." Unpublished Ph.D. Dissertation, Massachusetts Institute of Technology, 1967.

34. Cushing, Barry. "The Effects of Accounting Policy Decisions on Trends in Reported Corporate Earnings per Share." Ph.D. Dissertation, Michigan State University, 1969.

35. Dadekian, Zaven A. *The Strategy of Puts and Calls.* New York: Corinthian Editions, 1968.

36. Darling, P. G. "The Influence of Expectations and Liquidity on Dividend Policy," *Journal of Political Economy,* vol. 65, no. 3 (June 1957), pp. 209–24.

37. Darvas, Nicholas. *How I Made $2,000,000 in the Stock Market.* Larchmont (N.Y.): American Research Council, 1960.

38. Douglas, George W. "Risk in the Equity Market: An Empirical

Appraisal of Market Efficiency." Unpublished Ph.D. Dissertation, Yale University, 1967.

39. Driscoll, T. E. "Some Aspects of Corporate Insider Stock Holdings and Trading under Section 16 (b) of the Securities Exchange Act." M.B.A. Thesis, University of Pennsylvania, 1956.

40. Edwards, Robert D., and John Magee. *Technical Analysis of Stock Trends.* 4th ed. Springfield (Mass.) : John Magee, 1962.

41. Evans, John Leslie. "Diversification and the Reduction of Dispersion: An Empirical Analysis." Unpublished Ph.D. Dissertation, University of Washington, 1968.

42. Fama, Eugene F. "The Behavior of Stock Market Prices," *Journal of Business,* vol. 38, no. 1 (January 1965), pp. 34–105.

43. Fama, Eugene F., and H. Babiak. "Dividend Policy: An Empirical Analysis," *Journal of the American Statistical Association,* vol. 63, no. 12 (December 1968), pp. 1132–61.

44. Fama, Eugene F., L. Fisher, M. C. Jensen, and R. Roll. "The Adjustment of Stock Prices to New Information," *International Economic Review,* vol. 10, no. 2 (February 1969), pp. 1–21.

45. Fama, Eugene F. "Efficient Capital Markets: A Review of Theory and Empirical Work," *Journal of Finance,* vol. 25, no. 2 (May 1970), pp. 383–423.

46. Ferber, Robert. "Short-run Effects of Stock Market Services on Stock Prices," *Journal of Finance,* vol. 13, no. 1 (March 1958), pp. 80–95.

47. Filer, Herbert. *Understanding Put and Call Options.* New York: Crown Publishers, Inc., 1959.

48. Filter, Eunice. "Accounting Practices of Major Computer Companies," *Financial Analysts Journal,* vol. 27, no. 3 (May–June 1971), p. 44.

49. Fisher, Lawrence. "Outcomes for 'Random' Investments in Common Stocks Listed on the New York Stock Exchange," *Journal of Business,* vol. 3, no. 4 (April 1965), pp. 149–61.

50. Fisher, Lawrence, and James H. Lorie. "Rates of Return on Investments in Common Stocks," *Journal of Business,* vol. 37, no. 1 (January 1964), pp. 1–21.

51. Friedman, Milton, and Anna J. Schwartz. *Monetary History of the United States, 1867–1960.* Princeton (N.J.) : Princeton University Press, 1963.

52. Friend, Irwin, et al. *A Study of Mutual Funds.* Prepared for the Securities and Exchange Commission by the Securities Research Unit, The Wharton School, University of Pennsyl-

vania. Washington (D.C.) : U.S. Government Printing Office, 1962.

53. Friend, Irwin, and Douglas Vickers. "Portfolio Selection and Investment Performance," *Journal of Finance,* vol. 20, no. 2 (September 1965), pp. 391–415.

54. Friend, Irwin, James Longstreet, Ervin Miller, and Arleigh Hess. *Investment Banking and the New Issues Market.* New York: World Publishing Company, 1967.

55. Friend, Irwin, Marshall Blume, and Jean Crockett. *Mutual Funds and Other Institutional Investors: A New Perspective.* New York: McGraw-Hill Book Company, Inc., 1970.

56. Friend, Irwin, and Marshall Blume. "Risk and the Long-Run Rate of Return on NYSE Common Stocks." Working Paper No. 18–72, The Wharton School, Rodney L. White Center for Financial Research, p. 10.

57. Furst, R. W. "Does Listing Increase the Market Price of Common Stock?" *Journal of Business,* vol. 43, no. 4 (April 1970), pp. 174–80.

58. Gastineau, Gary L. *The Stock Options Manual.* New York: McGraw-Hill Book Company, Inc., 1975.

59. Gaumnitz, Jack E. "Investment Diversification under Uncertainty: An Examination of the Number of Securities in a Diversified Portfolio." Unpublished Ph.D. Dissertation, Stanford University, 1967.

60. Godfrey, Michael D., Clive W. J. Granger, and Oskar Morgenstern. "The Random-Walk Hypothesis of Stock Market Behavior," *Kyklos,* vol. 17, fasc. 1 (1964), pp. 1–30.

61. Graham, Benjamin, David L. Dodd, and Sidney Cottle. *Security Analysis.* 4th ed. New York: McGraw-Hill Book Company, Inc., 1951.

62. Granger, Clive W. J. "What the Random-Walk Model Does Not Say," *Financial Analysts Journal,* vol. 26, no. 3 (May–June 1970), pp. 91–93.

63. Granger, Clive W. J., and Oskar Morgenstern. "Spectral Analysis of New York Stock Market Prices," *Kyklos,* vol. 16 (1963), pp. 1–27.

64. Green, David, Jr., and Joel Segall. "The Predictive Power of First Quarter Earnings Reports," *Journal of Business,* vol. 40, no. 1 (January 1967), pp. 44–55.

65. ———. "Brickbats and Straw Men: A Reply to Brown and

Niederhoffer," *Journal of Business,* vol. 41, no. 4 (October 1968), pp. 498–502.

66. ———. "Return of Strawman," *Journal of Business,* vol. 43, no. 1 (January 1970), 63–65.

67. Gup, Benton E. "The Economics of the Security Option Markets." Unpublished Ph.D. Dissertation, University of Cincinnati, 1966.

68. Hagin, Robert L. "An Empirical Evaluation of Selected Hypotheses Related to Price Changes in the Stock Market." Unpublished Ph.D. Dissertation, University of California (Los Angeles), 1966.

69. Hamanda, R. S. "An Analysis of Diffusion Indices of Insiders' Transactions." Unpublished S.M. Thesis, Massachusetts Institute of Technology, 1961.

70. Hanna, M. "Short Interest: Bullish or Bearish?—Comment," *Journal of Finance,* vol. 23, no. 6 (June 1968), pp. 520–23.

71. Hausman, Warren H. "A Note on the Value Line Contest: A Test of the Predictability of Stock-Price Changes," *Journal of Business,* vol. 42, no. 3 (July 1969), pp. 317–20.

72. Hausman, Warren H., R. R. West, and J. A. Largay. "Stock Splits, Price Changes, and Trading Profits: A Synthesis." *Journal of Business,* vol. 44, no. 1 (January 1971), pp. 69–77.

73. Homa, Kenneth E., and Dwight M. Jaffee. "The Supply of Money and Common Stock Prices," *Journal of Finance,* vol. 26, no. 5 (December 1971) pp. 1045–66.

74. Houthakker, Hendrik S. "Systematic and Random Elements in Short-Term Price Movements," *American Economic Review,* vol. 51, no. 2 (May 1961), pp. 164–72.

75. Ibbotson, Roger G., and Rex A. Sinquefield. "Stocks, Bonds, Bills, and Inflation—The Past and the Future." Center for Research on Securities Prices, University of Chicago, 1974.

76. James, F. E., Jr. "Monthly Moving Averages—An Effective Investment Tool?" *Journal of Financial and Quantitative Analysis,* vol. 3, no. 3 (September 1968), pp. 315–26.

77. Jensen, Michael C. "Random Walks: Reality or Myth—Comment," *Financial Analysts Journal,* vol. 23, no. 6 (November–December 1967), pp. 77–85.

78. ———. "The Performance of Mutual Funds in the Period 1945–1964," *Journal of Finance,* vol. 23, no. 5 (May 1968), pp. 389–416.

79. Jiler, William L. *How Charts Can Help You in the Stock Market.* New York: Commodity Research Publication Corp., 1962.

80. Johnson, Paul R., and H. Marchman. "Moving Averages and Exponential Smoothing Applied to Common Stock Prices." Mimeographed, n.d.

81. Kaish, S. "Odd-lot Profit and Loss Performance," *Financial Analysts Journal,* vol. 25, no. 9 (September–October 1969), pp. 83–92.

82. Kaplan, Gilbert Edmund, and Chris Welles. *The Money Managers.* New York: Random House, 1969.

83. Kaplan, Robert S., and Richard Roll. "Investor Evaluation of Accounting Information: Some Empirical Evidence," *Journal of Business,* vol. 45, no. 2 (April 1972), pp. 225–57.

84. Kaplan, Robert S., and Roman L. Weil. "Risk and the Value Line Contest," *Financial Analysts Journal,* vol. 29, no. 4 (July–August 1973), pp. 56–62.

85. Katona, George. *Psychological Economics.* New York: American Elsevier Publishing Co., 1975.

86. Kendall, Maurice George. "The Analysis of Economic Time Series—Part I: Prices," *Journal of the Royal Statistical Society,* Series A (General), vol. 116, pt. 1 (1953), pp. 11–25.

87. Kewley, T. J., and R. A. Stevenson. "The Odd-Lot Theory as Revealed by Purchase and Sales Statistics for Individual Stocks," *Financial Analysts Journal,* vol. 23, no. 5 (September–October 1967), 103–6.

88. ———. "The Odd-lot Theory for Individual Stocks: A Reply," *Financial Analysts Journal,* vol. 25, no. 1 (January–February 1969), pp. 99–104.

89. King, Benjamin F. "The Latent Statistical Structure of Security Price Changes." Unpublished Ph.D. Dissertation, University of Chicago, 1964.

90. Kisor, Manown, Jr., and Van A. Messner. "The Filter Approach and Earnings Forecasts," *Financial Analysts Journal,* vol. 25, no. 1 (January 1969), pp. 109–15.

91. Kisor, Manown, Jr., and Victor Niederhoffer. "Odd-Lot Short Sales Ratio: It Signals a Market Rise." *Barron's* (September 1, 1969), p. 8.

92. Klein, D. J. "The Odd-Lot Stock Trading Theory." Ph.D. Dissertation, Michigan State University, 1964.

93. Kolin, Alexander. *Physics: Its Laws, Ideas, and Methods.* New York: McGraw-Hill Book Company, Inc., 1950.

94. Latané, Henry Allen, and Donald L. Tuttle. "An Analysis of

Common Stock Price Ratios," *Southern Economic Journal,* vol. 33, no. 1 (January 1967), pp. 343–54.

95. Lederman, David. "Put and Call Options with Special Emphasis on Option Portfolios." Unpublished Master's Thesis, Stanford University, 1969.

96. Levin, Jesse. "Prophetic Leaders," *Financial Analysts Journal,* vol. 26, no. 4 (July–August 1970), pp. 87–90.

97. Levine, Sidney. "Heuristic Determination of Optimum Filter for Use in a Rule of Speculative Market Action." Unpublished Master's Thesis, Massachusetts Institute of Technology, Cambridge, 1962.

98. Levy, Robert A. "An Evaluation of Selected Applications of Stock Market Timing Techniques, Trading Tactics, and Trend Analysis." Unpublished Ph.D. Dissertation, American University, Washington, D.C., 1966.

99. ———. "Random Walks: Reality or Myth," *Financial Analysts Journal,* vol. 23, no. 6 (November–December 1967), pp. 129–32.

100. ———. "Random Walks: Reality or Myth—Reply," *Financial Analysts Journal,* vol. 24, no. 1 (January–February 1968), pp. 129–32.

101. ———. "A Note on the Safety of Low P/E Stocks," *Financial Analysts Journal,* vol. 29, no. 1 (January–February 1973), p. 57.

102. Lintner, John. "Distribution of Incomes of Corporations among Dividends, Retained Earnings, and Taxes," *American Economic Review,* vol. 46, no. 5 (May 1956), pp. 97–113.

103. Lintner, John, and Robert Glauber. "Higgledy Piggledy Growth in America." Unpublished paper prepared for the Seminar on the Analysis of Security Prices, University of Chicago, May 1967.

104. Loeb, Gerald M. *The Battle for Investment Survival.* New York: Simon and Schuster, 1957.

105. ———. *The Battle for Stock Market Profits.* New York: Simon and Schuster, 1971.

106. Logue, Dennis Emhardt. "An Empirical Appraisal of the Market for First Public Offerings of Common Stock." Unpublished Ph.D. Dissertation, Cornell University, 1971.

107. Loll, Leo M., Jr., and Julian G. Buckley. *Questions and Answers on Securities Markets.* Englewood Cliffs (N.J.): Prentice-Hall, Inc., 1968.

108. Lorie, James H., and Victor Niederhoffer. "Predictive and Statistical Properties of Insider Trading," *Journal of Law and Economics,* vol. 11, no. 4 (April 1968), pp. 35–53.

109. Lorie, James H., and Mary T. Hamilton. *The Stock Market: Theories and Evidence.* Homewood (Ill.): Richard D. Irwin, Inc., 1973.

110. Malkiel, Burton G. *A Random Walk down Wall Street.* New York: W. W. Norton & Company, Inc., 1973.

111. Malkiel, Burton G., and Richard E. Quandt. *Strategies and Rational Decisions in the Securities Options Market.* Cambridge: Massachusetts Institute of Technology Press, 1969.

112. Mandelbrot, Benoit. "Forecasts of Future Prices, Unbiased Markets, and 'Martingale' Models," *Journal of Business,* vol. 39, no. 1, pt. 2 (January 1966), pp. 242–55.

113. ———. "The Variation of Some Other Speculative Prices," *Journal of Business,* vol. 40, no. 4 (October 1967), pp. 393–413.

114. Markowitz, Harry M. "Portfolio Selection," *Journal of Finance,* vol. 7, no. 1 (March 1952), pp. 77–91.

115. ———. *Portfolio Selection: Efficient Diversification of Investments.* New York: John Wiley and Sons, Inc., 1959.

116. May, A. Wilfred. "Current Popular Delusions about the Stock Split and Stock Dividend," *Commercial and Financial Chronicle,* vol. 184, no. 5586 (November 15, 1956), p. 5.

117. Mayor, T. H. "Short Trading Activities and the Price of Equities: Some Simulation and Regression Results," *Journal of Financial and Quantitative Analysis,* vol. 3, no. 9 (September 1968), pp. 283–98.

118. McDonald, J. G., and A. K. Fisher. "New Issue Stock Price Behavior," *Journal of Finance,* vol. 27, no. 1 (March, 1972), pp. 97–102.

119. Merjos, A. "Going on the Big Board: Stocks Act Better before Listing than Right Afterward," *Barron's* (January 29, 1962), pp. 54 ff.

120. ———. "Going on the Big Board," *Barron's* (May 1, 1967), pp. 9–10.

121. ———. "New Listings and Their Price Behavior," *Journal of Finance,* vol. 25, no. 9 (September 1970), pp. 783–94.

122. Miller, Paul F., Jr. *Institutional Service Report—Monthly Review.* Philadelphia: Drexel & Co., Inc., November 1965.

123. Modigliani, Franco, and Gerald Pogue. "An Introduction to Risk and Return," *Financial Analysts Journal*, vol. 30, no. 2 (March–April 1974), p. 68.

124. Moore, Arnold B. "A Statistical Analysis of Common Stock Prices." Unpublished Ph.D. Dissertation, University of Chicago, 1962.

125. Murphy, John Michael. "The Value Line Contest: 1969," *Financial Analysts Journal*, vol. 26, no. 3 (May–June 1970), pp. 94–100.

126. Murphy, Joseph E., Jr. "Relative Growth of Earnings per Share —Past and Future," *Financial Analysts Journal*, vol. 22, no. 6 (November–December 1966), pp. 73–76.

127. ———. "Return, Payout, and Growth," *Financial Analysts Journal*, vol. 23, no. 3 (May–June 1967), pp. 91–96.

128. Ney, Richard. *The Wall Street Jungle.* New York: Grove Press, Inc., 1970.

129. Niederhoffer, Victor. "Non-Randomness in Stock Prices: A New Model of Stock Price Movements." Unpublished Bachelor's Thesis, Department of Economics, Harvard University, 1965.

130. ———. "Clustering of Stock Prices," *Operations Research*, vol. 13, no. 2 (March–April 1965), pp. 258–65.

131. ———. "A New Look at Clustering of Stock Prices," *Journal of Business*, vol. 39, no. 2 (April 1966), pp. 309–13.

132. Niederhoffer, Victor, and M. F. M. Osborne. "Market Making and Reversal on the Stock Exchange," *Journal of the American Statistical Association*, vol. 61, no. 316 (December 1966), pp. 887–916.

133. Niederhoffer, Victor, and Patrick Regan. "Earnings Changes, Analysts' Forecasts, and Stock Prices," *Financial Analysts Journal*, vol. 28, no. 3 (May–June 1972), pp. 65–71.

134. Noddings, Thomas C. *The Dow Jones-Irwin Guide to Convertible Securities.* Homewood (Ill.): Dow Jones-Irwin, Inc., 1973.

135. Noddings, Thomas C., and Earl Zazove. *Listed Call Options: Your Daily Guide to Portfolio Strategy.* Homewood (Ill.): Dow Jones-Irwin, Inc., 1975.

136. O'Brien, John W. "How Market Theory Can Help Investors Set Goals, Select Investment Managers, and Appraise Investment Performance," *Financial Analysts Journal*, vol. 26, no. 4 (July–August 1970), pp. 91–103.

137. Osborne, M. F. M. "Brownian Motion in the Stock Market,"

Operations Research, vol. 7, no. 2 (March–April 1959), pp. 145–73.

138. ———. "Reply to 'Comments on Brownian Motion in the Stock Market,'" *Operations Research,* vol. 7 (1959); pp. 807–11.

139. ———. "Periodic Structure of Brownian Motion of Stock Prices," *Operations Research,* vol. 10, no. 3 (May–June 1962), pp. 345–79.

140. Pettit, Richardson R. "Dividend Announcements and Security Performance." Preliminary Working Paper, Rodney L. White Center for Financial Research, The Wharton School, University of Pennsylvania, February 19, 1971.

141. Pratt, Shannon P. "Relationship between Risk and Rate of Return for Common Stocks." Unpublished D.B.A. Dissertation, Indiana University, 1966.

142. Pratt, Shannon P., and C. W. DeVere. "Relationship between Insider Trading and Rates of Return for NYSE Common Stocks, 1960–1966." Unpublished paper prepared for the Seminar on the Analysis of Security Prices, University of Chicago (May 1968).

143. Reilly, F. K. "Price Changes in NYSE, AMEX, and OTC Stocks Compared," *Financial Analysts Journal,* vol. 27, no. 2 (March–April 1971), p. 54.

144. Reilly, F. K., and K. Hatfield. "Experience with New Stock Issues," *Financial Analysts Journal,* vol. 25, no. 5 (September–October 1969), pp. 73–82.

145. Rieke, R. C. "Selling on the News," *Barron's,* vol. 44, no. 48 (November 30, 1964), p. 9.

146. Roberts, Harry V. "Stock Market 'Patterns' and Financial Analysis," *Journal of Finance,* vol. 14, no. 1 (March 1959), pp. 1–10.

147. Rogoff, D. L. "The Forecasting Properties of Insiders' Transactions." Unpublished Ph.D. Dissertation, Michigan State University, 1964.

148. Rozeff, Michael. "The Money Supply and Common Stock Prices," *Journal of Financial Economics,* September 1974.

149. Rudolph, Allan. "The Money Supply and Common Stock Prices," *Financial Analysts Journal,* vol. 28, no. 2 (March–April 1972), p. 19.

150. Ruff, R. T. "The Effect of Selection and Recommendation of a Stock of the Month," *Financial Analysts Journal,* vol. 19, no. 2 (March–April 1965), pp. 41–43.

151. Samuelson, Paul A. "Proof that Properly Anticipated Prices Fluctuate Randomly," *Industrial Management Review,* vol. 6, no. 2 (Spring 1965), pp. 41–49.

152. Scholes, Myron. "A Test of the Competitive Hypothesis: The Market for New Issues and Secondary Offerings." Unpublished Ph.D. Dissertation, Graduate School of Business, University of Chicago, 1969.

153. Seneca, Joseph J. "Short Interest: Bearish or Bullish?" *Journal of Finance,* vol. 23, no. 3 (March 1967), pp. 67–70.

154. ———. "Short Interest: Bullish or Bearish?—Reply," *Journal of Finance,* vol. 23, no. 3 (March 1967), pp. 524–27.

155. Sharpe, William F. "Mutual Fund Performance," *Journal of Business,* vol. 39, no. 1, pt. 2 (January 1966), pp. 119–38.

156. ———. "Likely Gains from Market Timing," *Financial Analysts Journal,* vol. 31, no. 2 (March–April 1975).

157. Shelton, John P. "The Value Line Contest: A Test of the Predictability of Stock Price Changes," *Journal of Business,* vol. 40, no. 3 (July 1967), pp. 251–69.

158. Shenker, Israel. "Professors Top Wall Street's Stock Advice," *New York Times,* March 11, 1972, p. 37.

159. Shiskin, Julius. "Systematic Aspects of Stock Price Fluctuation." Unpublished paper prepared for the Seminar on the Analysis of Security Prices, University of Chicago (May 1967).

160. Slutsky, Eugen. "The Summation of Random Causes as the Source of Cyclic Processes," *Econometrica,* vol. 5, no. 2 (April 1937), pp. 105–46.

161. Smith, Adam. *An Inquiry into the Nature and Causes of the Wealth of Nations.* 2d ed., vol. 1, bk. 2. London: Methuen and Company, Ltd., 1904.

162. Smith, Adam. *The Money Game.* New York: Random House, 1968.

163. ———. *Supermoney.* New York: Random House, 1972.

164. Smith, Randall D. "Short Interest and Stock Market Prices," *Financial Analysts Journal,* vol. 24, no. 6 (November–December 1968), pp. 151–54.

165. Solnik, Bruno. "Why Not Diversify Internationally Rather than Domestically," *Financial Analysts Journal,* vol. 30, no. 4 (July–August 1974), p. 48.

166. Sprinkel, Beryl W. *Money and Stock Prices.* Homewood (Ill.): Richard D. Irwin, Inc., 1964.

167. ————. *Money and Markets: A Monetarist View.* Homewood (Ill.) : Richard D. Irwin, Inc., 1971.

168. *Standard Industrial Classification Manual.* Statistical Policy Division, Office of Management and Budget, Washington (D.C.) , 1971.

169. Stauffer, C. Hoff, Jr., and Robert C. Vogel. "Parameters of Mutual Fund Performance." Wesleyan University, Middletown, Conn., 1969 (mimeographed) .

170. Stern, Joel M. "The Case against Maximizing Earnings per Share," *Financial Analysts Journal,* vol. 26, no. 5 (September–October 1970) , pp. 107–12.

171. Stigler, George J. "Public Regulation of the Securities Markets," *Journal of Business,* vol. 37, no. 2 (April 1964) , pp. 117–42.

172. Stoffels, J. D. "Stock Recommendations by Investment Advisory Services: Immediate Effects on Market Pricing," *Financial Analysts Journal,* vol. 22, no. 3 (March 1966) , pp. 77–86.

173. *Survey of Current Business.* United States Department of Commerce, Washington (D.C.) , November 1974.

174. Tabell, Edmund W., and Anthony W. Tabell. "The Case for Technical Analysis," *Financial Analysts Journal,* vol. 20, no. 2 (March–April 1964) , pp. 67–76.

175. Taussig, F. W. "Is Market Price Determinate?" *Quarterly Journal of Economics,* vol. 35, no. 5 (May 1921) , pp. 394–411.

176. Thorp, Edward O., and Sheen T. Kassouf. *Beat the Market: A Scientific Stock Market System.* New York: Random House, 1967.

177. Treynor, Jack L. "How to Rate Management of Investment Funds," *Harvard Business Review,* vol. 43, no. 1 (January–February 1965) , pp. 63–76.

178. Van Horne, James C. "New Listings and Their Price Behavior," *Journal of Finance,* vol. 25, no. 9 (September 1970) , pp. 783–94.

179. von Neumann, John, and Oskar Morgenstern. *The Theory of Games and Economic Behavior.* New York: John Wiley and Sons, Inc., 1940.

180. Walter, James. "Dividend Policies and Common Stock Prices," *Journal of Finance,* vol. 11, pp. 29–41.

181. Welles, Chris. "The Beta Revolution: Learning to Live with Risk," *Institutional Investor,* vol. 5, no. 9 (September 1971) , pp. 21–27 ff.

182. Whitbeck, Volkert S., and Manown Kisor, Jr. "A New Tool in Investment Decision Making," *Financial Analysts Journal,* vol. 19, no. 3 (May–June 1963), pp. 55–62.

183. Working, Holbrook. "A Random-Difference Series for Use in the Analysis of Time Series," *Journal of the American Statistical Association,* vol. 29, no. 185 (March 1934), pp. 11–24.

184. ———. "New Ideas and Methods for Price Research," *Journal of Farm Economics,* vol. 38, no. 5 (December 1956), pp. 1427–36.

185. ———. "Note on the Correlation of First Differences of Averages in a Random Chain," *Econometrica,* vol. 28, no. 4 (October 1960), pp. 916–18.

186. Wu, Hsiu-Kwang. "Corporate Insider Trading, Profitability, and Stock Price Movement." Unpublished Ph.D. Dissertation, University of Pennsylvania, 1963.

187. Zieg, Kermit C., Jr. *The Profitability of Stock Options.* Larchmont (N.Y.): Investors Intelligence, Inc., 1970.

188. *Business Week,* December 18, 1971, p. 88.

189. *Business Week,* December 23, 1972, p. 111.

190. *Business Week,* November 3, 1975, p. 64.

191. *Forbes,* Special Report, 1967, p. 5.

192. *Fortune,* July 1966, p. 160.

193. *Fortune,* January 1970, p. 101.

194. *Fortune,* July 1975, p. 57.

195. *Fortune,* October 1975, p. 108.

196. *Investing,* October 1973, p. 22.

197. *Money,* July 1975, p. 53.

198. *Money,* September 1975, p. 10.

199. *Money,* September 1975, p. 29.

200. *Newsweek,* July 15, 1971, p. 46.

201. *Time,* June 27, 1969, p. 71.

202. *Wall Street Journal,* December 11, 1972, p. 14.

203. *Wall Street Journal,* "Heard on the Street," April 15, 1975.

204. *Wall Street Journal,* "Abreast of the Market," October 16, 1975.

205. *Wall Street Journal,* "Heard on the Street," November 14, 1975.

206. *Wall Street Journal,* December 5, 1975, p. 24.

index

Index